Security Analysis
&
Portfolio
Management
a casebook

Security Analysis & Portfolio Management

a casebook

Allan J. Twark
Kent State University

William P. Dukes
Texas Tech University

Oswald D. Bowlin
Texas Tech University

HOLDEN–DAY, INC.
San Francisco

Düsseldorf   *Johannesburg*   *London*   *Panama*
Singapore   *Sydney*   *Toronto*

Security Analysis and Portfolio Management: A Casebook

Copyright © 1973 by Holden-Day, Inc., 500 Sansome Street, San Francisco, California 94111. All rights reserved.

Library of Congress Catalog Card Number: 72-83245
ISBN: 0-8162-8946-8

Printed in the United States of America
1234567890 MP 8079876543

To Charlene, Janie, and Caroline

Preface

The field of securities investments has become considerably more scientific since Markowitz's pioneering works* in the portfolio selection process. Continued improvement in portfolio theory and greater knowledge of capital markets have made possible the establishment of more precise standards of performance for investments in securities. Despite growth in the application of many of the new ideas, however, students of investments and capital markets have been faced with limited availability of cases for study. The purpose of this casebook is to help fill the void.

A variety of cases will be presented in each of the important problem areas of common stock investments. The book has been designed for the first course in investments, but it may also be useful to the advanced undergraduate and graduate student because of the breadth of coverage and the varying degrees of complexity of the cases.

The amount of data presented in most instances has been limited in order to focus the attention of the student on the principal issues. In general, the questions found at the end of the cases are designed to help the beginning student to develop a knowledge of the step by step process of analysis required in determining a solution. Mathematical computations necessary for all solutions can be performed by hand. Limiting the cases in this way, even those dealing with portfolios, has not greatly reduced their effectiveness for pedagogical purposes, because the same type of analysis can be applied to situations involving a greater number of computations.

Although heavy emphasis in financial literature has been placed on the techniques of analysis, relatively little work has been published to date on the derivation of realistic inputs for portfolio models. In most instances, the inputs have been derived solely from historical data under the assumption that the future will be a continuation of the past. This simplistic approach severely limits the usefulness of the analysis. A significant percentage of the cases in this book

---

* Harry M. Markowitz, "Portfolio Selection," *The Journal of Finance,* Vol. VII, No. 1, March 1952, pp. 77–91. See also Harry M. Markowitz, *Portfolio Selection: Efficient Diversification of Investments*, New York: John Wiley & Sons, Inc., 1959.

will concentrate on obtaining the requisite inputs, namely, expected returns on investments and expected variances of those returns.

There are two "schools of thought" on how portfolio inputs should be obtained. One is the traditional, or fundamental, school which concentrates on value analysis: financial statements of firms are analyzed and related to other business and economic data to arrive at a current value for the securities. Benjamin Graham has been the long-time leader of this school, and its techniques of analysis have been rigorously applied by investment advisory services such as The Value Line. The second school, broadly defined as the "efficient capital market's school," postulates that the overall market digests new information as it becomes available and such information is quickly reflected in the price of the stock. Advocates of this theory contend that the market price of the security always reflects its proper value.

Part I of the casebook is concerned with the fundamental approach to obtaining portfolio inputs. The principal problems in this section focus on earnings and capitalization rate determination. Part II concentrates on deriving portfolio inputs under the assumptions of efficient capital markets and relatively constant systematic and random risks. Any or all of the cases in Parts I and II can be assigned in the first undergraduate course in investments. Part III includes cases dealing with the determination of efficient portfolios. Several portfolio models are to be applied, utilizing inputs developed by the student. Part III will be more useful in advanced courses.

The appendixes at the end of the casebook include most of the market data and analytical techniques required in developing the required solutions. Nevertheless, the student will gain breadth of knowledge of the topics covered if the casebook is used in conjunction with one of the many texts currently available.

The authors are indebted to a number of people for their help in completing the book. Students in investment courses at Texas Tech and at Kent State have played an indispensable role in the class testing of the cases. Special thanks go to Ruth Dilsworth and Hugh Bradberry for tabulating data for the exhibits. Mrs. LaVerna Hipp and Mrs. Jane Allison have done an outstanding job in typing the manuscript and in putting it together for publication. Despite the high quality of the help of all of the above people, however, errors doubtlessly remain for which the authors are entirely responsible.

Allan J. Twark
William P. Dukes
Oswald D. Bowlin

Contents

SECURITY ANALYSIS

1 Earnings Determination

Case 1: Accounting Factors

Midwestern Electric Power

Until the early Sixties, the traditional way of representing balance-of-payments surpluses and deficits was known as the "regular" transactions methods, which, so to speak, covered the waterfront. Under this system, however, the figures began to look so ugly that the New Frontier and Great Society, in what became known as "cosmetic transactions," sought to put a better face on the accounts . . . . Now, according to the Treasury, the Nixon Administration plans to go still further by developing two new methods of calculations, known as the "current account" and "basic" balances. Suffice to say, without getting too technical, that while the various methods of calculation may muddy the waters, they will scarcely alter the results. (Barron's, March 15, 1971, "Another Day, Another Dollar? The U.S. Can't Afford to be Complacent About Its Finances," p. 10.)

Midwestern Electric Power (MEP) is a medium-sized electric utility company which supplies electricity to approximately 2.3 million persons. The Federal Power Commission estimates that over the next decade the area serviced by MEP will experience a 5.6 percent annual average rate of increase in electric power requirements. This compares unfavorably with a 6.0 percent growth rate for the area over the past decade and a 6.15 percent growth rate expected nationally for the next decade.

MEP's revenue breakdown for major categories is currently as follows: residential, 38 percent; industrial, 31 percent; commercial, 24 percent. Percentages for the same categories for the nation as a whole are 30, 43, and 22, respectively. In general, residential sales are considerably more profitable than other sales in that MEP's residential rates are 2.42 cents per kilowatthour versus 2.09 cents per kilowatthour nationally. Annual average usage comparisons indicate 5,760 kilowatthours versus 6,570 kilowatthours for the company and the nation, respectively.

The rates of most electric utility firms are regulated by a state public utility commission. Since rate changes ordinarily lag behind price level changes, public utilities usually face rising costs and falling profit margins during inflationary periods. MEP is currently petitioning for rate increases on the basis of reduced profitability caused by large increases in both operating and financing costs. The company has operated for years at a target rate of earnings growth of approximately 8 percent per year; however, recent adverse factors have made this goal impractical at the present time. The 10 percent tax surcharge of 19x8 and 19x9, coupled with the suspension of the investment tax credit in 19x9, added further downward pressure on profit margins. This accumulation of adverse factors has encouraged many utility firms, including MEP, to resort to various accounting means to moderate the consequent effects on reported earnings.

The most significant accounting change utilized by firms has been the conversion from straight-line to accelerated depreciation for tax purposes. By continuing to report profits on the basis of straight-line depreciation the resultant tax savings "flow through" to current earnings. In 19x7, MEP revised its composite depreciation rate from 3.25 percent to 3.00 percent and then switched to the double declining balance method of depreciation. These changes resulted in federal income tax savings of $2.45 million for 19x7 and $3.20 million for 19x8. Other means used by utility firms to inflate reported earnings during recent years have been: increasing the rate at which new construction expenditures are capitalized, adjusting downward the rate of contribution to pension funds, and "flowing through" the balances of their investment tax credits.

MEP's management believes that it has always operated in the best interests of its stockholders. It believes further that when the company absorbs the current flurry of unexpectedly high costs, more efficient operating measures will enable the firm to return to its former 8 percent growth rate. MEP expects to report a decline in earnings per share for the current year to approximately $1.80 from $1.89 last year. An annual dividend increase of 4 cents per share, however, has already been approved by the board of directors.

Profit declines in 2 of the last 3 years have contributed to a decline in the market price of the common stock to as low as $21\frac{5}{8}$. The stock price has rebounded to the mid 20s during the past few weeks.

QUESTIONS

1. (a) Is there any evidence that MEP has stablized its reported earnings per share in recent years through accounting adjustments? Explain.
   (b) What would have been the impact on earnings per share if MEP had not changed the basis for calculating depreciation in 19x7?
   (c) Explain other accounting techniques that firms can use to moderate variations in their earnings.

2. Is there any evidence that investors have been aware of MEP's accounting changes and have, accordingly, discounted them? Substantiate your answer.

3. Can management rekindle its former 8 percent target growth in earnings? Why or why not?

4. (a) Compute the annual holding period returns and variances of the returns for both MEP and the industry average for the period 19x0-19x9.

(b) Explain briefly the factors other than earnings quality and growth that are instrumental in the pricing of MEP's common stock.

EXHIBIT 1

Balance Sheet Data (millions)

MIDWESTERN ELECTRIC POWER

	19x9	19x8	19x7	19x6	19x5	19x4	19x3	19x2	19x1	19x0
Assets:										
Current	57.54	35.24	31.31	77.49	88.41	79.28	61.38	47.31	39.16	27.47
Cash Items	27.57	7.15	6.91	55.06	68.36	60.22	43.43	27.94	20.78	7.34
Receivables	16.02	14.55	13.99	12.33	10.92	10.41	9.98	10.88	8.88	8.27
Inventory	13.95	13.54	10.41	10.10	9.13	8.65	7.97	8.49	9.50	11.86
Fixed	752.33	717.41	669.67	607.90	576.79	575.08	584.37	589.85	584.40	553.10
Other	39.33	38.17	37.90	35.57	43.50	39.27	32.84	30.77	29.03	25.95
Total Assets	849.20	790.82	738.88	720.96	708.70	693.63	678.59	667.93	652.59	606.52
Liabilities:										
Current	101.70	94.99	53.66	50.17	50.22	49.07	46.88	48.26	45.05	41.54
Bonds	317.54	277.54	277.54	277.54	277.54	277.54	277.54	277.54	277.54	277.54
Other	40.68	39.64	39.97	39.99	40.63	41.39	41.05	39.70	38.25	33.71
Preferred Stock	63.63	63.63	63.63	63.63	63.63	63.63	63.63	63.63	63.63	63.63
Common Stock	231.26	231.06	230.88	230.73	230.61	191.98	191.74	191.62	191.60	191.60
Surplus	94.39	83.96	73.20	58.90	46.07	70.02	57.75	47.18	36.52	28.50
Total Liabilities	849.20	790.82	738.88	720.96	708.70	693.63	678.59	667.93	652.59	606.52

EXHIBIT 2

Income Data (millions)

MIDWESTERN ELECTRIC POWER

	19x9	19x8	19x7	19x6	19x5	19x4	19x3	19x2	19x1	19x0
Sales	234.22	217.06	202.65	192.76	183.44	173.61	163.91	155.43	144.51	139.74
Operating Expense	115.20	105.83	95.30	88.78	83.06	79.56	74.52	71.72	68.23	67.13
Depreciation	26.84	24.49	24.20	23.55	22.98	22.53	22.19	21.08	17.83	16.44
Operating Income	92.18	86.74	83.15	80.43	77.40	71.52	67.20	62.63	58.45	56.17
Other Income	4.44	4.34	4.51	5.00	5.15	4.75	4.12	3.42	3.05	2.68
Earnings Before Interest & Taxes	96.62	91.08	87.66	85.43	82.55	76.27	71.32	66.05	61.50	58.85
Interest	11.43	10.75	9.76	9.77	9.76	9.76	9.90	9.87	9.17	8.34
Interest Charged to Construction	(2.78)	(4.36)	(3.87)	(1.17)	(.36)	(.20)	(.23)	(1.54)	(2.16)	(2.39)
Earnings Before Taxes	87.97	84.69	81.77	76.83	73.15	66.71	61.65	57.72	54.49	52.90
Taxes	36.57	34.99	31.61	30.44	29.14	27.14	25.51	23.05	24.04	23.32
Earnings After Taxes	51.40	49.70	50.16	46.39	44.01	39.57	36.14	34.67	30.45	29.58
Preferred Dividends	2.75	2.75	2.75	2.75	2.75	2.75	2.75	2.75	2.75	2.75
Common Earnings	48.65	46.95	47.41	43.64	41.26	36.82	33.39	31.92	27.70	26.83
Common Dividends	38.54	36.45	33.34	30.76	27.15	24.95	23.00	21.08	19.67	18.90
No. of Common Shares	25.7	25.7	25.7	25.6	25.6	25.6	25.6	25.5	25.5	25.5

EXHIBIT 3

Per Share Data

MIDWESTERN ELECTRIC POWER

	19x9	19x8	19x7	19x6	19x5	19x4	19x3	19x2	19x1	19x0
Sales	9.11	8.45	7.89	7.53	7.17	6.78	6.40	6.10	5.67	5.48
Operating Expense	4.48	4.12	3.71	3.47	3.25	3.11	2.91	2.81	2.68	2.64
Depreciation	1.04	.95	.94	.92	.90	.88	.87	.83	.70	.64
Operating Income	3.59	3.38	3.24	3.14	3.02	2.79	2.63	2.46	2.29	2.20
Other Income	.17	.16	.17	.20	.20	.19	.16	.13	.12	.11
Earnings Before Interest & Taxes	3.76	3.54	3.41	3.34	3.22	2.98	2.79	2.59	2.41	2.31
Interest	.45	.41	.38	.39	.37	.38	.39	.39	.35	.33
Interest Charged to Construction	(.11)	(.17)	(.15)	(.05)	(.01)	(.01)	(.01)	(.06)	(.08)	(.09)
Earnings Before Taxes	3.42	3.30	3.18	3.00	2.86	2.61	2.41	2.26	2.14	2.07
Taxes	1.42	1.36	1.23	1.19	1.14	1.06	1.00	.90	.94	.91
Earnings After Taxes	2.00	1.94	1.95	1.81	1.72	1.55	1.41	1.36	1.20	1.16
Preferred Dividends	.11	.11	.11	.11	.11	.11	.11	.11	.11	.11
Common Earnings	1.89	1.83	1.84	1.70	1.61	1.44	1.30	1.25	1.09	1.05
Common Dividends	1.50	1.42	1.30	1.20	1.06	.97	.90	.83	.77	.74

EXHIBIT 4

Index Values per Share

MIDWESTERN ELECTRIC POWER

	19x0	19x1	19x2	19x3	19x4	19x5	19x6	19x7	19x8	19x9
Total Assets	1.00	1.08	1.10	1.11	1.14	1.16	1.18	1.21	1.29	1.39
Sales	1.00	1.03	1.11	1.17	1.24	1.31	1.37	1.44	1.54	1.66
Operating Expense	1.00	1.02	1.07	1.11	1.18	1.23	1.32	1.41	1.56	1.70
Depreciation	1.00	1.08	1.28	1.34	1.37	1.39	1.43	1.46	1.48	1.62
Operating Income	1.00	1.04	1.12	1.19	1.27	1.37	1.43	1.47	1.53	1.63
Earnings Before Interest & Taxes	1.00	1.05	1.12	1.21	1.29	1.40	1.45	1.48	1.54	1.63
Interest	1.00	1.10	1.18	1.18	1.17	1.17	1.17	1.16	1.28	1.36
Earnings Before Taxes	1.00	1.03	1.09	1.16	1.26	1.38	1.45	1.53	1.59	1.65
Taxes	1.00	1.03	.99	1.09	1.16	1.24	1.30	1.34	1.49	1.56
Earnings After Taxes	1.00	1.03	1.17	1.22	1.33	1.48	1.56	1.68	1.67	1.72
Common Earnings	1.00	1.03	1.19	1.24	1.37	1.53	1.62	1.75	1.74	1.80
Common Dividends	1.00	1.04	1.12	1.21	1.31	1.43	1.62	1.75	1.91	2.02
No. of Common Shares	1.00	1.00	1.00	1.00	1.00	1.00	1.00	1.01	1.01	1.01

EXHIBIT 5

<u>Selected Data</u>

MIDWESTERN ELECTRIC POWER

	19x9	19x8	19x7	19x6	19x5	19x4	19x3	19x2	19x1	19x0
Return on Sales (%)	20.8	21.6	23.4	22.6	22.5	21.2	20.4	20.5	19.2	19.2
Return on Assets (%)	6.1	6.3	6.8	6.4	6.2	5.7	5.3	5.2	4.7	4.9
Return on Equity (%)	14.9	14.9	15.6	15.1	14.9	14.1	13.4	13.4	12.1	12.2
Capital Turnover	.28	.27	.27	.27	.26	.25	.24	.23	.22	.23
Average Collection Period (days)	25	24	25	23	21	22	22	25	22	21
Interest Coverage	8.70	8.88	9.38	8.68	8.49	7.83	7.23	6.85	6.94	7.34
Prior Charge Coverage	5.94	5.95	6.08	5.75	5.51	5.08	4.71	4.46	4.40	4.49
Total Debt to Equity	1.41	1.31	1.22	1.27	1.33	1.40	1.46	1.53	1.58	1.47
Preferred to Equity	.19	.20	.21	.22	.23	.24	.25	.27	.28	.29
Tax Rate (%)	41.6	41.3	38.7	39.6	39.8	40.7	41.4	39.9	44.1	44.1
Book Value Per Share	12.67	12.26	11.83	11.31	10.81	10.23	9.75	9.36	8.95	8.63
Dividend Payout (%)	79.2	77.6	70.3	70.5	65.8	67.8	68.9	66.0	71.0	70.4
Debt Leverage (dollars per share)	.93	.84	.82	.80	.78	.71	.65	.62	.54	.50
Preferred Leverage (dollars per share)	.06	.06	.07	.07	.07	.05	.05	.04	.02	.03
Relative Debt Leverage (%)	49.1	45.9	44.3	46.8	48.3	49.5	50.1	49.4	50.1	47.9
Relative Preferred Leverage (%)	3.0	3.3	4.0	4.1	4.1	3.8	3.5	3.2	2.2	2.6

EXHIBIT 6

Per Share Data

MIDWESTERN ELECTRIC POWER

	19x9	19x8	19x7	19x6	19x5	19x4	19x3	19x2	19x1	19x0
Price:										
High	30.50	30.50	29.38	30.00	32.88	30.38	26.50	24.63	26.13	19.38
Low	21.63	25.12	24.13	23.13	27.88	24.25	23.13	19.00	18.00	14.75
Average	26.07	27.81	26.76	26.56	30.38	27.31	24.81	21.81	22.06	17.06
Price-Earnings Ratio:										
High	16.1	16.7	15.9	17.6	20.4	21.1	20.3	19.7	24.0	18.4
Low	11.4	13.7	13.1	13.6	17.3	16.9	17.7	15.2	16.6	14.0
Average	13.7	15.2	14.5	15.6	18.8	19.0	19.0	17.4	20.3	16.2
Market-Book Value:										
High	2.41	2.49	2.49	2.65	3.04	2.97	2.72	2.63	2.92	2.24
Low	1.71	2.05	2.04	2.04	2.58	2.37	2.37	2.03	2.01	1.71
Average	2.06	2.27	2.26	2.35	2.81	2.67	2.55	2.33	2.47	1.98

EXHIBIT 7

Selected Industry Data per Share

MIDWESTERN ELECTRIC POWER

	19x9	19x8	19x7	19x6	19x5	19x4	19x3	19x2	19x1	19x0
Operating Revenues	24.36	23.03	21.67	20.60	19.15	18.12	17.40	16.72	15.75	15.10
Depreciation	2.64	2.50	2.37	2.23	2.10	1.98	1.91	1.79	1.66	1.55
Taxes	1.99	2.15	1.99	2.05	1.96	1.97	1.93	1.92	1.89	1.89
Net Operating Income	5.29	4.98	4.83	4.51	4.21	3.92	3.76	3.56	3.25	3.05
Common Earnings	3.38	3.25	3.28	3.09	2.90	2.65	2.45	2.34	2.11	2.01
Common Dividends	2.33	2.27	2.16	2.04	1.90	1.74	1.63	1.52	1.44	1.37
Price Index										
High	53.0	53.9	55.0	57.8	60.9	58.6	53.5	50.4	52.9	39.4
Low	41.2	49.3	46.2	45.6	57.3	52.1	48.7	39.1	39.5	32.9
Average	47.1	51.6	50.6	51.7	59.1	55.4	51.1	44.8	46.2	36.2
Price-Earnings Ratio:										
High	15.7	16.5	16.8	18.7	21.0	22.1	21.8	21.5	25.1	19.6
Low	12.2	15.2	14.7	14.8	19.7	19.7	19.9	16.7	18.7	16.4
Average	14.0	15.8	15.6	16.8	20.4	20.9	20.9	19.1	21.4	18.0

Source: *S & P Analyst's Handbook.*

Case 2:   Profit Trend

Southcentral Natural Gas

There are many unexpected reasons for the varied performance; the important thing is that performance trends do change and investment values with them. (Benjamin Graham.)

Southcentral Natural Gas (SNG) was incorporated in Delaware in 1928. Acquisition of several natural gas and fuel oil firms in the mid 1930s firmly established the company as the major distributor of natural gas in the southern states of Texas, Oklahoma, Arkansas, and Louisiana. In the late 1950s and early 1960s, SNG acquired firms in other lines of business, namely, air conditioning, chemicals, pipelines, finance, and fiberglass. Subsequently, firms producing engines and compressors were acquired. No acquisitions have been made within the past several years, however, and SNG seems to have abandoned, at least temporarily, its aggressive acquisition and diversification programs. The above nonutility operations have accounted for approximately 50 percent of SNG's net income in recent years.

The company holds mineral leases on approximately 400,000 acres of land of which 100,000 acres are currently producing. Natural gas reserves of the company are estimated at 8 trillion cubic feet; the American Gas Association estimates total U. S. reserves at about 300 trillion cubic feet. SNG maintains over 18,000 miles of transmission lines and plans to build a new 230-mile pipeline through its main producing areas at a cost in excess of $100 million. The latter project is to begin next year and is to be completed within 3 years. Additional capital outlays of nearly $100 million are also planned for the same period. Thus investment expenditures for the next 3 years compare favorably with the $35 million and $41 million spent during 19x8 and 19x9 respectively. The company recently floated a $40 million bond issue at $8\frac{7}{8}$ percent to finance part of the planned investments.

Natural gas pipeline and distributing is the sixth largest industry in the nation. Industry revenues have grown at a 6.3 percent annual rate and net income at a 5.6 percent annual rate during the past decade. However, sales growth for the industry is expected to decline in the future. Although sales are growing this year at an approximate 8.3 percent rate, the American Gas

Association has projected a 5.2 percent rate for the next decade. Future improvements in the growth rate can come from new family formations, industrial conversions to natural gas from other fuels, and increased use of gas turbines for heating, cooling, and electricity. The government's recent emphasis on ecology should increase industrial conversions since natural gas is essentially a nonpolluting fuel.

Natural gas provides 37 percent of the nation's total energy consumption and this proportion is expected to grow, although gas shortages could be a limiting factor. There is currently a severe shortage of natural gas in the northeast and midwest sections of the U. S. and the reduced growth rate of sales reflects predicted gas shortages. In 19x9, the industry used 2.5 times as much gas as was discovered. While the current reserve to production ratio is a comfortable 13:1, it is expected to drop to 10:1 in the near future. The Federal Power Commission has established a 12:1 ratio as a minimum. Well drilling this year was down by 40 percent when compared with the recent past. To encourage more well drilling, the Federal Power Commission has been expediting rate increase settlements, liberalizing depreciation allowances, and adopting a more flexible attitude toward problems of individual firms.

SNG's utility rates are under state jurisdiction in all states in which it operates except in Texas where rates are initially negotiated with cities. Rate increase applications are pending in Texas and Oklahoma; if approved, these increases will add about 1 million dollars to annual revenues.

Preliminary data reveal that operating revenues for the current year should increase 7.3 percent from 19x9. Net income per share, however, is expected to decline by 1.8 percent to $2.51 from $2.56 last year. The company recently announced that the regular quarterly dividend would be reduced from $42\frac{1}{2}$ cents to $32\frac{1}{2}$ cents beginning in the fourth quarter of the current year.

Current share price is $27.

QUESTIONS

1. (a) Compute the average annual rates of growth over the past decade for each of the following items for SNG: (1) sales per share, (2) operating income per share, (3) common earnings per share, and (4) common dividends per share.
(b) Identify the factors that contributed to the large differentials in the above growth rates.

2. (a) How can you explain the general increase in the rate of return on sales from 19x0 to 19x5, whereas the rate of return on assets declined steadily? (See Exhibit 5 for rates of return.)
(b) Evaluate SNG's sources of earnings from 19x0 to the present.

3. (a) How much would the proposed rate increases add to SNG's current earnings per share?

(b) Can the planned capital expenditures of $200 million over the next few years be justified from the standpoint of SNG's management? From the standpoint of the company's stockholders?

4. Estimate SNG's earnings per share over each of the next 5 years. Give high, low, and most probable figures for each year.

5. What factors other than those discussed above have significant implications for SNG's share price in the short run? In the long run?

EXHIBIT 1

SOUTHCENTRAL NATURAL GAS

Balance Sheet Data (millions)

	19x9	19x8	19x7	19x6	19x5	19x4	19x3	19x2	19x1	19x0
Assets:										
Current	83.1	74.2	68.6	77.3	55.8	52.2	47.6	36.3	39.4	37.7
Cash Items	7.4	7.1	6.6	6.6	7.7	6.9	5.0	4.1	5.7	3.7
Receivables	47.8	42.1	37.3	51.4	31.6	29.8	27.7	18.1	18.9	21.1
Inventory	27.9	25.0	24.7	19.3	16.5	15.5	14.9	14.1	14.8	12.9
Other	18.3	18.2	18.7	14.3	12.7	10.0	7.5	6.9	8.5	6.1
Fixed	360.3	334.9	314.2	288.8	271.0	240.9	214.8	190.6	180.1	154.7
Total Assets	461.70	427.3	401.5	380.4	339.5	303.1	269.9	233.8	228.0	198.5
Liabilities:										
Current	87.8	78.3	70.5	58.7	54.8	59.2	30.4	41.0	39.2	35.6
Bonds	174.9	163.2	161.1	167.4	141.7	114.0	115.6	72.2	71.5	64.4
Other	37.7	32.0	25.2	21.8	20.2	19.5	18.7	18.1	16.2	13.4
Preferred Stock	2.6	2.8	2.8	3.2	3.2	3.2	3.2	3.2	15.7	17.8
Common Stock	27.1	27.1	27.1	27.1	27.1	27.1	27.1	27.1	25.9	24.1
Surplus	131.6	123.9	114.8	102.2	92.5	80.1	74.9	72.2	59.5	43.2
Total Liabilities	461.7	427.3	401.5	380.4	339.5	303.1	269.9	233.8	228.0	198.5

EXHIBIT 2

Income Data (millions)

SOUTHCENTRAL NATURAL GAS

	19x9	19x8	19x7	19x6	19x5	19x4	19x3	19x2	19x1	19x0
Sales	219.2	202.3	171.6	163.7	155.7	153.9	146.6	135.5	128.1	114.4
Operating Expense	155.9	141.2	117.4	108.9	105.9	102.0	99.1	93.6	85.0	77.2
Depreciation	15.2	14.4	10.0	10.1	9.5	9.3	8.5	7.6	7.4	5.8
Operating Income	48.1	46.7	44.2	44.7	40.3	42.6	39.0	34.3	35.7	31.4
Other Income	1.7	1.3	2.1	1.3	1.5	.7	1.0	.4	.5	.5
Earnings Before Interest & Taxes	49.8	48.0	46.3	46.0	41.8	43.3	40.0	34.7	36.2	31.9
Interest	13.0	11.0	10.0	8.9	7.1	6.1	5.4	4.7	4.5	3.9
Interest Charged to Construction	(.6)	(.5)	(.5)	(.6)	(1.0)	(.2)	(.2)	0	(.1)	(.2)
Earnings Before Taxes	37.4	37.5	36.8	37.7	35.7	37.4	34.8	30.0	31.8	28.2
Taxes	11.5	11.1	7.4	9.7	10.4	13.3	12.7	11.5	12.9	11.8
Earnings After Taxes	25.9	26.4	29.4	28.0	25.3	24.1	22.1	18.5	18.9	16.4
Preferred Dividends	.1	.1	.1	.1	.1	.1	.1	.3	.7	.9
Common Earnings	25.8	26.3	29.3	27.9	25.2	24.0	22.0	18.2	18.2	15.5
Common Dividends	17.1	17.1	16.2	15.2	13.8	12.2	10.5	10.7	10.6	9.6
No. of Common Shares	10.1	10.1	10.1	10.2	10.2	10.5	10.5	11.2	10.7	9.9

EXHIBIT 3

Per Share Income Data

SOUTHCENTRAL NATURAL GAS

	19x9	19x8	19x7	19x6	19x5	19x4	19x3	19x2	19x1	19x0
Sales	21.70	20.03	16.99	16.05	15.26	14.66	13.96	12.10	11.97	11.55
Operating Expense	15.44	13.98	11.62	10.68	10.38	9.71	9.44	8.36	7.94	7.80
Depreciation	1.50	1.43	.99	.99	.93	.89	.81	.68	.69	.58
Operating Income	4.76	4.62	4.38	4.38	3.95	4.06	3.71	3.06	3.34	3.17
Other Income	.17	.13	.20	.13	.15	.06	.10	.04	.04	.05
Earnings Before Interest & Taxes	4.93	4.75	4.58	4.51	4.10	4.12	3.81	3.10	3.38	3.22
Interest	1.29	1.09	.99	.87	.70	.58	.52	.42	.42	.39
Interest Charged to Construction	(.06)	(.05)	(.05)	(.06)	(.10)	(.02)	(.02)	0	(.01)	(.02)
Earnings Before Taxes	3.70	3.71	3.64	3.70	3.50	3.56	3.31	2.68	2.97	2.85
Taxes	1.14	1.10	.73	.95	1.02	1.26	1.21	1.03	1.20	1.19
Earnings After Taxes	2.56	2.61	2.91	2.75	2.48	2.30	2.10	1.65	1.77	1.66
Preferred Dividends	.01	.01	.01	.01	.01	.01	.01	.03	.07	.10
Common Earnings	2.55	2.60	2.90	2.74	2.47	2.29	2.09	1.62	1.70	1.56
Common Dividends	1.69	1.69	1.60	1.49	1.35	1.16	1.00	.96	.99	.97

EXHIBIT 4

Index Values per Share

SOUTHCENTRAL NATURAL GAS

	19x9	19x8	19x7	19x6	19x5	19x4	19x3	19x2	19x1	19x0
Total Assets	2.28	2.11	1.98	1.86	1.66	1.44	1.28	1.04	1.06	1.00
Sales	1.88	1.73	1.47	1.39	1.32	1.27	1.21	1.05	1.04	1.00
Operating Expense	1.98	1.79	1.49	1.37	1.33	1.24	1.21	1.07	1.02	1.00
Depreciation	2.59	2.46	1.71	1.71	1.60	1.53	1.40	1.17	1.19	1.00
Operating Income	1.50	1.46	1.38	1.38	1.25	1.28	1.17	.97	1.05	1.00
Earnings Before Interest & Taxes	1.53	1.47	1.42	1.40	1.27	1.28	1.18	.96	1.05	1.00
Interest	3.28	2.78	2.52	2.22	1.77	1.48	1.31	1.07	1.07	1.00
Earnings Before Taxes	1.30	1.30	1.28	1.30	1.23	1.25	1.16	.94	1.04	1.00
Taxes	.96	.93	.62	.80	.86	1.07	1.02	.86	1.01	1.00
Earnings After Taxes	1.54	1.57	1.75	1.66	1.49	1.39	1.27	.99	1.07	1.00
Common Earnings	1.64	1.67	1.86	1.75	1.58	1.47	1.34	1.04	1.09	1.00
Common Dividends	1.75	1.75	1.66	1.54	1.40	1.20	1.03	.99	1.02	1.00
No. of Common Shares	1.02	1.02	1.02	1.03	1.03	1.06	1.06	1.13	1.08	1.00

SOUTHCENTRAL NATURAL GAS

EXHIBIT 5

Selected Data

	19x9	19x8	19x7	19x6	19x5	19x4	19x3	19x2	19x1	19x0
Return on Sales (%)	11.8	13.0	17.1	17.0	16.2	15.6	15.0	13.4	14.2	13.5
Return on Assets (%)	5.6	6.2	7.3	7.4	7.5	8.0	8.2	7.9	8.3	8.3
Return on Equity (%)	16.3	17.4	20.6	21.6	21.1	22.4	21.6	18.3	21.3	23.0
Capital Turnover	.48	.47	.43	.43	.46	.51	.54	.58	.56	.58
Average Collection Period (days)	78	75	78	113	73	70	68	48	53	66
Interest Coverage	3.88	4.41	4.68	5.24	6.03	7.13	7.44	7.38	8.07	8.23
Prior Charge Coverage	3.61	4.09	4.31	4.82	5.80	6.23	6.11	5.78	5.78	5.18
Total Debt to Equity	1.89	1.81	1.81	1.92	1.81	1.80	1.61	1.32	1.49	1.68
Preferred to Equity	.02	.02	.02	.02	.03	.03	.03	.03	.18	.26
Tax Rate (%)	30.8	29.6	20.1	25.7	29.1	35.4	36.5	38.4	40.4	41.8
Book Value Per Share	15.71	14.95	14.05	12.68	11.72	10.21	9.71	8.87	7.98	6.80
Dividend Payout (%)	66.3	65.0	55.3	54.5	54.8	50.8	47.7	58.8	58.2	61.9
Debt Leverage (dollars per share)	1.33	1.37	1.55	1.53	1.36	1.31	1.15	.81	.87	.84
Preferred Leverage (dollars per share)	.01	.01	.02	.02	.02	.02	.02	0	.07	.08
Relative Debt Leverage (%)	52.1	52.8	53.5	56.1	55.1	57.5	54.9	50.1	51.1	53.7
Relative Preferred Leverage (%)	.4	.5	.5	.7	.7	.8	.9	0	4.3	4.9

EXHIBIT 6

Per Share Data

SOUTHCENTRAL NATURAL GAS

	19x9	19x8	19x7	19x6	19x5	19x4	19x3	19x2	19x1	19x0
Price:										
High	36.88	39.88	43.00	46.38	48.13	41.38	37.13	43.00	44.88	39.00
Low	26.00	37.00	33.00	33.38	40.00	31.38	28.00	24.13	35.00	26.25
Average	31.44	38.44	38.00	39.88	44.06	36.38	32.56	33.56	39.94	32.62
Price-Earnings:										
High	14.4	15.3	14.8	17.0	19.5	18.1	17.7	26.5	26.4	25.0
Low	10.1	14.2	11.4	12.2	16.2	13.7	13.4	14.8	20.6	16.8
Average	12.2	14.7	13.1	14.6	17.8	15.9	15.5	20.6	23.5	20.9
Market-Book Value:										
High	2.35	2.67	3.06	3.66	4.10	4.05	3.83	4.86	5.63	5.72
Low	1.65	2.47	2.35	2.63	3.41	3.07	2.89	2.71	4.39	3.86
Average	2.00	2.57	2.70	3.14	3.76	3.56	3.36	3.78	5.00	4.79

EXHIBIT 7

Selected Natural Gas Distributors Industry Data per Share

SOUTHCENTRAL NATURAL GAS

	19x9	19x8	19x7	19x6	19x5	19x4	19x3	19x2	19x1	19x0
Sales	60.45	56.62	53.37	51.72	48.92	46.12	44.25	42.51	39.76	38.10
Depreciation	4.85	4.58	4.30	4.06	3.89	3.59	3.41	3.18	3.04	2.87
Income Taxes	3.50	3.42	3.35	3.28	3.67	3.60	3.47	3.53	3.40	3.40
Common Earnings	5.59	5.33	5.31	5.05	4.85	4.46	3.63	3.76	3.46	3.52
Common Dividends	3.63	3.57	3.40	3.17	2.95	2.81	2.68	2.52	2.47	2.29
Price Index:										
High	71.78	73.49	66.76	74.95	81.32	77.57	73.70	74.02	75.60	57.02
Low	54.35	61.01	60.48	59.72	73.73	69.48	67.66	59.87	56.80	46.84
Average	63.07	67.25	63.62	67.34	77.53	73.53	70.68	66.95	66.20	51.93
Price-Earnings Ratio:										
High	12.8	13.8	12.6	14.8	16.8	17.4	20.3	19.7	21.8	16.2
Low	9.7	11.4	11.4	11.8	15.2	15.6	18.6	15.9	16.4	13.3
Average	11.2	12.6	12.0	13.3	16.0	16.5	19.4	17.8	19.1	14.7

Source: S & P Analyst's Handbook.

Case 3: Leverage

Central Oil and Gas

Earnings can increase while productivity decreases—for awhile.

Central Oil and Gas (COG) was organized in 1887, and within several years it had become one of the largest producers of crude oil in the U. S. Beginning in 1911 the company embarked on an aggressive acquisition policy involving both horizontal and vertical integration. During the next 50 years subsidiaries were acquired on a planned and orderly basis. However, the company has stressed internal growth during the past decade.

COG is currently a medium-sized integrated oil company with domestic refining capacity in excess of 250,000 barrels of oil per day. In addition, the company has refineries in foreign countries with a total capacity of about 20 percent of its U. S. volume. Forty percent of its crude oil supply is derived at present from the U. S. and Canada, and 60 percent from Libya. The Libyan government has at times been a problem inasmuch as the tax imposed per barrel is subject to frequent negotiation. As one step to counter the foreign risk, COG has taken a strong position in Alaskan crude oil development. The company's current output in this development is 40,000 barrels daily, and steady increases are expected over the next several years.

The company has 1.7 million acres in land-lease holding in the U. S. and Canada, and foreign holdings of 40.5 million acres include extensive land rights in Ireland, Libya, Thailand, and England. The company's North American resources of crude and natural gas liquids are currently estimated at 924 million barrels, up from 911 million barrels last year. Its Libyan crude reserves are estimated at about 1 billion barrels. Net production of crude oil by the company has been averaging 165,000 barrels daily in the U. S. and Canada and 260,000 daily in Libya. Its Libyan crude is shipped to the U. S. by tanker. COG holds a 28 percent interest in a refinery in Spain and a 40 percent interest in a refinery in Germany with daily capacity of 80,000 and 72,000 barrels, respectively. In addition, a $100 million petroleum chemical refinery located in Germany is wholly owned.

The oil industry is characterized by intense competition both in the search for crude reserves and in the marketing of gasoline and gasoline products. The federal government has subsidized the oil industry for many years through a very favorable depletion allowance. This allowance was recently reduced from $27\frac{1}{2}$ percent to 23 percent by Congress. The reduction in the allowance has apparently satisfied, temporarily at least, the majority of those persons who believed that the oil industry was subsidized at an unnecessarily high level.

Current U. S. oil demand is 14.8 million barrels daily, and demand is expected to reach 23 million barrels daily over the next decade. Total demand in the free world is expected to increase from 40 to 80 million barrels daily. The breakdown of the major sources of energy in the U. S. is as follows: oil (44 percent), natural gas (32 percent), coal (20 percent), hydroelectric power (4 percent), and nuclear power (1 percent). Oil is expected to remain the dominant energy source for years to come due to its greater mobility and ease of handling, even though natural gas has the advantage of emitting less pollution.

Crude oil prices are relatively stable, but gasoline prices at times are very volatile. Gasoline price wars develop when supplies exceed demand by a substantial amount. A retail price war of long duration can significantly reduce company profits. COG markets its gasoline products through some 3,600 service stations located primarily in the central U. S. Refined product sales in 19x9 averaged 288,000 barrels per day, of which 16 percent were in European markets. Distribution in European markets, the fastest growing segment of COG's retail operations, was up approximately 40 percent from the previous year.

Gross revenue for the current year is expected to approach $1 billion, up 8 percent from 19x9, but earnings per share are estimated at $2.80, down from the $2.99 for last year. Operating costs and taxes are expected to increase more rapidly than sales this year, resulting in the first earnings reduction in several years.

As of December 31, 19x9, COG had outstanding $115 million in short-term notes; in addition, revolving credit agreements provided for additional borrowings of up to $185 million. Early this year COG marketed $100 million $8\frac{1}{2}$ percent sinking fund debentures, the proceeds of which were used to repay short-term bank notes. COG's present long-term debt includes $7.7 million of $4\frac{1}{2}$ percent debentures which are convertible into common at $31.50 per share.

Capital expenditures in the current year are expected to decline by $35 million from the $290 million in 19x9.

Share price of the company's common stock has recently been in the upper 30s.

QUESTIONS

1. (a) Briefly evaluate COG's operations and financial performance over the past decade.

(b) Are there any irregularities on the company's income statement? Explain.

(c) How can you explain the fact that the company's earnings before interest and taxes have increased much faster than its sales?

2. (a) What has been the main source of COG's earnings per share growth since 19x5?

(b) Would you consider the source in 2(a) to be temporary or permanent? Why?

3. Is COG faced with any special business risks? Explain.

4. (a) How would you expect COG's future stock price performance to compare with that of industry? Discuss.

(b) How would you expect COG's future $\overline{HPR}$s and HPR variances to compare with the $\overline{HPR}$s and HPR variances of the company during the past decade? Discuss.

EXHIBIT 1

Balance Sheet Data (millions)

CENTRAL OIL AND GAS

	19x9	19x8	19x7	19x6	19x5	19x4	19x3	19x2	19x1	19x0
Assets:										
Current										
Cash Items	331.4	318.5	247.2	238.5	204.7	172.1	162.7	155.8	120.1	123.4
Receivables	130.7	128.0	88.2	92.1	81.6	44.6	53.8	46.4	45.2	53.6
Inventory	130.1	121.8	98.8	88.2	72.0	68.8	56.5	64.0	44.0	40.4
Other	70.6	68.7	60.2	58.2	51.1	58.7	52.4	45.4	30.9	29.4
	74.1	82.5	69.3	91.5	104.4	65.4	49.8	32.8	22.8	19.7
Fixed	894.1	750.0	660.8	541.5	476.7	447.6	430.3	422.2	347.2	326.9
Total Assets	1299.6	1151.0	977.3	871.5	785.8	685.1	642.8	610.8	490.1	470.0
Liabilities:										
Current	264.2	217.0	222.5	178.4	104.3	66.3	57.5	60.5	43.3	44.1
Bonds	294.9	241.9	155.9	133.3	142.9	100.4	93.7	94.4	5.1	6.1
Other	36.6	34.8	2.9	-0-	8.0	4.9	10.1	-0-	-0-	-0-
Common Stock	176.7	171.2	151.7	152.8	153.6	154.6	153.2	136.8	125.0	107.0
Surplus	527.2	486.1	444.3	407.0	377.0	358.9	328.3	319.1	316.7	312.8
Total Liabilities	1299.6	1151.0	977.3	871.5	785.8	685.1	642.8	610.8	490.1	470.0

EXHIBIT 2

Income Data (millions)

CENTRAL OIL AND GAS

	19x9	19x8	19x7	19x6	19x5	19x4	19x3	19x2	19x1	19x0
Sales	924.3	797.4	695.6	621.8	549.4	496.4	466.2	416.7	352.1	352.0
Costs of Goods Sold	458.5	374.3	323.8	262.7	237.6	222.3	205.9	181.3	135.2	138.7
Depreciation	62.2	59.5	46.4	48.0	42.3	45.4	38.2	34.3	30.7	32.1
Operating Expense	206.5	198.3	173.3	163.6	152.5	141.0	145.6	139.8	127.3	121.2
Operating Income	197.1	165.3	152.1	147.5	117.0	87.7	76.5	61.3	58.9	60.0
Other Income	11.3	15.7	10.3	7.7	9.7	4.7	4.8	2.7	4.3	5.7
Other Expense	15.8	14.1	14.9	16.8	23.0	24.8	27.0	25.0	22.8	25.2
Earnings Before Interest & Taxes	192.6	166.9	147.5	138.4	103.7	67.6	54.3	39.0	40.4	40.5
Interest	19.0	11.6	8.8	7.5	6.3	4.4	4.2	3.3	.9	1.0
Earnings Before Taxes	173.6	155.3	138.7	130.9	97.4	63.2	50.1	35.7	39.5	39.5
Taxes	84.2	72.1	64.9	62.1	37.3	2.8	1.1	(2.2)	.6	.3
Common Earnings	89.4	83.2	73.8	68.8	60.1	60.4	49.0	37.9	38.9	39.2
Common Dividends	47.8	41.8	36.6	33.1	31.9	29.8	24.9	23.1	22.9	22.0
No. of Common Shares	29.9	29.6	29.3	29.3	29.5	29.8	29.7	29.6	29.7	29.3

EXHIBIT 3

Per Share Income Data

CENTRAL OIL AND GAS

	19x9	19x8	19x7	19x6	19x5	19x4	19x3	19x2	19x1	19x0
Sales	30.91	26.94	23.74	21.22	18.62	16.66	15.70	14.08	11.86	12.01
Cost of Goods Sold	15.33	12.65	11.05	8.97	8.05	7.46	6.93	6.13	4.55	4.73
Depreciation	2.08	2.01	1.58	1.64	1.43	1.52	1.29	1.16	1.03	1.10
Operating Expense	6.91	6.70	5.92	5.58	5.17	4.74	4.90	4.72	4.30	4.13
Operating Income	6.59	5.58	5.19	5.03	3.97	2.94	2.58	2.07	1.98	2.05
Other Income	.38	.54	.35	.26	.33	.16	.16	.09	.15	.19
Other Expense	.53	.48	.51	.57	.78	.83	.91	.84	.77	.86
Earnings Before Interest & Taxes	6.44	5.64	5.03	4.72	3.52	2.27	1.83	1.32	1.36	1.38
Interest	.63	.39	.30	.25	.22	.15	.14	.11	.03	.03
Earnings Before Taxes	5.81	5.25	4.73	4.47	3.30	2.12	1.69	1.21	1.33	1.35
Taxes	2.82	2.44	2.21	2.12	1.26	.09	.04	(.07)	.02	.01
Common Earnings	2.99	2.81	2.52	2.35	2.04	2.03	1.65	1.28	1.31	1.34
Common Dividends	1.60	1.41	1.25	1.13	1.08	1.00	.84	.78	.77	.75

EXHIBIT 4

Index Values per Share

CENTRAL OIL AND GAS

	19x0	19x1	19x2	19x3	19x4	19x5	19x6	19x7	19x8	19x9
Total Assets	1.00	1.03	1.29	1.35	1.43	1.66	1.85	2.08	2.42	2.71
Sales	1.00	.99	1.17	1.31	1.39	1.55	1.77	1.98	2.24	2.57
Cost of Goods Sold	1.00	.96	1.29	1.46	1.58	1.70	1.89	2.33	2.67	3.24
Depreciation	1.00	.94	1.06	1.17	1.39	1.31	1.50	1.45	1.83	1.90
Operating Expense	1.00	1.04	1.14	1.19	1.14	1.25	1.35	1.43	1.62	1.67
Operating Income	1.00	.97	1.01	1.26	1.44	1.94	2.46	2.53	2.73	3.22
Other Income	1.00	.74	.47	.84	.84	1.74	1.37	1.84	2.79	2.00
Other Expense	1.00	.90	.98	1.06	.97	.91	.66	.59	.56	.62
Earnings Before Interest & Taxes	1.00	.98	.95	1.32	1.64	2.54	3.42	3.64	4.08	4.66
Interest	1.00	.89	3.27	4.14	4.33	6.26	7.50	8.80	11.48	18.62
Earnings Before Taxes	1.00	.99	.89	1.25	1.57	2.45	3.31	3.51	3.89	4.31
Taxes	1.00	1.97	(7.26)	3.62	9.18	123.49	207.00	216.33	237.90	275.03
Common Earnings	1.00	.98	.96	1.23	1.51	1.52	1.76	1.88	2.10	2.23
Common Dividends	1.00	1.03	1.04	1.12	1.33	1.44	1.50	1.66	1.88	2.13

EXHIBIT 5

Selected Data

CENTRAL OIL AND GAS

	19x9	19x8	19x7	19x6	19x5	19x4	19x3	19x2	19x1	19x0
Return on Sales (%)	9.7	10.4	10.6	11.1	10.9	12.2	10.5	9.1	11.0	11.1
Return on Assets (%)	6.9	7.2	7.6	7.9	7.6	8.8	7.6	6.2	7.9	8.3
Return on Equity (%)	12.7	12.7	12.4	12.3	11.3	11.8	10.2	8.3	8.8	9.3
Capital Turnover	.71	.69	.71	.71	.70	.73	.73	.68	.72	.75
Inventory Turnover	6.49	5.45	5.38	4.51	4.65	3.79	3.93	3.99	4.38	4.72
Average Collection Period (days)	51	55	51	51	47	50	44	55	45	41
Interest Coverage	10.1	14.4	16.8	18.5	16.5	15.4	12.9	11.8	44.9	40.5
Total Debt to Equity (%)	84.6	75.1	64.0	55.7	48.1	33.4	33.5	34.0	11.0	12.0
Tax Rate (%)	48.5	46.4	46.8	47.4	38.3	4.4	2.2	–	1.5	.8
Book Value Per Share	23.54	22.21	20.34	19.11	17.99	17.23	16.21	15.40	14.87	14.33
Dividend Payout (%)	53.5	50.2	49.6	48.1	53.1	49.3	50.8	60.9	58.9	56.1
Debt Leverage (dollars per share)	1.19	1.09	.89	.75	.57	.40	.31	.24	.10	.11
Relative Debt Leverage (%)	39.9	38.6	35.1	32.1	28.1	19.8	18.8	18.5	7.8	8.4

EXHIBIT 6

Per Share Data

CENTRAL OIL AND GAS

	19x9	19x8	19x7	19x6	19x5	19x4	19x3	19x2	19x1	19x0
Price:										
High	59.75	57.88	41.63	32.25	33.63	34.38	29.75	22.25	21.75	18.75
Low	31.13	40.63	28.75	24.50	26.63	27.88	21.75	17.63	17.38	14.25
Average	45.44	49.25	35.19	28.38	30.13	31.13	25.75	19.94	19.56	16.50
Price-Earnings:										
High	20.0	20.6	16.5	13.7	16.5	17.0	18.0	17.4	16.6	14.0
Low	10.4	14.5	11.4	10.4	13.1	13.8	13.2	13.8	13.3	10.6
Average	15.2	17.5	14.0	12.1	14.8	15.4	15.6	15.6	14.9	12.3
Market-Book Value:										
High	2.54	2.61	2.05	1.69	1.87	2.00	1.84	1.45	1.46	1.31
Low	1.32	1.83	1.41	1.28	1.48	1.62	1.34	1.15	1.17	.99
Average	1.93	2.22	1.73	1.49	1.68	1.81	1.59	1.30	1.32	1.15

EXHIBIT 7

Selected Oil (Integrated, Domestic) Industry Data per Share

CENTRAL OIL AND GAS

	19x9	19x8	19x7	19x6	19x5	19x4	19x3	19x2	19x1	19x0
Sales	107.22	100.62	99.27	90.91	82.16	72.72	69.90	64.91	61.19	59.64
Depreciation	10.07	9.23	9.19	8.69	8.10	7.12	7.07	6.70	6.25	6.20
Income Taxes	2.63	2.57	2.72	2.43	1.66	.95	1.25	.91	.80	1.03
Common Earnings	8.00	8.22	8.50	7.69	6.66	5.56	5.17	4.57	4.13	4.20
Common Dividends	3.73	3.82	3.41	3.16	2.87	2.57	2.28	2.08	1.90	1.91
Price Index:										
High	141.66	142.60	121.99	105.51	101.06	89.03	73.46	63.84	66.30	58.27
Low	86.48	103.75	97.84	90.57	86.33	71.38	58.13	49.66	56.21	45.55
Average	114.07	123.18	109.92	98.00	93.70	80.21	65.80	56.75	61.25	51.91
Price-Earnings Ratio:										
High	17.7	17.4	14.4	13.7	15.2	16.0	14.2	14.0	16.1	13.9
Low	10.8	12.6	11.5	11.8	13.0	12.9	11.2	10.9	13.6	10.9
Average	14.3	15.0	12.9	12.7	14.1	14.4	12.7	12.4	14.8	12.4
Book Value Per Share	81.98	78.82	73.67	67.49	64.11	61.94	59.13	57.45	55.37	52.27
Book Value – % Return	9.76	10.43	11.54	11.39	10.39	8.98	8.74	7.95	7.46	8.04

Source: *S & P Analyst's Handbook.*

Case 4: Equity Dilution

Specialized Metals, Inc.

*For years some managements have been using current earnings per share as an investment decision-making guide because it attracts investors . . . . In reality, earnings per share is a game with costly consequences that fools not only the investor, but also the management of many companies. (*The Wall Street Journal.*)*

Specialized Metals (SM) was incorporated in Delaware on November 20, 1929, and immediately became a subsidiary of a tin plate firm which had been incorporated in 1901. The two companies were merged in 1941 to form the present entity. Since the merger, numerous other firms have been acquired, principally through exchanges of common or convertible preferred stock. In early 19x7, the company embarked on a very ambitious policy of external growth, mostly in its primary product area of metal containers but also into the related area of glass containers. In addition, the company has diversified vertically within the past 2 years by acquiring firms in the pet food and vegetable packing areas. Early this year SM created a plastics division which has expected annual sales of approximately $2 million.

Three-fourths of the total value of SM's sales last year came from sales of metal containers (two-thirds of which were for nonfood products), one-tenth from sales of food packaging, and the remainder from sales of glass containers and pet foods.

The "age of mergers" was born in the latter half of the past decade. Fostered by accelerating inflation and great investor interest, new incorporations increased at the rate of over 200,000 per year. In addition, many "undiscovered" over-the-counter and American Stock Exchange equities were selling at very low price-earnings ratios. Prompted by the desire to maximize reported earnings per share, managers of firms with high price-earnings ratios discovered they could accomplish their objective much faster by absorbing other companies than by internal expansion. Demand for firms whose common stock was selling at low price-earnings ratios subsequently became so great that the prices of these stocks rose sharply. Competition even developed between parent companies for "takeover" candidates.

Although the "merger craze" has been dampened somewhat due to various reasons as well as restrictions imposed by the federal government, SM plans to continue its external growth and diversification plans. In addition to expansion in the U. S., the company is acquiring firms in foreign countries in an effort to increase sales and profits. Acquisitions have been made recently in England, Greece, and Italy.

Industry sales of packaging materials in the current year should reach $20.6 billion versus $19.5 billion in 19x9. The expected sales breakdown for this year is as follows: metal containers, 20 percent of total sales; paper and paperboard, 37 percent; and glass containers, 9 percent. A variety of other types of packaging will comprise the remainder of sales, with plastics amounting to only about 3 percent. Container sales over the next decade are expected to reach a level of $30 billion, with the greatest percentage gains probably in plastics.

The consumer still prefers the convenience of disposable containers, and plastics are favored over other conventional packaging materials because of their lighter weight, flexible nature, and resistance to breakage. However, the government's recent antipollution push has increased the sales of returnable glass containers and recycled metal containers. Thus all nonreturnable containers are facing greater competition due to the ecology issue.

SM has long been an able competitor because of its numerous innovative production, distribution, and marketing policies. The company settled recent wage contract negotiations early and got the jump on competitors who had to contend with strikes by unions. The company has also granted price reductions to buyers who have purchased either as much as 1 million cans per year or a complete line of its products. Although competitors often match SM's activities after a period of time, the company has been able to increase its share of the market in many instances in the past by its innovative policies.

The container industry is currently experiencing a profit margin squeeze. The recently settled wage agreements amounted to a 14 percent increase in wages for the current year and an additional increase of 30 percent over the succeeding 2 years. However, since modern production lines are highly mechanized, the efficiency of capital equipment moderates the effect of labor cost increases. Direct labor constitutes less than 30 percent of the total value of shipments.

SM's total common stock earnings after taxes will fall approximately 2.5 percent this year, and share earnings are expected to decline to $1.94 from $2.04 in 19x9. Part of the decline in earnings can be attributed to the company's expansion plans; short-run profitability is being sacrificed for diversity. Through diversification and expansion of other existing lines, the firm plans to reduce the relative importance of its domestic sales of metal containers to about 50 percent of total sales within the next 5 years. Its annual sales objective is expected to be $500 million by the end of the fifth year.

SM began issuing convertible securities in 19x7 with the sale of 900,000 shares of a $1.50 Series A preferred, each convertible into 1.8 shares of common. In 19x8 the company sold an additional 350,000 shares of Series A preferred and $10,000,000 of 5 percent debenture bonds, the latter convertible into common at $31\frac{1}{8}$ per common share. In 19x9 80,000 shares of the Series A preferred were converted into common by shareholders, and the company issued 640,000 shares of a $.60 Series B preferred, the latter convertible into two-sevenths of one share of common. Early in the current year, another 70,000 shares of Series A preferred were exchanged for common.

The company has on occasion purchased its own common shares. In some cases the stock was purchased for use in acquisitions; however, in 19x6 the company purchased a large number of outstanding common shares because management felt the stock was highly undervalued in the market.

SM's investment tax credits, which totaled $910,000 in 19x9 and $884,000 in 19x8, will be negligible in the current year. The "flow-through" method of accounting for tax credits has been utilized in the past.

SM's common dividends are $11\frac{1}{4}$ cents quarterly, and current share price is $25.

QUESTIONS

1. (a) Appraise SM's overall performance record during the past decade.
   (b) Analyze carefully the sources of funds utilized by SM to finance its rapid growth. In your answer, explain the advantages and disadvantages the company obtained from utilizing these sources.

2. Adjust SM's reported earnings per share for each year since 19x6, assuming full conversion of all convertible securities.

3. What evidence exists to show that investors have been efficient in the pricing of SM's common stock? Inefficient?

4. (a) Discuss the implications revealed in the case concerning SM's future earnings growth.
   (b) Discuss the merits of external growth versus internal growth. Which do you believe represents superior management? Why?

5. Estimate SM's *HPR* for next year. Justify your answer.

EXHIBIT 1

Balance Sheet Data (millions)

SPECIALIZED METALS, INC.

	19x9	19x8	19x7	19x6	19x5	19x4	19x3	19x2	19x1	19x0
Assets:										
Current	105.19	99.09	67.71	51.64	60.81	41.35	41.39	36.20	34.37	31.95
Cash Items	10.77	5.95	4.91	5.22	4.03	6.92	8.88	6.09	4.72	7.32
Receivables	41.53	32.68	25.42	19.93	17.42	13.45	10.11	11.77	10.96	9.47
Inventory	52.89	60.46	37.38	26.49	39.36	20.98	22.40	18.34	18.69	15.16
Other	22.69	13.64	4.20	3.83	1.50	1.67	1.77	2.00	1.38	1.37
Fixed	71.92	52.46	38.49	30.21	27.97	23.92	21.27	21.13	22.12	22.79
Total Assets	199.80	165.19	110.40	85.68	90.28	66.94	64.43	59.33	57.87	56.11
Liabilities:										
Current	60.20	53.41	28.93	15.86	24.59	13.00	12.41	9.38	9.47	8.75
Bonds	38.70	36.98	16.86	17.70	19.05	12.50	13.70	14.90	16.32	21.74
Other	7.01	3.66	2.67	2.74	1.86	1.42	.59	.27	.01	-0-
Preferred Stock	12.10	12.54	13.21	-0-	-0-	-0-	-0-	-0-	-0-	-0-
Common Stock	37.01	27.31	32.11	37.48	35.38	32.85	31.21	29.68	28.06	22.24
Surplus	44.18	31.29	16.62	11.90	9.40	7.17	6.52	5.10	4.01	3.38
Total Liabilities	199.80	165.19	110.40	85.68	90.28	66.94	64.43	59.33	57.87	56.11

EXHIBIT 2

Income Data (millions)

SPECIALIZED METALS, INC.

	19x9	19x8	19x7	19x6	19x5	19x4	19x3	19x2	19x1	19x0
Sales	345.38	272.40	219.94	167.32	153.30	147.18	126.61	121.79	114.80	109.46
Cost of Goods Sold	283.73	227.87	185.12	143.29	132.12	129.91	111.36	108.53	102.39	99.40
Depreciation	6.83	5.07	5.38	4.33	3.85	3.32	3.07	3.04	3.07	2.93
Operating Expenses	18.90	16.00	12.30	7.89	7.42	6.14	5.57	4.67	3.83	3.93
Operating Income	35.92	23.46	17.14	11.81	9.91	7.81	6.61	5.55	5.51	3.20
Other Income	-0-	-0-	-0-	-0-	-0-	.26	.35	.62	.17	.57
Earnings Before Interest & Taxes	35.92	23.46	17.14	11.81	9.91	8.07	6.96	6.17	5.68	3.77
Interest	4.58	2.79	2.13	1.62	1.18	.98	.90	1.12	1.13	1.49
Earnings Before Taxes	31.34	20.67	15.01	10.19	8.73	7.09	6.06	5.05	4.55	2.28
Taxes	16.33	10.38	7.06	4.49	3.77	3.29	3.07	2.49	2.35	1.16
Earnings After Taxes	15.01	10.29	7.95	5.70	4.96	3.80	2.99	2.56	2.20	1.12
Preferred Dividends	1.82	1.44	.81	-0-	-0-	-0-	-0-	-0-	-0-	-0-
Common Earnings	13.19	8.85	7.14	5.70	4.96	3.80	2.99	2.56	2.20	1.12
Common Dividends	2.42	1.53	1.30	1.06	.92	.88	.22	-0-	-0-	-0-
No. of Common Shares	6.5	5.1	5.2	4.4	5.1	5.1	5.1	5.0	5.0	3.9

EXHIBIT 3
Per Share Income Data

SPECIALIZED METALS, INC.

	19x9	19x8	19x7	19x6	19x5	19x4	19x3	19x2	19x1	19x0
Sales	53.38	53.52	42.21	38.20	30.00	29.03	24.97	24.26	22.96	28.36
Cost of Goods Sold	43.85	44.77	35.53	32.71	25.86	25.62	21.96	21.62	20.48	25.75
Depreciation	1.06	1.00	1.03	.99	.75	.65	.61	.61	.61	.76
Operating Expenses	2.92	3.14	2.36	1.80	1.45	1.22	1.10	.92	.77	1.02
Operating Income	5.55	4.61	3.29	2.70	1.94	1.54	1.30	1.11	1.10	.83
Other Income	-0-	-0-	-0-	-0-	-0-	.05	.07	.12	.04	.15
Earnings Before Interest & Taxes	5.55	4.61	3.29	2.70	1.94	1.59	1.37	1.23	1.14	.98
Interest	.71	.55	.41	.37	.23	.19	.17	.22	.23	.39
Earnings Before Taxes	4.84	4.06	2.88	2.33	1.71	1.40	1.20	1.01	.91	.59
Taxes	2.52	2.04	1.35	1.03	.74	.65	.61	.50	.47	.30
Earnings After Taxes	2.32	2.02	1.53	1.30	.97	.75	.59	.51	.44	.29
Preferred Dividends	.28	.28	.16	-0-	-0-	-0-	-0-	-0-	-0-	-0-
Common Earnings	2.04	1.74	1.37	1.30	.97	.75	.59	.51	.44	.29
Common Dividends	.37	.30	.25	.24	.18	.17	.04	-0-	-0-	-0-

EXHIBIT 4

Index Values per Share

SPECIALIZED METALS, INC.

	19x9	19x8	19x7	19x6	19x5	19x4	19x3	19x2	19x1	19x0
Total Assets	2.12	2.23	1.46	1.35	1.22	.91	.87	.81	.80	1.00
Sales	1.88	1.89	1.49	1.35	1.06	1.02	.88	.86	.81	1.00
Cost of Goods Sold	1.70	1.74	1.38	1.27	1.00	1.00	.85	.84	.80	1.00
Depreciation	1.39	1.31	1.36	1.30	.99	.86	.80	.80	.81	1.00
Operating Expenses	2.87	3.09	2.32	1.77	1.43	1.19	1.08	.91	.75	1.00
Operating Income	6.70	5.56	3.97	3.25	2.34	1.86	1.57	1.33	1.33	1.00
Earnings Before Interest & Taxes	5.68	4.72	3.37	2.76	1.99	1.63	1.41	1.26	1.16	1.00
Interest	1.83	1.42	1.06	.96	.60	.50	.46	.58	.59	1.00
Earnings Before Taxes	8.20	6.88	4.88	3.94	2.89	2.36	2.02	1.70	1.54	1.00
Taxes	8.40	6.79	4.51	3.41	2.45	2.16	2.01	1.65	1.56	1.00
Earnings After Taxes	8.00	6.97	5.26	4.49	3.35	2.58	2.03	1.76	1.52	1.00
Common Earnings	7.03	5.99	4.72	4.49	3.35	2.58	2.03	1.76	1.52	1.00
No. of Common Shares	1.66	1.32	1.35	1.13	1.32	1.31	1.31	1.30	1.30	1.00

EXHIBIT 5

Selected Data

SPECIALIZED METALS, INC.

	19x9	19x8	19x7	19x6	19x5	19x4	19x3	19x2	19x1	19x0
Return on Sales (%)	3.8	3.2	3.2	3.4	3.2	2.6	2.4	2.1	1.9	1.0
Return on Assets (%)	7.5	6.2	7.2	6.7	5.5	5.7	4.6	4.3	3.8	2.0
Return on Equity (%)	16.2	15.1	14.7	11.5	11.1	9.5	7.9	7.4	6.9	4.4
Capital Turnover	1.73	1.65	1.99	1.95	1.70	2.20	1.97	2.05	1.98	1.95
Inventory Turnover	5.36	3.77	4.95	5.41	3.36	6.19	4.97	5.92	5.48	6.56
Average Collection Period (Days)	43	43	42	43	41	33	29	35	34	31
Interest Coverage	7.84	8.41	8.05	7.29	8.40	8.24	7.73	5.51	5.03	2.53
Total Debt to Equity	1.31	1.61	.99	.74	1.02	.67	.71	.71	.80	1.19
Preferred to Equity	.15	.21	.27	-0-	-0-	-0-	-0-	-0-	-0-	-0-
Tax Rate (%)	52.1	50.2	47.0	44.1	43.2	46.5	50.7	49.3	51.6	50.9
Book Value Per Share	12.55	11.51	9.35	11.27	8.76	7.89	7.44	6.93	6.41	6.64
Dividend Payout (%)	18.6	17.3	18.2	18.4	18.5	22.6	7.0	-0-	-0-	-0-
Debt Leverage, Dollars Per Share	1.08	1.03	.55	.43	.42	.24	.19	.15	.14	.07
Preferred Leverage, Dollars Per Share	(.12)	(.11)	.05	-0-	-0-	-0-	-0-	-0-	-0-	-0-
Relative Debt Leverage (%)	52.9	59.4	40.0	33.2	43.7	31.9	32.7	28.4	30.8	24.5
Relative Preferred Leverage (%)	(6)	(6)	.04	-0-	-0-	-0-	-0-	-0-	-0-	-0-

EXHIBIT 6

Per Share Data

SPECIALIZED METALS, INC.

	19x9	19x8	19x7	19x6	19x5	19x4	19x3	19x2	19x1	19x0
Price:										
High	37.63	31.38	19.63	15.75	13.25	8.63	7.63	7.25	6.50	3.88
Low	26.25	16.25	11.50	9.63	7.88	6.25	4.88	3.88	3.25	2.75
Average	31.94	23.81	15.56	12.69	10.56	7.44	6.25	5.56	4.88	3.31
Price-Earnings:										
High	18.5	18.0	14.3	12.1	13.6	11.5	12.9	14.2	14.8	13.4
Low	12.9	9.3	8.4	7.4	8.1	8.3	8.3	7.6	7.4	9.5
Average	15.7	13.6	11.3	9.7	10.8	9.9	10.6	10.9	11.1	11.4
Market-Book Value:										
High	3.00	2.73	2.10	1.40	1.51	1.09	1.03	1.05	1.01	.59
Low	2.09	1.41	1.23	.85	.90	.79	.66	.56	.51	.42
Average	2.55	2.07	1.66	1.13	1.21	.94	.84	.80	.76	.50

EXHIBIT 7

Selected Containers (Metal and Glass), Industry Data per Share

SPECIALIZED METALS, INC.

	19x9	19x8	19x7	19x6	19x5	19x4	19x3	19x2	19x1	19x0
Sales	71.51	63.76	58.55	55.47	50.26	47.18	44.59	44.41	42.56	42.14
Depreciation	2.58	2.33	2.08	1.91	1.78	1.78	1.69	1.61	1.50	1.39
Income Taxes	3.42	3.01	2.35	2.42	2.16	1.71	1.77	1.81	1.79	1.41
Common Earnings	3.29	3.11	2.93	2.92	2.56	2.01	1.70	1.70	1.59	1.30
Common Dividends	1.35	1.31	1.29	1.23	1.09	1.03	1.02	1.00	1.00	1.00
Price Index:										
High	52.47	52.18	44.96	42.02	40.38	32.14	28.98	29.52	30.22	28.49
Low	44.60	36.16	35.44	35.48	31.18	27.47	26.80	23.46	23.71	21.83
Average	48.54	44.17	40.20	38.75	35.78	29.81	27.89	26.49	26.97	25.16
Price/Earnings Ratio:										
High	15.9	16.8	15.3	14.4	15.8	16.0	17.0	17.4	19.0	21.9
Low	13.6	11.6	12.1	12.1	12.2	13.7	15.8	13.8	14.9	16.8
Average	14.7	14.2	13.7	13.2	14.0	14.8	16.4	15.6	16.9	19.3
Book Value Per Share	29.75	27.97	26.35	25.21	23.24	20.52	20.75	19.87	19.93	19.76
Book Value – % Return	11.06	11.12	11.12	11.58	11.02	9.80	8.19	8.56	7.98	6.58

Source: *S & P Analyst's Handbook.*

Case 5: Risk

National Aircraft, Inc.

I was gratified to be able to answer promptly, and I did. I said I didn't know.
(Mark Twain.)

National Aircraft, Inc. (NA), is a leading aircraft manufacturer which emphasizes airframe production. Approximately 67 percent of the company's sales and 85 percent of its income last year were derived from commercial aircraft. The remainder of its sales and operating income came from military aircraft, missiles, and the space program.

The growth in personal income in the U. S. has increased the mobility of individuals and concomitantly the demand for a rapid transportation system. The aircraft industry has taken an increasingly larger percentage of the total transportation business in recent years. This trend has been interpreted by the industry as a call for larger and faster aircraft, hence the trend toward the "jumbo" jets. In addition, the continued emphasis on defense by the U. S. and European countries has perpetuated the demand for military aircraft.

While all of these factors have combined to keep the airframe and aerospace industries growing, factors causing temporary disequilibria, such as the congressional debate over the SST and its subsequent demise, have plunged the industry into despair. More importantly, the attempts by the federal government to dampen the inflationary pressures in the economy have resulted in a substantial decline in the rate of growth of passenger air travel. Many airline companies have thus canceled or delayed deliveries of new aircraft, and some companies have even had to curtail the number of scheduled flights. Expenditures for wages and materials, research and development, and engineering have risen at the same time sales have been falling. This situation has resulted in the most severe profit squeeze the industry as a whole has ever experienced.

Last year, even with an investment tax credit amounting to $12.4 million, NA's earnings after taxes fell 88 percent from the previous year. The factors responsible were: increased operating costs, delayed deliveries, the federal surtax, accelerated depreciation, and higher financing costs.

NA has specialized in commercial aircraft production and has focused its attention recently on the production of a single large airplane for the immediate future. Preliminary findings indicate that the plane is living up to advance billings with respect to expected operating performance. Several other competing manufacturers have entered the "big-jet" market, but NA currently leads in the number of deliveries.

As more aircraft are delivered, management intends to accelerate amortization of deferred preproduction expenses. Hence, for the next 2 to 3 years, earnings will be held down relative to those in subsequent years.

Research and development activity is a prominent characteristic of the aerospace industry; a company is unable to compete effectively without a vigorous R & D program. Ninety percent of the total R & D spending has usually been funded by the federal government, although some companies also have invested heavily from their own funds. NA ranked tenth in 19x6 and seventh in 19x7 among the leading R & D contractors.

Although NA seemed unaffected by the merger fever which was prevalent especially within the past 6 years, other companies in the industry did enter nonaerospace fields. Such activity is expected to continue as firms in the industry explore applications of systems methodology to problems resulting from increased urbanization and welfare consciousness. Areas of interest are mass transit, waste disposal, Medicare, and juvenile delinquency.

Although the expected current year's sales and earnings for NA are higher than last year, the outlook continues to look gloomy. Dividends, which have been paid every year for the past 29 years, have been cut from a $.30 to a $.10 quarterly rate. Sales for the current year are expected to be in the vicinity of $3.6 billion with earnings per share expected to approach $1.15. Investment tax credits of $11.7 million will be taken this year. Sales for next year are expected to drop slightly from those expected for the current year. Profit margins may be wider, however, due to lower start-up costs. NA's profitability over the next several years will hinge upon the growth in passenger travel as well as upon the acceptance of its jumbo jet relative to the acceptance of competing products of other aircraft manufacturers.

The current price of NA's common stock is $23 per share.

QUESTIONS

1. (a) How was NA able to report a profit of $.47 per share for 19x9 when *EBT* was negative?

   (b) Evaluate the quality of the current year's expected earnings per share of $1.15.

2. Why did NA pay $1.20 in dividends in 19x9 when earnings before taxes were negative?

3. (a) Analyze management's apparent investment strategy since 19x5.

   (b) How does NA's current risk exposure compare with its exposure in the recent past? Discuss.

4. (a) Identify the elements that have to be taken into consideration in forecasting NA's earnings per share for next year? For the next 5 years?

(b) Prepare a subjective probability distribution which includes low-, average-, and high-valued estimates of NA's earnings for next year. Prepare the same type of distribution for the company's earnings 5 years hence.

(c) Calculate the expected values of your distributions in 4(b). How much reliability would you place in your estimates?

(d) Explain the relevance of subjective probability distributions in NA's situation.

5. Are there any factors other than those presented in the case which could have an important bearing on NA's future earnings? Discuss.

EXHIBIT 1

Balance Sheet Data (millions)

NATIONAL AIRCRAFT, INC.

	19x9	19x8	19x7	19x6	19x5	19x4	19x3	19x2	19x1	19x0
Assets:										
Current	1690.5	1256.1	1062.7	802.0	552.4	487.0	542.2	509.5	442.7	429.8
Cash Items	93.1	71.2	74.3	76.6	100.9	50.7	26.4	32.2	52.5	31.9
Receivables	201.8	160.8	204.4	223.7	235.7	241.0	197.7	167.8	194.1	164.1
Inventory	1395.6	1024.1	784.0	501.7	215.8	195.3	318.1	309.5	196.1	233.8
Other	4.2	4.5	3.4	6.0	3.8	3.2	3.1	3.9	3.3	3.1
Fixed	907.7	925.5	964.3	636.5	206.0	161.2	145.0	134.7	141.4	104.3
Total Assets	2602.4	2186.1	2030.4	1444.5	762.2	651.4	690.3	648.1	587.4	537.2
Liabilities:										
Current	1080.1	789.1	704.4	367.7	285.7	235.3	298.8	312.2	263.4	229.7
Bonds	632.5	470.5	480.5	466.5	98.3	109.7	115.1	65.1	64.6	70.6
Other	93.9	116.2	93.9	46.7	.3	-0-	-0-	-0-	-0-	-0-
Common Stock	447.0	445.6	443.9	315.2	136.0	128.6	127.9	127.1	126.9	126.5
Surplus	348.9	364.7	307.7	248.4	241.9	177.8	148.5	143.7	132.5	110.4
Total Liabilities	2602.4	2186.1	2030.4	1444.5	762.2	651.4	690.3	648.1	587.4	537.2

EXHIBIT 2

Income Data (millions)

NATIONAL AIRCRAFT, INC.

	19x9	19x8	19x7	19x6	19x5	19x4	19x3	19x2	19x1	19x0
Sales	2834.6	3274.0	2879.7	2356.6	2023.4	1969.5	1771.4	1768.5	1800.9	1554.6
Cost of Goods Sold	1391.4	1602.4	1342.1	1030.2	1038.8	1093.5	897.9	918.8	1076.8	916.8
Depreciation	105.3	93.8	72.3	40.2	25.5	24.7	21.6	21.1	20.6	19.4
Operating Expenses	1322.5	1411.4	1305.2	1147.7	813.0	759.2	802.7	768.2	628.7	557.8
Operating Income	15.4	166.4	160.1	138.5	146.1	92.1	49.2	60.4	74.8	60.6
Other Income	19.0	16.7	16.6	12.5	11.0	4.2	2.2	2.2	3.0	(1.4)
Earnings Before Interest & Taxes	34.4	183.1	176.7	151.0	157.1	96.3	51.4	62.6	77.8	59.2
Interest	48.7	33.5	32.3	10.4	7.5	7.3	6.5	6.3	3.9	7.4
Earnings Before Taxes	(14.3)	149.6	144.4	140.6	149.6	89.0	44.9	56.3	73.9	51.8
Taxes	(24.5)	66.7	60.4	64.5	71.2	43.6	23.1	29.1	38.2	27.3
Common Earnings	10.2	82.9	84.0	76.1	78.4	45.4	21.8	27.2	35.7	24.5
Common Dividends	26.0	26.0	25.9	21.5	20.5	16.1	16.0	16.0	13.6	8.3
No. of Common Shares	21.7	21.6	21.6	19.5	16.4	16.1	16.0	16.0	16.0	16.0

EXHIBIT 3
Per Share Income Data

NATIONAL AIRCRAFT, INC.

	19x9	19x8	19x7	19x6	19x5	19x4	19x3	19x2	19x1	19x0
Sales	130.63	151.57	133.32	120.85	123.38	122.33	110.71	110.53	112.56	97.16
Cost of Goods Sold	64.12	74.19	62.13	52.83	63.34	67.92	56.12	57.42	67.30	57.30
Depreciation	4.85	4.34	3.35	2.06	1.55	1.53	1.35	1.32	1.29	1.21
Operating Expenses	60.95	65.34	60.43	58.86	49.58	47.16	50.17	48.02	39.30	34.86
Operating Income	.71	7.70	7.41	7.10	8.91	5.72	3.07	3.77	4.67	3.79
Other Income	.88	.78	.77	.64	.67	.26	.14	.14	.19	(.09)
Earnings Before Interest & Taxes	1.59	8.48	8.13	7.74	9.58	5.98	3.21	3.91	4.86	3.70
Interest	2.25	1.55	1.49	.53	.46	.45	.40	.39	.24	.46
Earnings Before Taxes	(.66)	6.93	6.69	7.21	9.12	5.53	2.81	3.52	4.62	3.24
Taxes	(1.13)	3.09	2.80	3.31	4.34	2.71	1.45	1.82	2.39	1.71
Common Earnings	.47	3.84	3.89	3.90	4.78	2.82	1.36	1.70	2.23	1.53
Common Dividends	1.20	1.20	1.20	1.10	1.25	1.00	1.00	1.00	.85	.52

EXHIBIT 4

Index Values per Share

NATIONAL AIRCRAFT, INC.

	19x9	19x8	19x7	19x6	19x5	19x4	19x3	19x2	19x1	19x0
Total Assets	3.57	3.01	2.80	2.21	1.38	1.21	1.28	1.21	1.09	1.00
Sales	1.34	1.56	1.37	1.24	1.27	1.26	1.14	1.14	1.16	1.00
Cost of Goods Sold	1.12	1.29	1.08	.92	1.11	1.19	.98	1.00	1.17	1.00
Depreciation	4.00	3.58	2.76	1.70	1.28	1.27	1.11	1.09	1.06	1.00
Operating Expenses	1.75	1.87	1.73	1.69	1.42	1.35	1.44	1.38	1.13	1.00
Operating Income	.19	2.03	1.96	1.88	2.35	1.51	.81	1.00	1.23	1.00
Earnings Before Interest & Taxes	.43	2.29	2.21	2.09	2.59	1.62	.87	1.06	1.31	1.00
Interest	4.85	3.35	3.23	1.15	.99	.98	.88	.85	.53	1.00
Earnings Before Taxes	--	2.14	2.06	2.23	2.82	1.71	.87	1.09	1.43	1.00
Taxes	--	1.81	1.64	1.94	2.54	1.59	.85	1.07	1.40	1.00
Common Earnings	.31	2.51	2.54	2.55	3.12	1.84	.89	1.11	1.46	1.00
Common Dividends	2.31	2.31	2.31	2.13	2.41	1.93	1.93	1.93	1.64	1.00

NATIONAL AIRCRAFT, INC.

EXHIBIT 5
Selected Data

	19x9	19x8	19x7	19x6	19x5	19x4	19x3	19x2	19x1	19x0
Return on Sales (%)	.4	2.5	2.9	3.2	3.9	2.3	1.2	1.5	2.0	1.6
Return on Assets (%)	.4	3.8	4.1	5.3	10.3	7.0	3.2	4.2	6.1	4.6
Return on Equity (%)	1.3	10.2	11.2	13.5	20.7	14.8	7.9	10.0	13.8	10.3
Capital Turnover	1.09	1.50	1.42	1.63	2.66	3.02	2.57	2.73	3.07	2.89
Inventory Turnover	1.00	1.57	1.71	2.05	4.81	5.60	2.82	2.97	5.49	3.92
Average Collection Period (Days)	26	18	26	34	42	44	40	34	39	38
Interest Coverage	.71	5.47	5.47	14.52	20.95	13.19	7.91	9.94	19.95	8.00
Total Debt to Equity	2.27	1.70	1.70	1.56	1.02	1.13	1.50	1.39	1.26	1.27
Tax Rate (%)	--	44.6	41.8	45.9	47.6	49.0	51.4	51.7	51.7	52.7
Book Value Per Share	36.68	37.51	34.80	28.90	23.04	19.03	17.28	16.93	16.21	14.81
Dividend Payout (%)	254.9	31.4	30.8	28.3	26.1	35.5	73.4	58.8	38.1	33.9
Debt Leverage, Dollars Per Share	(.82)	2.10	2.13	2.27	2.29	1.38	.74	.91	1.19	.76
Relative Debt Leverage (%)	(173.6)	54.6	54.7	58.1	47.9	49.1	54.2	53.5	53.5	49.6

EXHIBIT 6

Per Share Data

NATIONAL AIRCRAFT, INC.

	19x9	19x8	19x7	19x6	19x5	19x4	19x3	19x2	19x1	19x0
Price:										
High	61.13	90.25	112.38	91.00	70.25	35.88	20.13	28.25	28.63	19.63
Low	27.25	52.50	61.75	44.00	30.13	18.00	15.25	17.50	17.75	11.50
Average	44.19	71.38	87.06	67.50	50.19	26.94	17.69	22.88	23.19	15.56
Price-Earnings:										
High	130.0	23.5	28.9	23.3	14.7	12.7	14.8	16.6	12.8	12.8
Low	58.0	13.7	15.9	11.3	6.3	6.4	11.2	10.3	8.0	7.5
Average	94.0	18.6	22.4	17.3	10.5	9.5	13.0	13.4	10.4	10.1
Market-Book Value:										
High	1.67	2.41	3.23	3.15	3.05	1.89	1.17	1.67	1.77	1.33
Low	.74	1.40	1.78	1.52	1.31	.95	.88	1.03	1.10	.78
Average	1.21	1.90	2.50	2.34	2.18	1.42	1.02	1.35	1.43	1.05

EXHIBIT 7

Selected Aerospace Industry Data per Share

NATIONAL AIRCRAFT, INC.

	19x9	19x8	19x7	19x6	19x5	19x4	19x3	19x2	19x1	19x0
Sales	260.16	277.48	251.25	218.11	202.45	208.99	212.25	215.87	204.01	221.53
Depreciation	6.89	6.14	5.16	3.95	3.74	4.00	3.76	3.59	3.46	3.58
Income Taxes	3.12	6.89	4.20	4.59	5.58	4.46	4.13	4.13	2.98	(.20)
Common Earnings	4.05	6.66	5.60	5.89	6.35	5.08	4.71	4.74	.24	(.12)
Common Dividends	2.54	2.56	2.34	2.29	2.28	1.93	1.85	1.76	1.63	1.75
Price Index:										
High	96.01	106.10	125.02	108.45	102.21	58.01	53.57	61.36	61.87	50.73
Low	51.60	87.92	86.50	70.06	57.71	45.38	44.94	44.21	49.90	39.66
Average	73.81	97.01	105.76	89.26	79.96	51.70	49.26	52.79	55.89	45.20
Price/Earnings Ratio:										
High	23.71	15.93	22.33	18.41	16.10	11.42	11.37	12.95	257.79	---
Low	12.74	13.20	15.45	11.89	9.09	8.93	9.54	9.33	207.92	---
Average	18.23	14.57	18.89	15.15	12.60	10.18	10.46	11.14	232.86	---

Source: *S & P Analyst's Handbook.*

Case 6: Comprehensive Case

United Auto Parts, Inc.

Charged with feeding the lions, one naturally considers the quality of his protection.

The management of United Auto Parts, Inc. (UAP), has recently begun a serious effort to reduce the company's dependence on the fortunes of the automobile manufacturers. The company, the largest auto frame manufacturer in the United States, has had a record of good earnings growth except in years when new car sales were down. The new policy of management is to increase the amount of diversification in its operations by expanding into new product areas.

UAP was formed by R. A. Thompson in 1901 to manufacture structural components of railroad locomotives. The company began manufacturing automobile and truck frames in 1938 and expanded gradually into other fields until last year when it increased its rate of diversification. The family of the founder has continued to maintain active control of the firm through the ownership of common stock. At the end of 19x9, the family holdings amounted to 54 percent of the common shares outstanding. The stock was held by United Automotive Investment Company, a holding company wholly owned by the Thompson family and close relatives.

The company's Automotive Division produces automobile, truck, bus, and trailer frames, automobile structural parts, and wheel suspension control arms. Almost all of the company's automobile frames are sold to various divisions of General Motors (GM). Truck frames manufactured by UAP are sold to all major truck producers. By the end of 19x9 UAP was producing, in addition to auto parts, the following products: electric motors and electrical control systems, steel pipe, road machinery accessories, sealed farm storage units, irrigation equipment, gasoline pumps, and various industrial products.

The output of firms in the auto parts industry is sold in the original equipment market, the replacement market or "aftermarket," and the nonautomotive market. The original equipment market is tied closely to the fortunes of the "Big Three" in the automobile assembly industry, i.e., GM, Ford, and Chrysler. The aftermarket is considerably more stable than the original equipment market and grows in importance as the number of older cars on the highways increases. Because of the effects of diversification, the nonautomotive market adds a degree of stability to the sales and earnings of firms in the auto parts industry. The long strike against GM this year is expected to reduce that company's market share to about 46 percent from the 52.5 percent in 19x9. Ford and Chrysler should increase their shares of the automobile market respectively to 31 percent from 27.6 percent and to 19 percent from 17.2 percent. However, deferred demand by loyal customers will probably increase GM's share of the market next year to its 19x9 level.

Automobile manufacturers contract parts from independent companies partially to protect themselves against interruption of supply. In addition, the parts companies have made heavy investments in research and specialized equipment and consequently are often able to make substantial improvements in auto components and to keep the costs of these products down. The parts manufacturers can spread the costs of their investments over several contracts, thereby obtaining a cost advantage over the "captive" shops of the automobile companies. For the above reasons the growth of parts manufacturers has approximately equaled the growth of the motor transportation industry. There appears to be no serious threat at the present time that auto manufacturers will decide to increase their percentage of the parts business.

Good gains were made by U. S. automobile and truck producers in the last decade although foreign competition became much more important. Factors that should lead to an increase in the domestic production of new cars in the future include the upward trend in automobile scrappage, a greater number of multicar families, and greater effort by U. S. companies to capture a larger share of the small car market of foreign competitors.

Most original equipment is sold under contracts with the independent parts firms for the model year, although subsequent changes can sometimes be made in prices and quantities purchased by the auto makers. However, the number of contracts for longer than one year has been increasing recently. Contract renewals are the general rule except when a change in design eliminates the need for a product, another parts company offers a lower price line, or the auto maker decides to build the item in its own shops. Thus the independent auto parts firm must be flexible in its operations and dealings or suffer a sudden loss of business.

Finished goods inventories normally do not involve high risks for the parts manufacturer because contracts are for specific orders. Inventories typically are carried at the lower of cost or market (FIFO).

Auto frames are produced by captive shops of the automobile assembly companies and four large independent firms. The trend during the early years of the past decade was for the use of unitized auto bodies. However, this trend was reversed in 19x4 when GM returned to the use of perimeter chassis frames on some of its models. Chevrolet returned to perimeter frame construction the following year. The perimeter frame construction is said to provide a quieter and safer ride.

Considerable variation in the annual production of both passenger cars and trucks is normal. During the past 8 years, production declines of 8, 14, and 6 percent from previous year levels occurred in 19x6, 19x7, and 19x9 respectively. The number of cars produced increased in each of the 5 other years during the period, with the largest increases occurring in 19x2, 19x5, and 19x8 when the percentages were 26, 21, and 19 percent respectively. Production is expected to decline approximately 6 percent in the current year.

Swings in truck production have followed a pattern similar to that of automobile production except in 19x9 when the number of trucks produced increased slightly. Truck production this year is expected to be down from last year.

Increases in both car and truck assemblies are likely next year because of improved economic conditions, deferred demand resulting from strikes this year, and because of the introduction of subcompact cars by GM and Ford.

UAP's revenues and profits in the past have come primarily from the production of automobile frames. Since most of the company's sales have been to the various divisions of GM, UAP earnings for the current year will be adversely affected by the prolonged strike against that giant auto maker. Earnings per share are expected to decline to approximately $2.95 from $5.85 last year. Despite rising production costs, earnings should make significant improvements next year, primarily because of the favorable outlook for production by GM.

The company's nonautomotive products have not made significant contributions to the company's profits in the past. However, management expects expansion of its present nonautomotive divisions and future acquisitions, both domestic and foreign, to add to future earnings. In addition, the greater degree of diversification should have a stabilizing effect on the company's sales and earnings.

UAP has made two acquisitions in the past 6 months through pooling of interest arrangements. New products include a complete line of residential food waste disposers and electrical control systems. Additional acquisitions are currently being studied, but auto frames will continue to be the company's principal product in the forseeable future. Management plans to finance future investments in such a way as to leave the company's capital structure approximately the same as it was at the end of 19x9.

UAP has followed the policy of consolidating the statements of all wholly owned domestic subsidiaries. The company's equity in the earnings of unconsolidated subsidiaries and affiliates is included in other income.

The current share price of UAP's common stock is in the mid 40s.

QUESTIONS

1. (a) Based upon per share data, compute the average annual growth rates since 19x0 of UAP's assets, equity, sales, operating income, and earnings.

(b) Explain the wide differences in the above growth rates.

2. (a) Identify the factors that have been primarily responsible for the increases in the return on assets and the return on equity from 19x0 through 19x9.
    (b) Do you believe that these factors will persist? Why or why not?
    (c) Explain any new factors on the horizon which may affect significantly the earnings of the firm in the future.

3. Estimate the company's earnings per share for each of the next 5 years. Give high, low, and most probable figures for each year.

4. Identify the major risks with which the company is faced.

5. Why has the company's ratio of market to book value per share been less than 1.0 on the average? Explain.

6. Do you believe that the company has been justified in retaining over 60 percent of its earnings since 19x0? Why or why not?

EXHIBIT 1

Balance Sheet Data (millions)

UNITED AUTO PARTS, INC.

	19x9	19x8	19x7	19x6	19x5	19x4	19x3	19x2	19x1	19x0
Assets:										
Current	139.94	134.64	117.28	116.84	108.85	110.11	99.51	87.30	77.58	82.34
Cash Items	13.00	30.72	10.20	15.71	14.95	9.27	14.03	9.64	16.33	12.25
Receivables	50.02	42.77	41.60	39.42	35.52	43.73	36.32	33.47	26.10	31.14
Inventory	76.92	61.15	65.48	61.71	58.38	57.11	49.16	44.19	35.15	38.95
Other	28.09	13.02	9.00	8.73	14.17	9.71	8.23	1.64	2.74	3.73
Fixed	69.30	64.02	65.65	65.25	50.68	58.87	54.29	51.81	53.70	54.10
Total Assets	237.33	211.68	191.93	190.82	173.70	178.69	162.03	140.75	134.02	140.17
Liabilities:										
Current	65.51	49.90	37.55	38.51	31.51	42.87	22.51	19.54	15.32	16.59
Bonds	28.87	28.48	30.35	33.60	31.00	32.44	32.57	25.00	26.00	27.00
Other	4.95	4.35	4.59	6.09	4.74	5.69	7.81	.62	.40	--
Common Stock	36.80	38.82	33.13	30.15	26.18	26.18	26.09	26.08	26.08	24.58
Surplus	101.20	90.13	86.31	82.47	80.27	71.51	73.05	69.51	66.22	72.00
Total Liabilities	237.33	211.68	191.93	190.82	173.70	178.69	162.03	140.75	134.02	140.17

EXHIBIT 2

Income Data (millions)

UNITED AUTO PARTS, INC.

	19x9	19x8	19x7	19x6	19x5	19x4	19x3	19x2	19x1	19x0
Sales	354.52	372.80	330.00	318.43	358.44	299.85	286.20	249.10	221.95	265.18
Cost of Goods Sold	298.07	323.79	292.97	280.48	320.17	175.92	243.58	213.53	201.82	231.86
Depreciation	8.53	9.87	10.17	8.84	9.57	8.87	8.30	8.58	8.17	7.38
Operating Expenses	20.44	17.58	15.31	16.51	15.78	15.00	22.19	17.10	16.49	16.67
Operating Income	27.48	21.56	11.55	12.60	12.92	.06	12.13	9.89	(4.53)	9.27
Other Income	4.04	3.94	5.43	2.20	1.67	3.15	2.23	2.10	1.76	2.90
Earnings Before Interest & Taxes	31.52	25.50	16.98	14.80	14.59	3.21	14.36	11.99	(2.77)	12.17
Interest	1.45	1.76	1.85	1.76	2.10	1.85	1.27	1.11	1.21	1.27
Earnings Before Taxes	30.07	23.74	15.13	13.04	12.49	1.36	13.09	10.88	(3.98)	10.90
Taxes	15.51	12.10	5.50	4.30	4.57	(.53)	5.80	5.20	(3.11)	4.45
Common Earnings	14.56	11.64	9.63	8.74	7.92	1.89	7.29	5.68	(.87)	6.45
Common Dividends	3.49	3.20	2.81	2.57	2.14	2.15	2.15	2.15	3.42	4.17
No. of Common Shares	2.5	2.5	2.5	2.5	2.5	2.5	2.5	2.5	2.5	2.5

EXHIBIT 3

Per Share Income Data

UNITED AUTO PARTS, INC.

	19x9	19x8	19x7	19x6	19x5	19x4	19x3	19x2	19x1	19x0
Sales	142.38	149.72	132.53	127.88	143.95	120.42	115.40	100.44	89.50	106.93
Cost of Goods Sold	119.71	130.04	117.66	112.64	128.58	110.81	98.22	86.10	81.38	93.49
Depreciation	3.43	3.98	4.08	3.55	3.84	3.56	3.35	3.46	3.29	2.98
Operating Expenses	8.20	7.04	6.15	6.63	6.34	6.03	8.94	6.89	6.66	6.72
Operating Income	11.04	8.66	4.64	5.06	5.19	.02	4.89	3.99	(1.83)	3.74
Other Income	1.62	1.58	2.18	.88	.67	1.27	.90	.84	.71	1.17
Earnings Before Interest & Taxes	12.66	10.24	6.82	5.94	5.86	1.29	5.79	4.83	(1.12)	4.91
Interest	.58	.71	.74	.70	.84	.74	.51	.44	.48	.51
Earnings Before Taxes	12.08	9.53	6.08	5.24	5.02	.55	5.28	4.39	(1.60)	4.40
Taxes	6.23	4.86	2.21	1.73	1.84	(.21)	2.34	2.10	(1.25)	1.80
Common Earnings	5.85	4.67	3.87	3.51	3.18	.76	2.94	2.29	(.35)	2.60
Common Dividends	1.40	1.29	1.13	1.03	.86	.86	.87	.87	1.38	1.68

UNITED AUTO PARTS, INC.

EXHIBIT 4

Index Values per Share

	19x9	19x8	19x7	19x6	19x5	19x4	19x3	19x2	19x1	19x0
Total Assets	1.69	1.50	1.36	1.36	1.23	1.27	1.16	1.00	.96	1.00
Sales	1.33	1.40	1.24	1.20	1.35	1.13	1.08	.94	.84	1.00
Cost of Goods Sold	1.28	1.39	1.26	1.20	1.38	1.19	1.05	.92	.87	1.00
Depreciation	1.15	1.33	1.37	1.19	1.29	1.20	1.12	1.16	1.11	1.00
Operating Expenses	1.22	1.05	.91	.99	.94	.90	1.33	1.03	.99	1.00
Operating Income	2.95	2.32	1.24	1.35	1.39	.01	1.31	1.07	(.49)	1.00
Earnings Before Interest & Taxes	2.58	2.09	1.39	1.21	1.19	.26	1.18	.99	(.23)	1.00
Interest	1.14	1.38	1.45	1.38	1.65	1.45	1.00	.87	.95	1.00
Earnings Before Taxes	2.75	2.17	1.38	1.19	1.14	.12	1.20	1.00	(.37)	1.00
Taxes	3.47	2.71	1.23	.96	1.02	(.12)	1.30	1.17	(.70)	1.00
Common Earnings	2.25	1.80	1.49	1.35	1.22	.29	1.13	.88	(.13)	1.00
Common Dividends	.83	.76	.67	.61	.51	.51	.52	.52	.82	1.00

EXHIBIT 5

Selected Data

UNITED AUTO PARTS, INC.

	19x9	19x8	19x7	19x6	19x5	19x4	19x3	19x2	19x1	19x0
Return on Sales (%)	4.1	3.1	2.9	2.7	2.2	.6	2.5	2.3	(.4)	2.4
Return on Assets (%)	6.1	5.5	5.0	4.6	4.6	1.1	4.5	4.0	(.6)	4.6
Return on Equity (%)	10.6	9.0	8.1	7.8	7.4	1.9	7.4	5.9	(.9)	6.7
Capital Turnover	1.49	1.76	1.72	1.67	2.06	1.68	1.77	1.77	1.66	1.89
Inventory Turnover	3.88	5.30	4.47	4.55	5.48	4.83	4.96	4.83	5.74	5.95
Average Collection Period (Days)	51	41	45	45	36	52	46	48	42	42
Interest Coverage	21.74	14.49	9.18	8.41	6.95	1.74	11.31	10.80	(2.29)	9.58
Total Debt to Equity(%)	72.0	64.2	60.7	69.4	63.2	82.9	63.4	47.2	45.2	45.1
Tax Rate (%)	51.6	51.0	36.4	33.0	36.6	--	44.3	47.8	--	40.8
Book Value Per Share	55.42	51.79	47.97	45.23	42.75	39.23	39.98	38.54	37.22	38.94
Dividend Payout (%)	24.0	27.5	29.2	29.4	27.0	113.8	29.5	37.9	--	64.7
Debt Leverage, Dollars Per Share	2.28	1.62	1.17	1.16	.90	(.22)	.97	.58	(.18)	.60
Relative Debt Leverage (%)	39	35	30	33	28	(29)	33	25	52	23

UNITED AUTO PARTS, INC.

EXHIBIT 6
Per Share Data

	19x9	19x8	19x7	19x6	19x5	19x4	19x3	19x2	19x1	19x0
Price:										
High	50.00	52.50	35.00	38.63	32.38	33.25	29.50	30.50	32.63	48.13
Low	37.13	32.25	21.50	19.25	24.38	23.00	19.75	16.76	22.75	26.25
Average	43.56	42.38	28.25	28.94	28.38	28.13	24.63	23.63	27.69	37.19
Price–Earnings:										
High	8.6	11.2	9.1	11.0	10.2	43.8	10.0	13.3	--	18.5
Low	6.4	6.9	5.6	5.5	7.7	30.3	6.7	7.3	--	10.1
Average	7.5	9.1	7.4	8.3	9.0	37.1	8.4	10.3	--	14.3
Market–Book Value:										
High	.90	1.01	.73	.85	.76	.85	.74	.79	.88	1.23
Low	.67	.62	.45	.43	.57	.59	.49	.44	.61	.67
Average	.79	.82	.59	.64	.66	.72	.62	.61	.74	.95

EXHIBIT 7

Selected Auto Accessories Industry Data per Share

UNITED AUTO PARTS, INC.

	19x9	19x8	19x7	19x6	19x5	19x4	19x3	19x2	19x1	19x0
Sales	100.32	87.07	75.08	75.12	68.38	59.17	55.56	58.08	49.58	58.99
Depreciation	2.48	2.29	2.19	1.80	1.76	1.67	1.65	1.83	1.87	1.88
Income Taxes	5.25	4.97	3.56	4.39	4.06	3.65	3.72	3.40	2.54	3.69
Common Earnings	5.00	4.84	4.02	5.14	4.59	3.95	3.64	3.35	2.37	3.26
Common Dividends	2.74	2.66	2.60	2.65	2.51	2.31	2.15	2.07	1.99	2.17
Price Index:										
High	68.38	72.58	60.42	62.15	58.99	54.61	48.58	48.98	47.77	54.30
Low	55.26	54.11	45.40	44.45	51.76	47.06	42.88	7.80	40.81	39.31
Average	61.82	63.35	52.91	53.30	55.38	50.84	45.73	43.39	44.29	46.81
Price/Earnings Ratio:										
High	13.7	15.0	15.0	12.1	12.9	13.8	13.4	14.6	20.2	16.7
Low	11.1	11.2	11.3	8.7	11.3	11.9	11.8	11.3	17.2	12.1
Average	12.4	13.1	13.2	10.4	12.1	12.9	12.6	13.0	18.7	14.4
Book Value Per Share	35.66	33.16	34.83	33.00	30.58	29.02	28.85	30.23	29.39	28.62
Book Value – % Return	14.02	14.60	11.54	15.58	15.01	13.61	12.62	11.08	8.06	11.39

Source: *S & P Analyst's Handbook.*

Case 7: Comprehensive Case

National Industries

*Thanks to this adjustment, American Life was able to report $1.41 a share in earnings for '70. Without adjustments, earnings would have been a bit less — more specifically, they would have totaled something like 32 cents a share. (*Barron's.*)*

National Industries (NI) was incorporated in Michigan in 1934 as the State Bumper Corporation. The principal business of the company during the following 3 decades was the manufacture of a wide variety of auto parts. The company's first external expansion was in 1957, when a manufacturer of electrical products was acquired. Two years later the company began acquiring other firms at a rapid rate and one or more firms have been acquired each year since that time. Most of the early acquisitions were related to the auto parts industry, but by 19x7, the company had diversified so widely that it was in reality a major conglomerate. Accordingly, the company's name was changed to National Industries.

The company's external expansion through 19x5 was consumated primarily by the exchange of common stock for the assets of other firms. In 19x6, the company began issuing convertible preferred stock or convertible subordinate debenture bonds in exchange for the outstanding common stock of other firms. The pooling of interest method of accounting was often used. The primary objective of the growth program has been to seek out those companies which are expertly managed and already staffed with proven executives. However, no major acquisition is currently planned by management.

Beginning in 19x7, NI began selling shares of some of the companies acquired earlier. A sizable capital gains was realized in 19x9 from the sale of stock of two of the subsidiaries, one of which was acquired in 19x6 and the other in 19x9. The company will probably continue to spin off some of its less profitable operations during the next 12 months.

The company at present groups its operations into eleven major areas: distribution of auto replacements parts; manufacture of industrial products, primarily including metalworking machinery, auto parts (both original equipment and replacements), and components for electrical appliances; metal forming.

primarily for auto and air conditioning parts and assemblies; systems development related to defense and numerous industrial products; precision engineering; leisure time, primarily including the production of movie and television films; production of consumer products, primarily including cigars; manufacture of agricultural chemicals; manufacture of paper products; manufacture of food products, including a wide variety of individual items; and financial services, primarily including banking activities. The majority of these activities are handled by wholly owned subsidiaries whose statements are consolidated with those of NI. Statements of subsidiaries not wholly owned are not consolidated, and the equity in the earnings of these firms is shown as other income in NI's income statement. The relative importance of the company's various current operating areas is indicated in Exhibit 1.

NI's sales and earnings are usually tied closely to general economic conditions, although special conditions in a particular industry in which the company does a substantial amount of business can sometimes affect results significantly. The national economy is currently experiencing an extraordinary situation. Economic indicators suggest a mild recession, but wholesale and consumer prices have been rising rapidly. Although there is some indication that both the unemployment and inflation rates will be reduced in the second half of next year, the possibility of significant improvement in the economic situation is still highly uncertain. A brief description of the prospects in the company's major areas of activity follows.

Auto Parts

Auto production this year has been reduced from 19x9 levels because of weak consumer demand in the first half and strikes at assembly plants in the second half. Total automobile and truck production for the entire year will probably be down by approximately 6 percent. Consumer demand should improve substantially next year because of better economic conditions and demand deferrals caused by current year strikes. Total auto, including truck, production should rise by about 30 percent from the current year levels. The increase in production next year is expected to increase earnings of major auto parts manufacturers by about 25 percent.

Sales and earnings of original equipment parts closely parallel those of the auto industry. On the other hand, the volume of replacement, or aftermarket, parts production is dependent upon the public's buying power and the number, usage, average age, and average size of the cars on the road. Since older cars require more replacement parts, a decline in auto production tends to benefit the replacement business because the average age of cars on the road increases. In spite of the fact that many replacement parts have been improved in recent years, and thus last longer, the long run outlook is favorable for the replacement parts business because of a growing number of vehicles in use and because of stricter requirements by states for motor vehicle inspections. The production of replacement parts is more stable than the production of original equipment.

Metalworking Machinery

Sales of machine tools are very volatile and usually reach their peak in periods of high production for defense purposes. Orders have been declining since 19x6. Total sales for this year are expected to be significantly below 19x9 levels, perhaps by as much as 20 percent, and no improvement is in prospect for next year. Profits are highly levered in the industry because of heavy fixed costs.

In recent years approximately 11 percent of machine tool sales of U. S. companies have been to foreign markets. This percentage will probably increase in the future because of various U. S. aid programs and because of the technical superiority and quality of domestic products compared to the products of most other major producing countries. Imports in recent years have been running about 9 percent of the sales of the U. S. companies.

Consumer Electrical Products

Aided by the increasing affluence in the U. S., sales in the consumer electrical products market have been growing at an average annual rate of 5.7 percent during the past decade. Sales this year are expected to be slightly over $8 billion, an increase of about 5 percent over the 19x9 level, and they are expected to reach the $10 billion level in 5 years. Earnings have been growing at a faster rate than sales except in recession years. The rate of growth in earnings over the long run is expected to equal or better the growth in sales.

Air Conditioning and Refrigeration

Sales in the air conditioning and commercial and industrial refrigeration industry have grown at an average annual rate of 9 percent since 19x5. Although sales for this year are expected to be only about 4 percent above those for last year, a growth rate of 10 percent is forecast for the next year.

The ratio of exports to imports for the industry currently is 10:1, but the ratio has been in a declining trend. Packaged air conditioning equipment leads the export market for the products of the industry.

Movie and Television Films

Production budgeting has been the most important factor affecting success in the motion picture industry. Substantial losses from big-budget films in the past have made many production companies more careful in their selection of projects. Furthermore, large profits from some low-budget films will probably result in an emphasis on cost reduction in the big projects.

Prospects for the movie industry as a whole over the next few years are fairly good. In spite of the fact that the movie industry's share of each leisure-time dollar spent in the U. S. has declined in recent years, there is ample evidence that good films can still provide excellent profits. Furthermore, moderate increases in the number of film releases are expected to occur in the next few years. Feature films also have a highly profitable aftermarket in the television industry. The "best" features may return close to $1 million for two network appearances, and syndication can result in approximately $500,000 additional income to the film's owner. Overall movie industry profits for this year should be up about 5 percent over those of last year.

Some of the major movie studios are producing feature films, film series, and original film specials for television. On the other hand, the television networks are beginning to produce some of their own feature films, but this practice is currently under litigation as being monopolistic.

Cigars

Cigar consumption in the U. S. increased significantly in 19x4, presumably as a result of the decrease in cigarette sales which occurred after the Surgeon General's *Report on Smoking and Health*. However, consumption of cigars declined from 19x5 through 19x8 as cigarette sales increased. Since the strong anticigarette smoking campaign began again in 19x9, cigar consumption has increased almost every month. Moderate increases of perhaps 5 percent in cigar consumption are expected next year and in the longer run. No major change is expected in profit margins.

Agricultural Chemicals

The chemical industry is faced with serious problems during the next decade. In addition to the pressure on prices caused by heavy competition, the industry is faced with expenditures for pollution control, government restrictions on pesticides, and high interest and construction costs. Earnings from the production and sale of agricultural chemicals look particularly dismal for some producers because of the apparent inability to control costs. Earnings for the current year in this sector may be off by as much as 10 percent.

Paper and Paperboard Products

Since the demand for paper and paperboard products is highly correlated with the rate of economic activity, long-term prospects for the industry in the U.S. are good. Production has grown in each of the last 10 years except in 19x7 when dampened economic activity caused a reduction. In the first 6 months of the current year, paper production was up only .9 of 1 percent, while paperboard production was down by .75 of 1 percent from the same period last year. The sluggish economy was the principal cause of these poor growth rates, and no significant improvement is expected in the near future.

Food Processing

With growing affluence in the U. S., the percentage of disposable income spent for food has been decreasing for the past 15 years. Currently the percentage is running about 16.7 percent. However, the total dollar expenditures for food have continued to increase each year. The growth has been from $70.1 billion in 19x0 to $114.0 billion estimated for this year, or a 63 percent increase.

The above estimate for food consumption for the current year is an 8.5 percent increase over 19x9 consumption, the largest rise from one year to the next in almost 20 years. Although the major part of this growth will have been caused by price increases, price-adjusted expenditures are expected to rise by 3 percent. Average annual increases of 5 percent in dollar expenditures for food and food products are projected by the Department of Commerce for the next decade.

Financial Services

Earnings of commercial banks have grown at a rate in excess of 10 percent since 19x2 due primarily to rapid increase in loan demand and higher interest rates. Since banks have been able to reduce their cost of money faster than the recent decline in interest rates on loans, earnings are expected to be up this year by approximately 9 percent over last year's level. This favorable situation may end by late next year. However, if economic activity has improved by that time, loan volume may more than offset pressures on profit margins, and earnings may again be up significantly.

QUESTIONS

1. Explain the reasons for the wide differences in the per share growth rates of each of the following during the past decade:
   (a) Assets
   (b) Sales
   (c) Earnings before interest and taxes
   (d) Earnings before taxes
   (e) Earnings after taxes
   (f) Common earnings

2. (a) Identify the items on the income statement that had the effect of reducing earnings per share in 19x9.
   (b) Identify the items that had the effect of increasing earnings per share in 19x9.

(c) Will the items you have indicated in your answers to 2(a) and 2(b) have the same effect this year and next year? Explain.

(d) Are there any new factors that will affect earnings this year and next year? Explain.

3. (a) Compute NI's *EPS* in 19x9, assuming that all convertible securities had been converted.

(b) Will dilution of *EPS* via conversion of any of the preferred stock issues be likely to occur in the near future? Explain.

4. (a) Using the growth trend information in the case text and the data in Exhibit 1, estimate the expected net change in NI's operating income for the next year.

(b) How much reliability would you place in your answer to 4(a)? Explain.

5. Estimate NI's earnings per share for this year and next year. Justify your answer.

6. Explain how each of the following can affect reported earnings per share:

(a) The pooling of interest method of acquisition as opposed to the purchase of assets method.

(b) Differentials between the price-earnings ratios of the previously outstanding common stock of an acquired company and the common stock of the parent company.

(c) Exchange of bonds for the common stock of another firm.

7. Have the risks with which NI is faced increased significantly during the past 5 years? Explain.

EXHIBIT 1

Sales and Earnings by Operating Group   NATIONAL INDUSTRIES

	19x9	
Group Name	Percent of Co. Sales	Percent of Co. Operating Income
1. Distribution of Auto Replacement Parts	6.5	5.9
2. Industrial Products	16.5	15.2
3. Metals Forming	9.8	11.0
4. Systems	9.4	10.2
5. Precision Engineering	4.7	4.1
6. Leisure Time	13.2	2.6
7. Consumer Products	8.3	8.3
8. Chemicals	6.3	2.8
9. Paper Products	12.3	5.5
10. Food Products	4.6	14.2
11. Financial Services	8.4	20.2

EXHIBIT 2

Composition of Operating Group   NATIONAL INDUSTRIES

<u>19x9</u>

Group and Component Areas	Percent of Group Sales
1. Distribution of auto replacement parts	<u>100</u>
2. Industrial Products	
Machine tools	41
Auto parts (original equipment and replacement)	39
Electrical appliance components	18
Other	<u>2</u>
	100
3. Metals Forming	
Auto parts and assemblies	52
Air Conditioning parts and assemblies	44
Other	<u>4</u>
	100
4. Systems	
Defense	42
Industrial products	<u>58</u>
	100
5. Precision Engineering	<u>100</u>
6. Leisure Time	
Movie and TV films	<u>100</u>
7. Consumer Products	
Cigars	99
Other	<u>1</u>
	100
8. Chemicals	
Agricultural	<u>100</u>
9. Paper Products	<u>100</u>
10. Food Products	<u>100</u>
11. Financial Services	
Banking	98
Other	<u>2</u>
	100

EXHIBIT 3

Balance Sheet Data (millions)

NATIONAL INDUSTRIES

	19x9	19x8	19x7	19x6	19x5	19x4	19x3	19x2	19x1	19xU
Assets:										
Current	1041.39	935.39	388.01	141.15	71.71	49.73	37.07	29.23	17.04	9.17
Cash Items	280.06	213.29	56.46	39.14	9.26	5.93	4.69	3.84	1.48	1.06
Receivables	248.13	224.86	110.41	35.65	22.61	16.60	11.24	9.02	6.05	2.42
Inventory	513.20	497.24	221.14	66.36	39.84	27.20	21.14	16.37	9.51	5.69
Other	605.58	601.72	80.50	37.43	3.60	4.15	3.42	2.10	1.41	.64
Fixed	525.06	518.22	280.93	115.66	28.79	14.48	7.62	6.28	4.12	1.72
Total Assets	2172.03	2055.33	749.44	294.24	104.10	68.36	48.11	37.61	22.57	11.53
Liabilities:										
Current	464.88	465.80	174.82	74.55	33.31	25.04	17.01	13.68	6.78	3.76
Bonds	962.40	461.47	267.99	102.37	29.94	11.53	8.52	6.90	5.00	1.80
Other	154.69	590.19	77.39	9.73	3.58	2.18	2.03	1.24	.41	.03
Preferred Stock	46.89	47.54	44.14	1.67	-0-	-0-	-0-	-0-	-0-	-0-
Common Stock	263.52	226.64	59.18	46.91	20.40	17.07	12.08	8.51	5.06	2.59
Surplus	279.65	263.69	125.92	59.01	16.87	12.54	8.47	7.28	5.32	3.35
Total Liabilities	2172.03	2055.33	749.44	294.24	104.10	68.36	48.11	37.61	22.57	11.53

EXHIBIT 4

Capitalization   NATIONAL INDUSTRIES

LONG TERM DEBT: $922,915,000, including $509,103,000 in debentures
convertible into a total of 9,256,418 shares of common stock. Average
coupon rate on the convertibles is approximately 6 percent.

$1.75 SERIES A CUMULATIVE CONVERTIBLE PREFERRED STOCK:
368,439 shares ($2.50 par); redeemable in Feb. 1974, at $65;
each convertible into 3.367 shares common.

$3.50 SERIES B CUMULATIVE CONVERTIBLE PREFERRED STOCK:
657,665 shares ($2.50 par); redeemable in Feb. 1974, at $100;
convertible into 4.208 shares common.

$3.875 SERIES C CUMULATIVE CONVERTIBLE PREFERRED STOCK:
823,441 shares ($2.50 par); redeemable in Feb. 1974, at $105;
convertible into 1.743 shares common.

$5.75 CUMULATIVE PREFERRED STOCK:
406,888 shares ($2.50 par); redeemable at $105 beginning Nov. 1, 1971.

COMMON STOCK: 15,010,401 shares ($1 par).

WARRANTS: To buy 7,418,556 common shares until 1978 and 1986 at total
exercise price of $388,555,000 (an average exercise price of $52.38 per
share).

EXHIBIT 5

Income Data (millions)

NATIONAL INDUSTRIES

	19x9	19x8	19x7	19x6	19x5	19x4	19x3	19x2	19x1	19x0
Sales	1563.56	1313.94	644.92	317.53	182.08	117.25	92.54	65.65	33.84	24.05
Cost of Goods Sold	1205.43	983.61	453.35	230.25	136.68	85.71	64.43	47.02	25.10	18.32
Depreciation	41.45	28.90	14.12	9.32	2.43	1.26	.94	.72	.45	.27
Operating Expenses	246.63	190.56	103.97	43.83	31.64	24.06	21.41	14.38	6.54	4.50
Operating Income	70.05	110.87	73.48	34.13	11.33	6.22	5.76	3.53	1.75	.96
Other Income*	58.85	19.63	10.12	3.29	.55	.74	.07	.18	.11	(.02)
Earnings Before Interest & Taxes	128.90	130.50	83.60	37.42	11.88	6.96	5.83	3.71	1.86	.94
Interest	64.00	26.76	11.52	7.27	1.87	.95	.68	.42	.19	.13
Earnings Before Taxes	64.90	103.74	72.08	30.15	10.01	6.01	5.15	3.29	1.67	.81
Taxes	13.92	33.90	25.88	10.03	4.50	2.55	2.52	1.52	.67	.38
Earnings After Taxes	50.98	69.84	46.20	20.12	5.51	3.46	2.63	1.77	1.00	.43
Preferred Dividends	9.45	8.13	3.90	1.11	-0-	-0-	-0-	-0-	-0-	-0-
Common Earnings	41.53	61.71	42.30	19.01	5.51	3.46	2.63	1.77	1.00	.43
Gains on Security Sales After Taxes	21.07	2.63	1.30	1.36	-0-	-0-	-0-	-0-	-0-	-0-
Common Dividends	7.20	3.86	2.43	.90	.85	-0-	-0-	-0-	-0-	-0-
No. of Common Shares Outstanding	19.3	20.6	16.3	11.3	4.4	5.8	5.5	4.7	3.7	2.5

*Includes primarily NI's share of earnings of unconsolidated subsidiaries. Excludes gains and losses on sales of securities.

EXHIBIT 6

Per Share Income Data

NATIONAL INDUSTRIES

	19x9	19x8	19x7	19x6	19x5	19x4	19x3	19x2	19x1	19x0
Sales	80.97	63.88	39.64	28.05	41.67	20.32	16.89	14.09	9.14	9.51
Cost of Goods Sold	62.43	47.82	27.86	20.34	31.28	14.85	11.76	10.09	6.78	7.24
Depreciation	2.15	1.40	.87	.82	.56	.22	.17	.15	.12	.11
Operating Expenses	12.76	9.27	6.39	3.87	7.24	4.17	3.91	3.09	1.78	1.78
Operating Income	3.63	5.39	4.52	3.02	2.59	1.08	1.05	.76	.47	.38
Other Income*	3.05	.95	.62	.29	.13	.13	.01	.04	.03	(.01)
Earnings Before Interest & Taxes	6.68	6.34	5.14	3.31	2.72	1.21	1.06	.80	.50	.37
Interest	3.32	1.30	.71	.65	.43	.17	.12	.09	.05	.05
Earnings Before Taxes	3.36	5.04	4.43	2.66	2.29	1.04	.94	.71	.45	.32
Taxes	.72	1.64	1.59	.88	1.03	.44	.46	.33	.13	.15
Earnings After Taxes	2.64	3.40	2.84	1.78	1.26	.60	.48	.38	.27	.17
Preferred Dividends	.49	.40	.24	.10	-0-	-0-	-0-	-0-	-0-	-0-
Common Earnings	2.15	3.00	2.60	1.68	1.26	.60	.48	.38	.27	.17
Gains On Security Sales After Taxes	1.09	.13	.08	.12	-0-	-0-	-0-	-0-	-0-	-0-
Common Dividends	.44	.28	.23	.17	.12	-0-	-0-	-0-	-0-	-0-

*Includes primarily NI's share of earnings of unconsolidated subsidiaries. Excludes gains and losses on sales of securities.

EXHIBIT 7

Index Values per Share

NATIONAL INDUSTRIES

	19x0	19x1	19x2	19x3	19x4	19x5	19x6	19x7	19x8	19x9
Total Assets	1.00	1.34	1.77	1.93	2.60	5.23	5.70	10.11	21.92	24.68
Sales	1.00	.96	1.48	1.78	2.14	4.38	2.95	4.17	6.72	8.52
Cost of Goods Sold	1.00	.94	1.39	1.62	2.05	4.32	2.81	3.85	6.60	8.62
Depreciation	1.00	1.14	1.45	1.61	2.05	5.21	7.71	8.13	13.16	20.11
Operating Expenses	1.00	.99	1.73	2.20	2.34	4.07	2.18	3.59	5.21	7.18
Operating Income	1.00	1.25	2.00	2.77	2.84	6.83	7.95	11.90	14.20	9.56
Earnings Before Interest & Taxes	1.00	1.35	2.14	2.86	3.25	7.32	8.90	13.83	17.08	17.97
Interest	1.00	1.00	1.75	2.41	3.20	8.33	12.50	13.78	25.32	64.50
Earnings Before Taxes	1.00	1.41	2.21	2.94	3.25	7.15	8.32	13.84	15.75	10.50
Taxes	1.00	1.21	2.17	3.06	2.94	6.86	5.90	10.59	10.97	4.80
Earnings After Taxes	1.00	1.59	2.23	2.82	3.53	7.42	10.46	16.71	19.98	15.53
Common Earnings	1.00	1.59	2.23	2.82	3.53	7.42	9.88	15.30	17.65	12.65
No. of Common Shares and equivalents	1.00	1.46	1.84	2.17	2.28	1.73	4.47	6.43	8.13	7.63

EXHIBIT 8

Selected Data

NATIONAL INDUSTRIES

	19x9	19x8	19x7	19x6	19x5	19x4	19x3	19x2	19x1	19x0
Return on Sales (%)	2.7	4.7	6.6	6.0	3.0	3.0	2.8	2.7	3.0	1.8
Return on Assets (%)	2.3	3.4	6.2	6.8	5.3	5.1	5.5	4.7	4.4	3.7
Return on Equity (%)	7.6	12.6	22.9	17.9	14.8	11.7	12.8	11.2	9.6	7.2
Capital Turnover	.72	.64	.86	1.08	1.75	1.72	1.92	1.75	1.50	2.09
Inventory Turnover	2.35	1.98	2.05	3.47	3.43	3.15	3.05	2.87	2.64	3.22
Average Collection Period (Days)	57	62	62	40	45	51	44	49	64	36
Interest Coverage	2.01	4.88	7.26	5.15	6.35	7.33	8.57	8.83	9.79	7.23
Prior Charge Coverage	1.57	3.08	4.39	3.98	6.35	7.33	8.57	8.83	9.70	7.23
Total Debt to Equity	2.91	3.10	2.81	1.76	1.79	1.31	1.34	1.38	1.17	.94
Preferred to Equity	.09	.10	.24	.02	-0-	-0-	-0-	-0-	-0-	-0-
Tax Rate (%)	21.4	32.7	35.9	33.3	45.0	42.4	48.9	46.2	40.1	46.9
Book Value Per Share	28.13	23.84	11.38	9.36	8.53	5.13	3.75	3.39	2.81	2.35
Dividend Payout (%)	17	6	6	5	15	-0-	-0-	-0-	-0-	-0-
Debt Leverage, Dollars Per Share	1.22	2.28	1.83	.97	.72	.30	.25	.20	.13	.07
Preferred Leverage, Dollars Per Share	(.38)	(.30)	(.05)	(.09)	-0-	-0-	-0-	-0-	-0-	-0-
Relative Debt Leverage (%)	57	76	71	58	58	50	52	53	49	40
Relative Preferred Leverage (%)	(18)	(10)	(2)	(5)	-0-	-0-	-0-	-0-	-0-	-0-

EXHIBIT 9

Per Share Data

NATIONAL INDUSTRIES

	19x9	19x8	19x7	19x6	19x5	19x4	19x3	19x2	19x1	19x0
Price:										
High	50.25	64.25	58.88	38.88	31.25	9.25	9.63	12.13	8.88	3.63
Low	17.50	37.75	28.13	16.50	9.13	6.88	6.88	5.38	2.38	2.63
Average	33.87	51.00	43.50	27.69	20.19	8.06	8.25	8.75	5.63	3.13
Price-Earnings:										
High	23.4	21.4	22.6	23.1	24.8	15.4	20.1	31.9	32.9	20.4
Low	8.1	12.6	10.8	9.8	7.2	11.5	14.3	14.2	8.8	15.5
Average	15.7	17.0	16.7	16.4	16.0	13.4	17.2	23.0	20.8	17.9
Market-Book Value:										
High	1.79	2.70	5.18	4.16	3.66	1.80	2.57	3.58	3.17	1.48
Low	.62	1.58	2.47	1.76	1.07	1.34	1.84	1.59	.85	1.10
Average	1.20	2.14	3.82	2.96	2.36	1.57	2.20	2.58	2.01	1.29

EXHIBIT 10

Market Prices of Capital Stock (Recent Close)   NATIONAL INDUSTRIES

Common	25 5/8
$1.75 Series A Cumulative Convertible Preferred	86 3/4
$3.50 Series B Cumulative Convertible Preferred	107 7/8
$3.875 Series C Cumulative Convertible Preferred	56 3/4
$5.75 Cumulative Preferred	68 1/4

2 Capitalization Rates

Case 8:   Earnings Quality

American Food Products

The president stated that the company will grow rapidly as before, however, at a somewhat slower pace.

The current year is the eighteenth consecutive year that American Food Products (AF), one of the nation's leading food processors, has increased its sales and the forty-seventh consecutive year that the company has paid dividends on its common stock. AF operates more than 50 processing plants worldwide and sells some 500 food items under 40 nationally known brand names. The company also owns and operates more than 200 fast-food outlets in the U. S. and abroad; an additional 800 fast-service restaurants are currently under franchise agreements. In the last 2 years grocery products and coffee averaged 40 and 28 percent respectively of the company's total sales. Overseas operations accounted for 14 percent of total sales.

The company's growth has been through a combination of internal and external means. While a precise breakdown is not available, internal growth has been responsible for more than 50 percent of the company's total increase in sales and assets. Acquisitions complementing AF's product lines have been made on an orderly and planned basis. The company continually updates its product lines with several new products being introduced each year. Research expenditures amounted to $20 million last year.

The packaged foods industry is expected to show modest gains during the next 2 years. Overall, a 7 percent gain in domestic food expenditures is forecast for the current year, and an 8-9 percent gain is forecast for next year. Demand for convenience items—especially frozen foods—is expected to be very good. Profits of firms in the industry should increase due to a shift to both higher volume and higher margin items. In the past, consumers in the U. S. have tended to spend a declining percentage of their incomes on food items. Aggressive firms have been able to offset this trend, however, by developing new products and especially by appealing to the consumer's desire for convenience items.

The FTC is currently investigating concentration in the cereal industry, but no serious problems for producers are expected.

81

AF sold $75 million $8\frac{7}{8}$ percent 20-year debentures and $50 million $8\frac{3}{4}$ percent 5-year notes during the current year. An additional $125 million debenture sale is being planned for next year. The company has also embarked on a stock repurchase program with repurchases to be made at irregular intervals. Management was recently reorganized for the expressed purpose of developing a more diversified and internationalized organization over the next decade.

Increased investment spending is being channelled into new plant and warehouse facilities, fast-food service, business expansion both domestic and international, and into additional product lines. A small high-fashion cosmetics firm with sales of $5 million annually was acquired in late 19x9. AF is also seeking to acquire a restaurant and hotel supply operation, and leisure-time industries are being surveyed for possible acquisitions. Unprofitable operations such as a corn mill and a system of grain elevators have been sold.

AF is assuming a more active role in contemporary social problems. It has incorporated members of minority groups into its advertising ($135 million was spent in advertising last year), and it refuses to sponsor TV programs which use violence as their central theme. The company is attempting to minimize pollution from its production operations and has provided employment for the hard-core unemployed as well as for disadvantaged youths. Through its research program, the company now is developing low-cost, nutritious foods for the undernourished people in this country and abroad. AF contributes financial support to causes considered worthy and encourages company personnel to serve in governmental, civic, charitable, and political posts.

Although the company's capital turnover has declined during the economic inflation that has persisted since 19x6, net common stock earnings have continued to increase. Both sales and earnings rose in 19x8 and 19x9 despite huge nonrecurring losses on products which included cyclamates and a 10 percent federal income surtax. A substantial profit resulting from the acquisition and subsequent sale of a household product manufacturer in 19x8 is currently under litigation.

Total sales and per share earnings are expected to increase to $2.05 billion and $4.46 respectively this year and to $2.50 billion and $4.80 respectively next year. The quarterly dividend expectation is $.65 for this year.

The current price of the common stock is $80 per share.

QUESTIONS

1. (a) Plot the following data for AF on semilog graph paper for the past 10 years: (1) sales per share, (2) earnings per share, (3) dividends per share, and (4) average price-earnings ratio.

   (b) Calculate the rates of growth for each of the above.

2. Plot the following on arithmetic graph paper:

   (a) Return on sales

   (b) Return on assets

(c) Return on equity

(d) Debt-equity ratio

3. (a) Briefly evaluate AF's performance record over the past decade.

(b) Why has AF's stock price generally declined over the past 9 years? Do you expect the decline to continue? Why or why not?

(c) As a prospective stockholder, what is your opinion of AF's participation in social problems?

4. (a) Calculate the value of AF's stock via (1) Gordon's dividend model and (2) Graham and Dodd's earnings multipliers.

(b) Which of the above methods of valuation do you believe is the most appropriate in valuing AF's stock? Why?

EXHIBIT 1

Balance Sheet Data (millions)

AMERICAN FOOD PRODUCTS

	19x9	19x8	19x7	19x6	19x5	19x4	19x3	19x2	19x1	19x0
Assets:										
Current	673.7	622.2	563.9	526.9	443.9	436.0	410.9	386.8	360.4	356.5
Cash Items	137.3	151.8	123.3	106.7	69.7	38.6	80.3	95.8	76.9	113.1
Receivables	225.0	199.2	180.0	158.9	159.9	140.8	125.9	107.5	94.4	86.0
Inventory	311.4	271.2	260.6	261.3	214.3	256.6	204.7	183.50	189.1	157.4
Other	63.4	58.5	33.2	22.3	22.6	25.9	26.2	22.3	15.6	8.3
Fixed	439.1	380.4	331.9	307.6	283.5	263.9	221.2	193.2	173.2	147.8
Total Assets	1176.2	1061.1	929.0	856.8	750.0	725.8	658.3	602.3	549.2	512.6
Liabilities:										
Current	330.8	292.2	231.1	218.7	173.2	201.5	162.0	141.4	128.0	126.2
Bond	101.1	103.5	61.0	54.4	37.4	23.4	34.1	42.1	37.4	39.7
Other	31.8	21.1	17.4	-0-	-0-	-0-	-0-	-0-	-0-	-0-
Common Stock	138.2	144.1	161.9	163.6	162.4	161.1	159.4	157.4	155.1	149.9
Surplus	574.3	500.2	457.6	420.1	377.0	339.8	302.8	261.4	228.7	196.8
Total Liabilities	1176.2	1061.1	929.0	856.8	750.0	725.8	658.3	602.3	549.2	512.6

EXHIBIT 2

Income Data (millions)

AMERICAN FOOD PRODUCTS

	19x9	19x8	19x7	19x6	19x5	19x4	19x3	19x2	19x1	19x0
Sales	1893.8	1739.7	1651.6	1554.7	1478.1	1338.0	1216.2	1189.5	1160.2	1087.1
Cost of Goods Sold	1152.9	1058.2	1012.2	964.6	937.3	837.5	773.7	769.0	763.6	724.8
Depreciation	39.7	36.7	34.4	31.9	29.5	26.1	26.2	21.8	18.6	16.2
Operating Expenses*	483.3	448.4	414.5	373.7	332.9	295.8	247.6	245.6	242.0	218.7
Operating Income	217.9	196.4	190.5	184.5	178.4	178.6	168.7	153.1	136.0	127.4
Other Income	9.1	8.8	6.1	2.7	1.5	2.2	3.3	4.6	3.7	3.6
Earnings Before Interest and Taxes	227.0	205.2	196.6	187.2	179.9	180.8	172.0	157.7	139.7	131.0
Interest	10.4	6.2	3.9	2.7	2.5	1.9	1.7	1.8	1.5	1.4
Earnings Before Taxes	216.6	199.0	192.7	184.5	177.4	178.9	170.3	155.9	138.2	129.6
Taxes	113.2	97.7	94.0	90.5	91.1	95.3	91.7	83.6	71.4	68.5
Common Earnings	103.4	101.3	98.7	94.0	86.3	83.6	78.6	72.3	66.8	61.1
Common Dividends	60.9	60.0	55.3	52.8	50.2	50.1	44.9	39.8	34.7	31.9
No. of Common Shares	24.8	24.9	25.1	25.1	25.1	25.1	25.0	24.9	24.8	24.6
*The following lease charges are included in operating expenses:	18.6	8.1	6.8	6.2	5.8	5.0	4.8	4.8	4.7	4.1

EXHIBIT 3

Per Share Income Data

AMERICAN FOOD PRODUCTS

	19x9	19x8	19x7	19x6	19x5	19x4	19x3	19x2	19x1	19x0
Sales	76.36	69.87	65.80	61.94	58.89	53.31	48.65	47.77	46.78	44.19
Cost of Goods Sold	46.49	42.50	40.33	38.43	37.34	33.37	30.95	30.88	30.79	29.46
Depreciation	1.60	1.47	1.37	1.27	1.18	1.04	1.05	.88	.75	.66
Operating Expenses	19.51	18.01	16.51	14.89	13.26	11.78	9.90	9.86	9.76	8.89
Operating Income	8.76	7.89	7.59	7.35	7.11	7.12	6.75	1.15	5.48	5.18
Other Income	.37	.35	.24	.11	.06	.09	.13	.18	.15	.15
Earnings Before Interest & Taxes	9.13	8.24	7.83	7.46	7.17	7.21	6.88	6.33	5.63	5.33
Interest	.42	.25	.16	.11	.10	.08	.07	.07	.06	.06
Earnings Before Taxes	8.71	7.99	7.67	7.35	7.07	7.13	6.81	6.26	5.57	5.27
Taxes	4.56	3.92	3.75	3.61	3.63	3.80	3.67	3.36	2.88	2.78
Common Earnings	4.15	4.07	3.92	3.74	3.44	3.33	3.14	2.90	2.69	2.49
Common Dividends	2.46	2.41	2.20	2.10	2.00	2.00	1.80	1.60	1.40	1.30

EXHIBIT 4

Index Values per Share

AMERICAN FOOD PRODUCTS

	19x0	19x1	19x2	19x3	19x4	19x5	19x6	19x7	19x8	19x9
Total Assets	1.00	1.06	1.16	1.26	1.39	1.43	1.64	1.78	2.05	2.28
Sales	1.00	1.06	1.08	1.10	1.21	1.33	1.40	1.49	1.58	1.73
Cost of Goods Sold	1.00	1.05	1.05	1.05	1.13	1.27	1.30	1.37	1.44	1.58
Depreciation	1.00	1.14	1.33	1.59	1.58	1.78	1.93	2.08	2.24	2.43
Operating Expense	1.00	1.10	1.11	1.11	1.33	1.49	1.67	1.86	2.03	2.19
Operating Income	1.00	1.06	1.19	1.30	1.37	1.37	1.42	1.47	1.52	1.70
Earnings Before Interest & Taxes	1.00	1.06	1.19	1.29	1.35	1.35	1.40	1.47	1.55	1.72
Interest	1.00	1.06	1.27	1.19	1.33	1.75	1.89	2.73	4.38	7.37
Earnings Before Taxes	1.00	1.06	1.19	1.29	1.35	1.34	1.40	1.46	1.52	1.66
Taxes	1.00	1.03	1.21	1.32	1.36	1.30	1.29	1.34	1.41	1.64
Earnings After Taxes	1.00	1.08	1.17	1.27	1.34	1.38	1.51	1.58	1.64	1.68
Common Dividends	1.00	1.08	1.23	1.39	1.54	1.54	1.62	1.70	1.86	1.89

EXHIBIT 5

Selected Data

AMERICAN FOOD PRODUCTS

	19x9	19x8	19x7	19x6	19x5	19x4	19x3	19x2	19x1	19x0
Return on Sales (%)	5.5	5.8	6.0	6.0	5.8	6.2	6.5	6.1	5.8	5.6
Return on Assets (%)	8.8	9.5	10.6	11.0	11.5	11.5	11.9	12.0	12.2	11.9
Return on Equity (%)	14.5	15.7	15.9	16.1	16.0	16.7	17.0	17.3	17.4	17.6
Capital Turnover	1.61	1.64	1.78	1.82	1.97	1.84	1.85	1.98	2.11	2.12
Inventory Turnover	3.70	3.90	3.88	3.69	4.37	3.26	3.78	4.19	4.04	4.61
Average Collection Period (days)	43	41	39	37	39	38	37	32	29	28
Interest Coverage	21.83	33.10	50.41	69.33	71.96	95.16	101.18	87.61	93.13	93.57
Prior Charge Coverage	8.47	14.92	19.01	21.73	22.37	26.93	27.20	24.62	23.29	24.56
Total Debt to Equity (%)	65.1	64.7	50.0	46.8	39.0	44.9	42.4	43.8	43.1	47.9
Tax Rate (%)	52.3	49.1	48.8	49.1	51.4	53.3	53.8	53.6	51.7	52.9
Book Value Per Share	28.73	25.88	24.68	23.26	21.49	19.96	18.49	16.82	15.48	14.09
Dividends Payout (%)	58.9	59.2	56.0	56.2	58.2	59.9	57.1	55.0	51.9	52.2
Debt Leverage (dollars per share)	1.52	1.52	1.26	1.16	.93	1.01	.91	.86	.79	.79
Relative Debt Leverage (%)	36.5	37.4	32.0	30.9	27.1	30.3	29.1	29.7	29.4	31.6

EXHIBIT 6

Per Share Data

AMERICAN FOOD PRODUCTS

	19x9	19x8	19x7	19x6	19x5	19x4	19x3	19x2	19x1	19x0
Price:										
High	86.25	93.88	81.75	83.00	89.88	93.25	90.50	96.00	107.75	75.50
Low	71.50	65.00	65.25	62.75	77.50	78.25	77.63	57.75	68.63	61.50
Average	78.88	79.44	73.50	72.88	83.69	85.75	84.07	76.88	88.19	68.50
Price-Earnings:										
High	20.7	23.1	20.8	22.2	26.1	28.0	28.8	33.1	40.0	30.4
Low	17.1	16.0	16.6	16.8	22.5	23.5	24.7	19.9	25.5	24.8
Average	18.9	19.5	18.7	19.5	24.3	25.7	26.7	26.5	32.7	27.6
Market-Book Value:										
High	3.00	3.63	3.31	3.57	4.18	4.67	4.89	5.80	6.96	5.36
Low	2.49	2.51	2.64	2.70	3.61	3.92	4.20	3.49	4.44	4.36
Average	2.75	3.07	2.98	3.13	3.90	4.30	4.55	4.65	5.70	4.86

EXHIBIT 7

Selected Industry Data per Share

AMERICAN FOOD PRODUCTS

	19x9	19x8	19x7	19x6	19x5	19x4	19x3	19x2	19x1	19x0
Sales	103.97	91.52	84.11	77.73	70.66	66.41	60.26	56.37	54.63	52.97
Depreciation	1.81	1.74	1.63	1.54	1.37	1.22	1.13	1.12	.97	.87
Income Taxes	5.41	5.16	4.34	4.13	3.79	3.90	3.90	3.68	3.48	2.97
Common Earnings	5.16	4.81	4.75	4.42	4.13	3.84	3.55	3.30	3.05	2.74
Common Dividends	2.90	2.84	2.67	2.48	2.36	2.19	2.07	1.87	1.68	1.52
Price Index:										
High	99.40	97.90	86.31	88.89	98.57	95.06	89.37	90.78	100.00	66.80
Low	84.44	75.39	66.68	88.16	88.04	74.17	61.72	64.28	61.72	45.56
Average	91.92	86.64	76.49	88.52	93.30	84.61	75.54	77.53	80.86	56.18
Price-Earnings Ratio:										
High	19.3	20.3	18.1	20.1	23.9	24.8	25.2	27.5	32.8	24.4
Low	16.4	15.7	15.8	15.1	21.3	22.9	20.9	18.7	21.1	16.6
Average	17.8	18.0	16.9	17.6	22.6	23.8	23.0	23.1	26.9	20.5
Book Value Per Share	29.21	29.39	26.20	24.83	24.59	22.94	21.28	19.64	18.33	17.55
Book Value – % Return	17.67	16.37	18.13	17.80	16.80	16.74	16.68	16.80	16.64	15.61

Source: *S & P Analyst's Handbook.*

Case 9:   Valuation of a Utility

Great Lakes Lighting

A man must now swallow more beliefs than he can digest. (Havelock Ellis.)

Great Lakes Lighting (GL) was incorporated in 1892 in Ohio. After a merger with two other companies in 1893, the company's growth during the next 30 years was primarily internal. During the period 1924 to 1929, however, GL acquired some 22 privately and municipally owned utilities. Over the next 25 years, its acquisition program included the purchase of additional utility companies within a 50-mile radius of its main operation. The company currently supplies electricity to over 2 million persons in an area which is heavily industrialized. Electric utility revenues last year were 35 percent residential, 26 percent commercial, and 35 percent industrial, compared with percentages of 30, 22, and 43 percent, respectively, for the nation as a whole. Average residential rates and usage for the year were 2.46 cents per kilowatthour and 5,532 kilowatthours versus 2.10 cents and 7,066 kilowatthours nationally.

Rates are negotiated directly with municipalities but are subject ultimately to the Ohio Public Utility Commission. Utility properties in Ohio are evaluated on the basis of reproduction cost new less depreciation. Early this year GL was granted a rate increase which is expected to add about $14 million to its annual revenues. The company is now permitted to earn 5.31 percent on a rate base of $995 million. Flow-through accounting is used by the company for tax purposes.

Utility firms are currently experiencing their most depressed stock prices in over 20 years. One of the major factors that has contributed to this situation has been the decline in profit margins caused by the economic inflation. During periods of inflation utility costs usually increase at a faster pace than rates. In addition high financing costs have dampened common earnings; the gains normally resulting from financial leverage have been significantly reduced, and have been negative in some instances. Although the earnings of electric utility companies have grown at an average annual rate of about 6 percent for many years, growth rates for this year and next year are expected to be 1.5 and 3 percent respectively. When these earnings growth rates are compared with expectations of kilowatthour sales increases of 6.3 and 7.5 percent for the 2 years, the squeeze on profit margins is obvious.

Over the next decade electric power requirements are expected to grow at about a 6.6 percent rate nationwide. The industry as a whole is currently suffering from a severe power shortage because of poor forecasts during the past decade when customer demand increased faster than expected. Capital outlays, therefore, must be sharply increased to meet the future demand. Accordingly, some $10 billion in capital outlays are planned for the current year and $12 billion are planned for next year. Since only about one-fourth of these funds can be raised internally, electric utility firms must enter the capital markets during a period of historically high interest rates.

GL is fortunate in that its generating capability of 3.2 million kilowatthours substantially surpasses its peak load thus far of 2.5 million kilowatthour. However, construction expenditures of $106 and $140 million are planned for the latter part of the current year and next year respectively. In addition, over $500 million will probably be spent by the company in the subsequent 5 years. In June of this year, $75 million 5-year 9 percent bonds were sold to refund $40 million of 3 percent bonds coming due in July and to provide a portion of the additional funds required for capital expenditures.

Estimates for the current year indicate that due largely to the rate increase, GL's operating revenues will advance 15 percent from those of a year ago. Operating income is expected to increase 20 percent, reflecting both the rate increase and lower income taxes. However, earnings per share of common stock are estimated at $3.02, up only 3 percent from last year due to a sharp increase in interest payments. Interest charged to construction is estimated at $.54 for the current year and is expected to remain at about that level next year.

Revenue gains for next year are forecast at 17 percent, and earnings per share expectations fall in the range of $3.15 to $3.20. A substantial increase in industrial activity from the current depressed levels should greatly enhance GL's earnings prospects over the longer term.

GL's quarterly dividend has been increased this year to $.54 and the company is expected to continue its past policy of annual dividend increases.

GL's share price is currently in the mid 30s.

QUESTIONS

1. (a) Is there any evidence that GL has used accounting adjustments to maintain its earnings per share growth and stability?

   (b) Has the market been efficient in pricing GL's common stock? Explain.

2. Do you agree with GL's dividend increase this year in view of its funds requirements and the current high interest costs on long-term bonds? Discuss.

3. Calculate on a per share basis the annual average growth rates over the past decade for each of the following:
   (a) Sales
   (b) Common earnings
   (c) Common dividends
   (d) Book value

4. (a) Value GL's stock based upon Gordon's dividend model, assuming investor required returns of 8, 10, and 12 percent.
   (b) Which of these returns on equity is the most realistic? Discuss.

5. Value GL's stock based upon Graham and Dodd's earnings multipliers for public utilities.

6. Which valuation method is more appropriate to GL's case? Explain.

7. How would you expect GL's *HPR*s for the next 5 years to compare with those of the past 5 years? Discuss.

EXHIBIT 1

Balance Sheet Data (millions)

GREAT LAKES LIGHTING

	19x9	19x8	19x7	19x6	19x5	19x4	19x3	19x2	19x1	19x0
Assets:										
Current	56.04	54.03	55.78	73.02	83.59	72.79	57.24	67.95	59.06	57.16
Cash Items	26.74	24.12	24.99	46.59	60.02	50.48	35.21	45.05	36.18	34.62
Receivables	17.18	15.37	15.45	13.06	11.32	11.42	10.52	10.83	10.71	9.35
Inventory	12.12	14.54	15.34	13.37	12.25	10.89	11.51	12.07	12.17	13.19
Other	53.19	12.22	10.27	9.89	3.79	5.41	4.58	4.43	4.10	4.41
Fixed	631.40	551.73	462.52	437.98	424.92	424.70	427.76	429.74	426.16	408.26
Total Assets	740.63	617.98	528.57	520.89	512.30	502.90	489.58	502.12	489.32	469.83
Liabilities:										
Current	145.10	120.38	60.23	61.02	57.43	55.08	52.58	50.58	51.20	44.63
Bonds	290.00	195.00	195.00	195.00	195.00	195.00	195.00	195.00	195.00	195.00
Other	32.31	42.89	32.76	33.77	30.71	31.56	30.25	28.87	35.92	32.78
Preferred Stock	—	—	—	—	—	—	—	25.75	25.73	25.71
Common Stock	182.69	180.72	179.94	139.59	141.07	140.69	139.83	107.97	106.15	104.67
Surplus	90.53	78.99	60.64	91.51	88.09	80.57	71.92	93.95	75.32	67.04
Total Liabilities	740.63	617.98	528.57	520.89	512.30	502.90	489.58	502.12	489.32	469.83

EXHIBIT 2

Income Data (millions)

GREAT LAKES LIGHTING

	19x9	19x8	19x7	19x6	19x5	19x4	19x3	19x2	19x1	19x0
Sales	218.50	203.84	189.02	184.25	168.97	161.40	154.22	146.52	139.05	136.37
Operating Expense	126.48	113.76	103.17	100.41	90.45	85.97	83.27	80.22	72.42	72.83
Depreciation	19.93	20.05	20.63	20.19	20.17	20.01	19.50	18.70	16.15	15.74
Operating Income	72.09	70.03	65.22	63.65	58.35	55.42	51.45	47.60	50.48	47.80
Other Income	.62	.42	1.19	1.66	1.78	1.45	1.55	1.45	1.23	1.16
Earnings Before Interest & Taxes	72.71	70.45	66.41	65.31	60.13	56.87	53.00	49.05	51.71	48.96
Interest	14.05	7.46	6.50	6.49	6.50	6.50	6.50	6.50	6.50	6.50
Interest Charged to Construction	(6.83)	(3.74)	(1.30)	(.51)	(.31)	(.19)	(.50)	(1.05)	(.90)	(.32)
Earnings Before Taxes	65.49	66.73	61.21	59.33	53.94	50.56	47.00	43.60	46.11	42.78
Taxes	26.25	29.42	25.44	25.55	22.89	23.18	21.04	18.93	21.75	21.43
Earnings After Taxes	39.24	37.31	35.77	33.78	31.05	27.38	25.96	24.67	24.36	21.35
Preferred Dividends	–	–	–	–	–	–	.87	1.16	1.16	1.16
Common Earnings	39.24	37.31	35.77	33.78	31.05	27.38	25.09	23.51	23.20	20.19
Common Dividends	27.42	25.36	23.40	21.89	18.14	16.60	15.25	13.75	12.97	11.14
No. of Common Shares	13.4	13.4	13.4	13.5	13.7	13.8	13.9	13.7	13.6	12.4

EXHIBIT 3

Per Share Income Data

GREAT LAKES LIGHTING

	19x9	19x8	19x7	19x6	19x5	19x4	19x3	19x2	19x1	19x0
Sales	16.26	15.19	14.05	13.64	12.30	11.67	11.13	10.66	10.19	11.02
Operating Expenses	9.42	8.48	7.67	7.44	6.58	6.21	6.01	5.84	5.31	5.89
Depreciation	1.48	1.49	1.53	1.49	1.47	1.45	1.41	1.36	1.18	1.27
Operating Income	5.36	5.22	4.85	4.71	4.25	4.01	3.71	3.46	3.70	3.86
Other Income	.05	.03	.09	.12	.13	.10	.11	.11	.09	.09
Earnings Before Interest & Taxes	5.41	5.25	4.94	4.83	4.38	4.11	3.82	3.57	3.79	3.95
Interest	1.05	.56	.49	.48	.47	.46	.47	.48	.48	.53
Interest Charged to Construction	(.51)	(.28)	(.10)	(.04)	(.02)	(.01)	(.04)	(.08)	(.07)	(.03)
Earnings Before Taxes	4.87	4.97	4.55	4.39	3.93	3.66	3.39	3.17	3.38	3.46
Taxes	1.95	2.19	1.89	1.89	1.67	1.68	1.52	1.38	1.60	1.74
Earnings After Taxes	2.92	2.78	2.66	2.50	2.26	1.98	1.87	1.79	1.78	1.72
Preferred Dividends	–	–	–	–	–	–	.06	.08	.08	.09
Common Earnings	2.92	2.78	2.66	2.50	2.26	1.98	1.81	1.71	1.70	1.63
Common Dividends	2.04	1.89	1.74	1.62	1.32	1.20	1.10	1.00	.95	.90

EXHIBIT 4

Index Values per Share

GREAT LAKES LIGHTING

	19x9	19x8	19x7	19x6	19x5	19x4	19x3	19x2	19x1	19x0
Total Assets	1.45	1.21	1.04	1.02	.98	.96	.93	.96	.94	1.00
Sales	1.48	1.38	1.28	1.24	1.12	1.06	1.01	.97	.92	1.00
Operating Expenses	1.60	1.44	1.30	1.26	1.12	1.06	1.02	.99	.90	1.00
Depreciation	1.17	1.18	1.21	1.18	1.15	1.14	1.11	1.07	.93	1.00
Operating Income	1.39	1.35	1.26	1.22	1.10	1.04	.96	.90	.96	1.00
Earnings Before Interest & Taxes	1.37	1.33	1.25	1.22	1.11	1.04	.97	.90	.96	1.00
Interest	1.99	1.06	.92	.91	.90	.90	.89	.90	.91	1.00
Earnings Before Taxes	1.41	1.44	1.32	1.27	1.14	1.06	.98	.92	.98	1.00
Taxes	1.13	1.27	1.09	1.09	.96	.97	.88	.80	.92	1.00
Earnings After Taxes	1.69	1.61	1.54	1.45	1.31	1.15	1.09	1.04	1.03	1.00
Common Earnings	1.79	1.70	1.63	1.53	1.39	1.21	1.11	1.05	1.04	1.00
Common Dividends	2.27	2.10	1.93	1.80	1.47	1.33	1.22	1.11	1.06	1.00

EXHIBIT 5

Selected Data

GREAT LAKES LIGHTING

	19x9	19x8	19x7	19x6	19x5	19x4	19x3	19x2	19x1	19x0
Return on Sales (%)	18.0	18.3	18.9	18.3	18.4	17.0	16.3	16.0	16.7	14.8
Return on Assets (%)	5.3	6.0	6.8	6.5	6.1	5.4	5.3	4.9	5.0	4.5
Return on Equity (%)	14.4	14.4	14.9	14.6	13.5	12.4	11.8	11.6	12.8	11.8
Capital Turnover	.30	.33	.36	.35	.33	.32	.32	.29	.28	.29
Average Collection Period (Days)	28	27	29	25	24	25	25	27	28	25
Interest Coverage	5.66	9.94	10.42	10.14	9.30	8.78	8.23	7.71	8.09	7.58
Total Debt to Equity	1.71	1.38	1.20	1.25	1.24	1.27	1.31	1.36	1.56	1.59
Tax Rate (%)	40.1	44.1	41.6	43.1	42.4	45.8	44.8	43.4	47.2	50.1
Book Value Per Share	20.33	19.35	17.89	17.11	16.68	16.00	15.28	14.69	13.30	13.87
Dividend Payout (%)	69.9	68.0	65.4	64.8	58.4	60.6	60.8	58.5	55.9	55.2
Debt Leverage, Dollars Per Share	1.42	1.39	1.29	1.26	1.12	.99	.94	.84	.90	.88
Relative Debt Leverage (%)	48.6	50.0	48.5	50.3	49.6	50.1	51.9	48.9	53.1	54.1

EXHIBIT 6

Per Share Data

GREAT LAKES LIGHTING

	19x9	19x8	19x7	19x6	19x5	19x4	19x3	19x2	19x1	19x0
Price:										
High	43.00	43.00	41.63	44.25	44.25	40.63	34.88	35.13	36.88	29.88
Low	30.00	35.13	34.50	35.50	38.50	31.00	30.50	26.50	26.75	23.88
Average	36.50	39.06	38.06	39.88	41.38	35.81	32.69	30.81	31.81	26.88
Price/Earnings:										
High	14.7	15.5	15.6	17.7	19.6	20.5	19.3	20.5	21.7	18.3
Low	10.3	12.6	13.0	14.2	17.0	15.6	16.8	15.5	15.7	14.6
Average	12.5	14.0	14.3	15.9	18.3	18.1	18.1	18.0	18.7	16.5
Market/Book Value:										
High	2.12	2.22	2.33	2.59	2.65	2.54	2.28	2.39	2.77	2.15
Low	1.48	1.82	1.93	2.08	2.31	1.94	2.00	1.81	2.01	1.72
Average	1.80	2.02	2.13	2.33	2.48	2.24	2.14	2.10	2.39	1.94

EXHIBIT 7

GREAT LAKES LIGHTING

Selected Industry Data per Share

	19x9	19x8	19x7	19x6	19x5	19x4	19x3	19x2	19x1	19x0
Operating Revenues	24.36	23.03	21.67	20.60	19.15	18.12	17.40	16.72	15.75	15.10
Depreciation	2.64	2.50	2.37	2.23	2.10	1.98	1.91	1.79	1.66	1.55
Taxes	1.99	2.15	1.99	2.05	1.96	1.97	1.93	1.92	1.89	1.89
Net Operating Income	5.29	4.98	4.83	4.51	4.21	3.92	3.76	3.56	3.25	3.05
Common Earnings	3.38	3.25	3.28	3.09	2.90	2.65	2.45	2.34	2.11	2.01
Common Dividends	2.33	2.27	2.16	2.04	1.90	1.74	1.63	1.52	1.44	1.37
Price Index:										
High	53.03	53.92	55.03	57.77	60.90	58.61	53.51	50.39	52.91	39.35
Low	41.22	49.33	46.16	45.63	57.26	52.14	48.66	39.06	39.47	32.87
Average	47.13	51.63	50.60	51.70	59.08	55.38	51.09	44.73	46.19	36.11
Price/Earnings Ratio:										
High	15.7	16.6	16.8	18.7	21.0	22.1	21.8	21.5	25.1	19.6
Low	12.2	15.2	14.1	14.8	19.7	19.7	19.9	16.7	18.7	16.3
Average	13.9	15.9	15.4	16.7	20.3	20.9	20.8	19.1	21.9	17.9
Net Property Per Share	86.54	80.17	74.37	69.03	64.16	60.72	58.97	56.98	54.99	52.62
% Earned on % Return	6.11	6.21	6.50	6.53	6.56	6.46	6.38	6.25	5.78	5.80

Source: *S & P Analyst's Handbook.*

Case 10:   Mature Growth

Computer Systems, Inc.

While earnings prospects are essential to all investment decisions, they
must be viewed in perspective. As indicated, historical patterns must be taken
into account. And it is necessary to determine whether the stock's price is
*already amply reflecting the improvement that is expected. (*The Outlook.*)*

Computer Systems, Inc. (CS), was incorporated in New York in 1911 as the Data Recording Company. After several name changes and numerous mergers and acquisitions, the company adopted its present name in 1941.

The company was originally formed to produce commercial scales, tabulating machines, and time recording equipment. The line was later expanded to include such items as typewriters, dictation equipment, computers, data processing systems, and peripheral equipment for data recorders. The company is now organized into 12 main divisions and three wholly owned subsidiaries, one of which specializes in world trade. In addition to its U. S. operations, the company has locations in 108 foreign countries. It is the largest of eight companies producing office equipment.

CS had little competition in the computer field for many years, but today the company operates in a highly competitive environment. Nevertheless CS has been able to stay ahead of its competition in most areas of technology, equipment, and applications because of its outstanding research and development programs. A new line of computers was recently introduced which management believes will be as successful as those of the past decade. The company has also introduced a full line of new peripheral equipment. In addition, CS has embarked on a diversification program beginning with the introduction of an office copying machine.

Sales have grown fairly steadily over the past decade with the exception of sharp increases in 19x4 and 19x8. An abnormally high volume of "outright" sales as opposed to rentals was responsible for the sharp increases in those 2 years. Management normally keeps its stockholders informed of customer shifts from rentals to sales, noting that increased rentals usually enhance future earnings while outright sales enhance current earnings. The sales breakdown for

CS last year was as follows: 79 percent, data processing machines; 17 percent, other; and 4 percent, government-related activities.

Industry sales have grown in excess of 25 percent per year over the past decade. Since growth over the next 5 years is expected to be only 17 percent per year, price competition will probably become more severe.

During the current year the European market was the single most important profit center for computers. For many firms, the sharply improved profitability of foreign markets offset a severe profit decline from domestic operations; this was true also for CS. Thus future developments in foreign markets are of great interest to American firms, although the current tide of nationalism may result in the foreign market reducing its consumption of many American made products, including computers.

CS's foreign operations have been growing much more rapidly than its domestic operations. The company's foreign sales for the current year are estimated at $2.93 billion and earnings at $512.5 million, versus $2.50 billion and $114.7 million, respectively, in 19x9. Furthermore, the company's backlog of foreign orders for data processing equipment is at a record high.

CS continues to be the dominant firm in the office equipment field, but competition is expected to increase as other firms obtain better footholds in the market. Even though CS's share of the market has been declining gradually over the past several years, shipments this year are expected to comprise 65 percent of the U. S. total sales. Whether the company's diversification program will successfully combat its recent declining rate of growth in earnings remains to be seen.

Sales revenues are expected to rise somewhat more than shipments because of a trend toward leasing. CS's sales for the current year are estimated at $7.5 billion, up from $7.2 billion in 19x9, and sales for next year are expected to rise moderately from the current year as well. Much of the increase in both years is expected to come from the foreign market, which should more than offset expected weaknesses in domestic shipments. Margins are expected to narrow slightly due to competitive pressure on prices and heavier promotion and start-up costs.

Earnings per share in the current year are estimated at $8.90, up from $8.21 in 19x9. The average number of shares currently outstanding is 114.1 million versus 113.7 million in 19x9.

The current quarterly dividend has been raised to $1.20 from $.90 last year. Next year's dividend is also expected to be increased, but by a smaller amount than this year's increase.

The current share price of common stock is about $310.

QUESTIONS

1. (a) Plot the per share data on semilog graph paper for each of the following for the period 19x0 through the current year: (1) sales, (2) earnings, (3) dividends, and (4) average market price.

   (b) Project each of the above values for the next 5 years.

   (c) Based upon your results of 1(b), estimate the implicit annual growth rates for each of the variables. How do these growth rates compare with those over the past decade?

2. Based upon Holt's model, estimate the investor's growth horizon for CS's common stock. Use the Standard and Poor's Industrial Stock Index and historical data in your computations.

3. (a) Discuss the applicability of Malkiel's finite horizon model to the valuation of CS's stock.

   (b) What complications arise if one attempts to solve, via Malkiel's model, for the implicit growth rate accorded to CS's earnings by investors?

4. Value the stock via Graham and Dodd's earnings multipliers.

5. Based upon the case text, compare CS's current return/risk position with the company's return/risk position of the past decade. Does the comparison reveal any implications about the future *HPR*s for CS's common stock? Explain.

EXHIBIT 1

COMPUTER SYSTEMS, INC.

Balance Sheet Data (millions)

	19x9	19x8	19x7	19x6	19x5	19x4	19x3	19x2	19x1	19x0
Assets:										
Current	3250.0	3301.1	2078.6	1540.1	1414.7	1537.7	1134.4	795.1	627.8	572.2
Cash Items	1431.4	1873.3	851.1	546.9	694.3	873.2	719.3	470.3	327.2	320.5
Receivables	1550.6	1201.5	1013.4	803.0	573.7	546.1	367.7	280.7	258.8	214.3
Inventory	268.0	226.3	214.1	190.2	146.7	118.4	47.4	44.1	41.8	37.4
Fixed	3863.5	3415.0	3496.3	3098.6	2303.5	1747.9	973.6	960.4	936.9	849.7
Other	276.5	27.3	23.8	22.1	26.7	23.6	265.9	229.0	203.9	113.5
Total Assets	7390.0	6743.4	5598.7	4660.8	3744.9	3309.2	2373.9	1984.5	1768.6	1535.4
Liabilities:										
Current	1435.9	1531.0	1162.2	816.9	716.1	637.7	357.1	178.9	154.5	137.6
Bonds	554.8	545.1	521.5	458.9	398.8	370.4	425.0	425.0	425.0	425.0
Other	122.3	97.8	83.4	62.3	51.9	47.0	.1	-0-	3.9	-0-
Common Stock	2277.4	2095.6	1936.9	1311.3	862.2	804.3	753.9	715.4	678.6	651.0
Surplus	2999.6	2473.9	1894.7	2011.4	1715.9	1449.8	837.8	665.2	506.6	321.8
Total Liabilities	7390.0	6743.4	5598.7	4660.8	3744.9	3309.2	2373.9	1984.5	1768.6	1535.4

EXHIBIT 2

Income Data (millions)

COMPUTER SYSTEMS, INC.

	19x9	19x8	19x7	19x6	19x5	19x4	19x3	19x2	19x1	19x0
Sales	7197.3	6888.5	5345.3	4247.7	3572.8	3299.4	2059.6	1925.2	1694.3	1436.1
Cost of Goods Sold	2692.6	2676.1	2260.6	1756.4	1363.1	1224.6	818.3	848.4	776.6	643.4
Depreciation	1008.6	975.2	863.6	640.6	523.3	475.3	283.0	278.1	249.2	218.0
Operating Expenses	1577.3	1390.0	913.4	805.0	741.0	655.4	413.8	336.8	264.8	245.9
Operating Income	1918.8	1847.2	1307.7	1045.7	945.4	884.1	544.5	461.9	403.7	328.8
Other Income	95.0	58.1	27.2	32.2	32.6	36.2	59.9	47.7	37.2	32.3
Earnings Before Interest & Taxes	2013.8	1905.3	1334.9	1077.9	978.0	920.3	604.4	509.6	440.9	361.1
Interest	34.9	40.8	37.4	23.8	18.1	23.1	15.0	15.2	15.2	15.2
Earnings Before Taxes	1978.9	1864.5	1297.5	1054.1	959.9	897.2	589.4	494.4	425.7	345.9
Taxes	1045.0	993.0	646.0	528.0	483.0	466.0	298.9	253.0	218.5	177.7
Common Earnings	933.9	871.5	651.5	526.1	476.9	431.2	290.5	241.4	207.2	168.2
Common Dividends	407.8	292.6	243.2	230.7	210.8	166.0	118.0	83.0	63.3	54.9
No. of Common Shares	113.7	113.0	112.1	111.7	108.4	107.8	106.8	106.3	106.2	105.8

EXHIBIT 3

Per Share Income Data

COMPUTER SYSTEMS, INC.

	19x9	19x8	19x7	19x6	19x5	19x4	19x3	19x2	19x1	19x0
Sales	63.27	60.94	47.67	38.03	32.96	30.05	19.28	18.10	15.95	13.58
Cost of Goods Sold	23.67	23.67	20.16	15.72	12.58	11.36	7.66	7.98	7.31	6.08
Depreciation	8.87	8.63	7.70	5.74	4.83	4.41	2.65	2.62	2.35	2.06
Operating Expenses	13.86	12.30	8.15	7.21	6.83	6.08	3.87	3.16	2.49	2.33
Operating Income	16.87	16.34	11.66	9.36	8.72	8.20	5.10	4.34	3.80	3.11
Other Income	.83	.52	.24	.29	.30	.34	.56	.45	.35	.30
Earnings Before Interest & Taxes	17.70	16.86	11.90	9.65	9.02	8.54	5.66	4.79	4.15	3.41
Interest	.30	.37	.33	.21	.16	.22	.14	.14	.14	.14
Earnings Before Taxes	17.40	16.49	11.57	9.44	8.86	8.32	5.52	4.65	4.01	3.27
Taxes	9.19	8.78	5.76	4.73	4.46	4.32	2.80	2.38	2.06	1.68
Common Earnings	8.21	7.71	5.81	4.71	4.40	4.00	2.72	2.27	1.95	1.59
Common Dividends	3.60	2.60	2.17	2.07	1.94	1.54	1.10	.78	.60	.52

EXHIBIT 4

Index Values per Share

COMPUTER SYSTEMS, INC.

	19x9	19x8	19x7	19x6	19x5	19x4	19x3	19x2	19x1	19x0
Total Assets	4.48	4.11	3.44	2.87	2.38	2.12	1.53	1.29	1.15	1.00
Sales	4.66	4.49	3.51	2.80	2.43	2.21	1.42	1.33	1.17	1.00
Cost of Goods Sold	3.89	3.89	3.31	2.59	2.07	1.87	1.26	1.31	1.20	1.00
Depreciation	4.30	4.19	3.74	2.78	2.34	2.14	1.29	1.27	1.14	1.00
Operating Expenses	5.97	5.29	3.50	3.10	2.94	2.62	1.67	1.36	1.07	1.00
Operating Income	5.43	5.26	3.75	3.01	2.81	2.64	1.64	1.40	1.22	1.00
Earnings Before Interest & Taxes	5.19	4.94	3.49	2.83	2.64	2.50	1.66	1.40	1.22	1.00
Interest	2.14	2.51	2.32	1.48	1.16	1.49	.98	.99	1.00	1.00
Earnings Before Taxes	5.32	5.04	3.54	2.89	2.71	2.55	1.69	1.42	1.23	1.00
Taxes	5.47	5.23	3.43	2.81	2.65	2.57	1.67	1.42	1.22	1.00
Earnings After Taxes	5.16	4.85	3.65	2.96	2.77	2.52	1.71	1.43	1.23	1.00
Common Earnings	5.16	4.85	3.65	2.96	2.77	2.52	1.71	1.43	1.23	1.00
Common Dividends	6.91	4.99	4.18	3.98	3.75	2.97	2.13	1.50	1.15	1.00

COMPUTER SYSTEMS, INC.

EXHIBIT 5
Selected Data

	19x9	19x8	19x7	19x6	19x5	19x4	19x3	19x2	19x1	19x0
Return on Sales (%)	13.0	12.7	12.2	12.4	13.3	13.3	14.1	12.5	12.2	11.7
Return on Assets (%)	12.6	12.9	11.6	11.3	12.7	13.0	12.2	12.2	11.7	11.0
Return on Equity (%)	17.7	19.1	17.0	15.8	18.5	19.1	18.3	17.5	17.5	17.3
Capital Turnover	.97	1.02	.96	.91	.95	.98	.87	.97	.96	.94
Inventory Turnover	10.05	11.83	10.56	9.23	9.29	10.34	17.26	19.24	18.58	17.20
Average Collection Period (Days)	78	63	68	68	58	61	64	52	55	54
Interest Coverage	57.70	46.70	35.69	45.29	54.03	39.84	40.29	33.53	29.01	23.76
Total Debt to Equity(%)	40.0	47.6	46.1	40.3	45.3	46.8	49.1	43.7	49.2	57.8
Tax Rate (%)	52.8	53.3	49.8	50.1	50.3	51.9	50.7	51.2	51.3	51.4
Book Value Per Share	46.39	40.42	34.17	29.75	23.79	20.91	14.90	12.98	11.16	9.20
Dividend Payout (%)	43.7	33.6	37.3	43.9	44.2	38.5	40.6	34.4	30.6	32.6
Debt Leverage, Dollars Per Share	2.24	2.37	1.72	1.28	1.31	1.20	.85	.64	.60	.54
Relative Debt Leverage (%)	27.3	30.8	29.6	27.1	29.9	30.1	31.2	28.3	30.6	33.9

EXHIBIT 6

Per Share Data

COMPUTER SYSTEMS, INC.

	19x9	19x8	19x7	19x6	19x5	19x4	19x3	19x2	19x1	19x0
Price:										
High	368.75	375.00	324.00	188.38	178.50	160.75	132.63	152.88	153.13	104.00
Low	291.75	280.00	176.75	141.13	131.38	132.00	99.88	78.13	116.38	70.63
Average	330.25	327.50	250.38	164.75	154.94	146.38	116.25	115.50	137.25	87.31
Price-Earnings:										
High	44.9	48.6	55.8	40.0	40.6	40.2	48.8	67.3	81.1	65.4
Low	35.5	36.3	30.4	30.0	29.9	33.0	36.7	34.4	59.7	44.2
Average	40.2	42.4	43.1	35.0	35.2	36.6	42.7	50.8	70.4	54.8
Market-Book Value:										
High	7.95	9.28	9.48	6.33	7.51	7.69	8.90	11.78	14.18	11.31
Low	6.29	6.93	5.17	4.74	5.52	6.31	6.70	6.02	10.43	7.68
Average	7.12	8.10	7.33	5.54	6.51	7.00	7.80	8.90	12.31	9.50

EXHIBIT 7

Selected Office and Business Equipment – Excluding IBM – Industry Data per Share   COMPUTER SYSTEMS, INC.

	19x9	19x8	19x7	19x6	19x5	19x4	19x3	19x2	19x1	19x0
Sales	139.90	124.30	109.84	85.55	70.87	66.74	60.90	95.55	97.17	90.75
Depreciation	12.45	9.77	9.90	7.47	6.09	4.70	3.83	4.11	4.11	3.56
Income Taxes	9.55	7.37	5.99	5.04	4.46	3.98	3.27	4.30	4.89	4.47
Common Earnings	9.27	7.96	6.89	5.66	4.50	3.71	2.95	3.86	3.82	3.71
Common Dividends	2.52	2.35	1.95	1.73	1.52	1.51	1.32	1.97	1.94	1.83
Price Index:										
High	415.41	387.67	358.76	263.04	217.03	150.51	124.67	163.92	178.29	117.02
Low	322.17	284.05	212.47	168.74	126.04	108.87	93.43	92.54	113.73	89.99
Average	368.79	335.86	285.62	215.89	171.54	129.69	109.05	128.23	146.01	103.51
Price/Earnings Ratio:										
High	44.8	48.7	52.1	46.5	48.2	40.6	42.3	42.5	46.7	31.5
Low	34.8	35.7	30.8	29.8	28.0	29.4	31.7	24.0	29.8	24.3
Average	39.8	42.2	41.5	38.2	38.1	35.0	37.0	33.3	38.3	27.9
Book Value Per Share	71.50	56.19	44.06	34.22	29.05	27.90	25.85	37.73	36.90	34.89
Book Value – % Return	12.97	14.17	15.64	16.54	15.15	13.07	11.25	10.11	10.24	10.56

Source: *S & P Analyst's Handbook.*

Case 11:   Management

Proprietary Drug Co.

*We do not underestimate the challenges that be ahead, but we know that challenges are, more often than not, disguised opportunities. (*J. Mark Hiebert.*)*

Proprietary Drug (PD) was incorporated in Delaware in 1932. Its original name, Proprietary Products, was changed to its present one in 1942. The company has followed an aggressive policy of strengthening its position in the pharmaceutical field by acquiring firms which manufacture products with nationally recognized reputations.

The company's divisions and subsidiaries are engaged in the manufacture, packaging, and sale of two main groups of products: proprietary and ethical drugs. Proprietary drugs are nonprescription medicine products for general use, whereas ethical drugs are medicines which are promoted through professional channels and which require a prescription by a licensed physician. The company, through its subsidiaries, also produces a variety of other products used in the home, such as home cleaners, disinfectants, flavorings, dyestuffs, and food enrichments. In addition, the company has developed a process which eliminates the pollution of streams caused by industrial waste; the process also recovers usable chemicals from the waste.

PD's sales breakdown for last year was as follows: 35 percent pharmaceutical specialties, 33 percent proprietary medicines, 20 percent other consumer products, and 12 percent industrial products.

PD has extensive business interests in several foreign countries, namely Canada, Mexico, England, Germany, Australia, and South Africa. The company's foreign operations, which accounted for approximately 37 percent of total sales last year, are conducted through subsidiaries.

Total sales of the drug industry are expected to increase on the average, by 10 percent per year over the next decade. On an annual basis, domestic growth is forecast at 8 percent and foreign growth at 12 percent.

Research expenditures are considered vital to a firm's success in meeting competition in the drug industry. The importance of research in this area is indicated by the fact that seven out of 10 ethical drug prescriptions written today are filled with medicines unknown 15 years ago. Last year research spending in the U. S. totaled $556 million, and these expenditures are also expected to grow at 10 percent per year over the next decade. Currently research expenditures for drugs and drug sundries are financed almost entirely by private firms.

Proposals have been made to expand Medicare to include outpatient drugs. There is a high probability that the hospital care benefits will be extended to a greater number of people and that payments for drugs will be substantially expanded but it is not yet certain when Congress will act on these matters. New drug approvals are becoming increasingly more difficult to obtain because of more rigorous standards set by the Federal Drug Administration. In addition, Congressional action relating to the drug industry is becoming more stringent and the Justice Department has been attempting, through its antitrust cases, to bring the prices of prescription drugs down. With the Government's role as a purchaser of drugs increasing, more attempts at regulation are likely. Currently the Federal Government accounts for almost 15 percent of all pharmaceutical sales. According to a task force on prescription drugs of the Department of Health, Education, and Welfare, this proportion could rise to as high as 45 percent over the next 5 years.

Worldwide sales of ethical drugs produced in the U. S. grew at an annual rate of 8.6 percent in the past decade. Domestic sales grew at a 6.5 percent rate and foreign sales at a 13 percent rate. Sales of domestic ethical drugs are expected to grow at just over a 5 percent annual rate during the next 5 years, and sales in foreign markets should grow by more than 10 percent annually. While there is currently a declining trend in new drug introduction, the older established products continue to return high profits.

PD has proven itself an able competitor in the drug industry. The company's sales for the current year are expected to increase by 9 percent in spite of a lengthy strike at some of its facilities. Although operating income will probably increase by only about 6.5 percent, a lower tax rate should help net common stock earnings increase by nearly 11 percent. The dividend rate is expected to increase to $.19 quarterly. PD's sales next year are expected to increase by at least 10 percent. Sales of the company's main products, particularly in foreign markets, will be counted on to produce these gains.

Dividends have been paid each year by PD for the past 70 years, and recent policy has been to pay out approximately 50 percent of earnings.

Capital expenditures of $19.0 million are planned for the current year compared with $16.6 million in 19x9.

The company's current capital structure consists of $17.4 million long-term debt; 940,000 shares of $1.50 preferred, convertible into $1\frac{7}{8}$ shares of common and redeemable at $55 per share; and 37.1 million shares of common stock.

The current share price of PD's common stock is $43.

QUESTIONS

1. Appraise PD's overall performance over the past decade. Identify the company's strengths and weaknesses.

2. (a) Using the log-trend equations in Exhibit 7, forecast sales per share earnings per share, and dividends per share for PD for next year and for 5 years hence.
   (b) How much reliability would you place in the above forecasts? Why?
   (c) Are these forecasts consistent with the information given in the text of the case? Explain.

3. Value PD's common stock based upon:
   (a) Graham and Dodd's earnings multipliers
   (b) Walter's model

4. Is Gordon's basic dividend model applicable to the valuation of PD's stock? Why or why not?

5. Compute the growth horizon for PD's common stock based upon Holt's model. Use the Standard and Poor's Industrial Stock Index in your computations.

6. Based upon your analyses above, how would you expect PD's *HPR* next year to compare with those of the past 5 years? Explain.

EXHIBIT 1

PROPRIETARY DRUG CO.

Balance Sheet Data (millions)

	19x9	19x8	19x7	19x6	19x5	19x4	19x3	19x2	19x1	19x0
Assets:										
Current	242.1	220.3	190.8	180.4	144.6	124.8	114.2	103.2	97.6	95.7
Cash Items	56.8	62.6	45.6	50.5	41.7	37.4	33.8	30.4	26.6	26.7
Receivables	91.9	78.7	71.9	58.7	53.8	43.0	37.1	31.6	29.9	28.5
Inventory	93.4	79.0	73.3	71.2	49.1	44.4	43.3	41.2	41.1	40.5
Other	38.3	37.6	34.7	29.6	25.2	26.3	30.6	31.3	30.4	27.1
Fixed	90.4	83.6	77.0	70.0	51.4	47.3	47.0	43.4	43.1	42.8
Total Assets	370.8	341.5	302.5	280.0	221.2	198.4	191.8	177.9	171.1	165.6
Liabilities:										
Current	78.5	75.5	60.2	60.2	41.7	31.1	30.8	29.9	33.1	35.5
Bonds	17.9	19.1	19.4	19.9	15.9	19.0	19.9	20.8	21.6	22.9
Other	8.4	8.8	8.3	8.2	7.6	7.1	6.7	5.5	5.7	6.3
Preferred Stock	16.6	18.2	18.6	19.3	-0-	-0-	-0-	-0-	-0-	-0-
Common Stock	79.0	78.4	47.7	47.3	50.5	52.6	60.0	39.9	39.8	39.7
Surplus	170.4	141.5	148.3	125.1	105.5	88.6	74.4	81.8	70.9	61.2
Total Liabilities	370.8	341.5	302.5	280.0	221.2	198.4	191.8	177.9	171.1	165.6

EXHIBIT 2

PROPRIETARY DRUG CO.

Income Data (millions)

	19x9	19x8	19x7	19x6	19x5	19x4	19x3	19x2	19x1	19x0
Sales	546.8	490.9	448.9	417.3	303.3	268.5	252.5	239.3	229.2	218.5
Cost of Goods Sold	209.5	185.0	173.9	157.6	114.1	103.5	98.1	95.2	91.4	86.4
Depreciation	7.1	6.4	5.5	5.2	4.1	3.7	3.6	3.6	3.4	3.3
Operating Expenses*	231.7	211.1	191.8	181.8	123.2	105.8	98.5	91.5	88.1	84.8
Operating Income	98.5	88.4	77.7	72.7	61.9	55.5	52.3	49.0	46.3	44.0
Other Income	5.0	2.5	2.9	2.8	2.3	1.3	1.1	.6	1.6	2.2
Earnings Before Interest & Taxes	103.5	90.9	80.6	75.5	64.2	56.8	53.4	49.6	47.9	46.2
Interest	1.3	1.3	1.3	1.2	.8	.8	.8	.8	.9	1.0
Earnings Before Taxes	102.2	89.6	79.3	74.3	63.4	56.0	52.6	48.8	47.0	45.2
Taxes	50.3	42.5	35.1	33.9	29.7	26.8	26.2	24.8	23.5	23.0
Earnings After Taxes	51.9	47.1	44.2	40.4	33.7	29.2	26.4	24.0	23.5	22.2
Preferred Dividends	1.6	1.7	1.8	.9	-0-	-0-	-0-	-0-	-0-	-0-
Common Earnings	50.3	45.4	42.4	39.5	33.7	29.2	26.4	24.0	23.5	22.2
Common Dividends	26.0	24.4	22.2	20.4	18.2	16.5	15.3	14.3	14.3	14.3
No. of Common Shares	36.7	36.3	36.0	35.8	35.8	34.8	36.0	35.9	35.8	35.7
*The following lease charges have been included in operating expenses:	8.5	7.3	5.8	5.5	3.9	1.5	1.2	1.3	1.2	1.2

PROPRIETARY DRUG CO.

EXHIBIT 3

Per Share Income Data

	19x9	19x8	19x7	19x6	19x5	19x4	19x3	19x2	19x1	19x0
Sales	14.90	13.52	12.47	11.66	8.47	7.72	7.01	6.67	6.40	6.12
Cost of Goods Sold	5.71	5.10	4.83	4.40	3.19	2.97	2.72	2.65	2.55	2.42
Depreciation	.19	.18	.15	.15	.11	.11	.10	.10	.09	.09
Operating Expenses	6.32	5.80	5.33	5.08	3.44	3.05	2.74	2.56	2.47	2.38
Operating Income	2.68	2.44	2.16	2.03	1.73	1.59	1.45	1.36	1.29	1.23
Other Income	.14	.06	.08	.08	.06	.04	.03	.02	.05	.06
Earnings Before Interest & Taxes	2.82	2.50	2.24	2.11	1.79	1.63	1.48	1.38	1.34	1.29
Interest	.04	.03	.04	.03	.02	.02	.02	.02	.03	.02
Earnings Before Taxes	2.78	2.47	2.20	2.08	1.77	1.61	1.46	1.36	1.31	1.27
Taxes	1.37	1.17	.97	.95	.83	.77	.73	.69	.65	.65
Earnings After Taxes	1.41	1.30	1.23	1.13	.94	.84	.73	.67	.66	.62
Preferred Dividends	.04	.05	.05	.03	-0-	-0-	-0-	-0-	-0-	-0-
Common Earnings	1.37	1.25	1.18	1.10	.94	.84	.73	.67	.66	.62
Common Dividends	.71	.67	.62	.57	.51	.47	.42	.40	.40	.40

EXHIBIT 4

Index Values per Share

PROPRIETARY DRUG CO.

	19x0	19x1	19x2	19x3	19x4	19x5	19x6	19x7	19x8	19x9
Total Assets	1.00	1.03	1.07	1.15	1.23	1.33	1.69	1.81	2.03	2.18
Sales	1.00	1.05	1.09	1.15	1.26	1.38	1.90	2.04	2.21	2.43
Cost of Goods Sold	1.00	1.05	1.10	1.13	1.23	1.32	1.82	2.00	2.11	2.36
Depreciation	1.00	1.03	1.08	1.08	1.15	1.24	1.57	1.65	1.91	2.09
Operating Expenses	1.00	1.04	1.07	1.15	1.28	1.45	2.14	2.24	2.45	2.66
Operating Income	1.00	1.05	1.11	1.18	1.29	1.40	1.65	1.75	1.98	2.18
Earnings Before Interest & Taxes	1.00	1.03	1.07	1.15	1.26	1.39	1.63	1.73	1.94	2.18
Interest	1.00	.90	.80	.79	.82	.80	1.20	1.29	1.28	1.26
Earnings Before Taxes	1.00	1.04	1.07	1.15	1.27	1.40	1.64	1.74	1.95	2.20
Taxes	1.00	1.02	1.07	1.13	1.20	1.29	1.47	1.51	1.82	2.13
Earnings After Taxes	1.00	1.06	1.08	1.18	1.35	1.51	1.81	1.97	2.09	2.27
Common Earnings	1.00	1.06	1.08	1.18	1.35	1.51	1.77	1.89	2.01	2.20
Common Dividends	1.00	1.00	.99	1.06	1.18	1.27	1.42	1.54	1.68	1.77
No. of Common Shares	1.00	1.00	1.01	1.01	.97	1.00	1.00	1.01	1.02	1.03

EXHIBIT 5

PROPRIETARY DRUG CO.

Selected Data

	19x9	19x8	19x7	19x6	19x5	19x4	19x3	19x2	19x1	19x0
Return on Sales (%)	9.2	9.2	9.4	9.5	11.1	10.9	10.5	10.0	10.3	10.2
Return on Assets (%)	14.0	13.8	14.6	14.4	15.2	14.7	13.8	13.5	13.7	13.4
Return on Equity (%)	20.2	20.6	21.6	22.9	21.6	20.7	19.6	19.7	21.2	22.0
Capital Turnover	1.48	1.44	1.48	1.49	1.37	1.35	1.32	1.35	1.34	1.32
Inventory Turnover	2.24	2.34	2.37	2.21	2.32	2.33	2.27	2.31	2.22	2.13
Average Collection Period (Days)	60	58	58	51	64	58	53	47	47	47
Interest Coverage	79.62	69.92	62.00	62.92	81.25	71.00	66.75	62.00	53.22	46.20
Prior Charge Coverage	8.68	8.25	8.15	9.64	14.49	25.35	27.30	24.24	23.38	21.54
Total Debt to Equity (%)	42.0	47.0	44.8	51.2	41.8	40.5	42.7	46.2	54.6	64.1
Preferred to Equity (%)	6.7	8.3	9.5	11.2	-0-	-0-	-0-	-0-	-0-	-0-
Tax Rate (%)	49.2	47.4	44.3	45.6	46.8	47.9	49.8	50.8	50.0	50.9
Book Value Per Share	6.80	6.06	5.44	4.82	4.36	4.06	3.73	3.39	3.09	2.83
Dividend Payout (%)	51.7	53.7	52.4	51.6	54.0	56.5	58.0	59.6	60.9	64.4
Debt Leverage, Dollars Per Share	.39	.38	.34	.34	.27	.23	.21	.20	.22	.23
Preferred Leverage, Dollars Per Share	.02	.02	.03	.05	-0-	-0-	-0-	-0-	-0-	-0-
Relative Debt Leverage (%)	28.2	30.4	29.1	31.1	28.6	27.8	28.9	30.5	34.1	37.7
Relative Preferred Leverage (%)	1.5	1.9	2.3	4.9	-0-	-0-	-0-	-0-	-0-	-0-

EXHIBIT 6

Per Share Data

PROPRIETARY DRUG CO.

	19x9	19x8	19x7	19x6	19x5	19x4	19x3	19x2	19x1	19x0
Price:										
High	44.75	40.38	35.63	27.88	27.50	22.25	23.38	20.38	22.13	15.88
Low	32.38	27.38	25.63	21.50	18.63	18.00	15.88	12.25	14.88	9.88
Average	38.56	33.88	30.63	24.69	23.06	20.13	19.63	16.31	18.50	12.88
Price–Earnings:										
High	32.7	32.3	30.2	25.3	29.2	26.5	32.0	30.4	33.5	25.6
Low	23.6	21.9	21.7	19.5	19.8	21.4	21.7	18.3	22.5	15.9
Average	28.1	27.1	26.0	22.4	24.5	23.9	26.8	24.4	28.0	20.7
Market–Book Value:										
High	6.59	6.67	6.54	5.79	6.31	5.48	6.26	6.01	7.13	5.62
Low	4.77	4.52	4.71	4.47	4.28	4.44	4.25	3.62	4.82	3.50
Average	5.68	5.59	5.63	5.13	5.29	4.96	5.26	4.82	5.97	4.56

EXHIBIT 7

Log-trend Equations of per Share Data

PROPRIETARY DRUG CO.

19x0-19x9
Log y = a + bx

Sales	Common Earnings	Common Dividends
y = .738 + .048x	y = -.241 + .044x	y = -.439 + .032x
x - 1 year	x = 1 year	x = 1 year
origin = 19x0	origin = 19x0	origin = 19x0
Sy.x = .077	Sy.x = .048	Sy.x = .039
r - .88	r - .91	r = .90

EXHIBIT 8

Selected Drugs Industry Data per Share

PROPRIETARY DRUG CO.

	19x9	19x8	19x7	19x6	19x5	19x4	19x3	19x2	19x1	19x0
Sales	56.00	51.04	44.27	47.47	40.41	35.33	34.87	32.87	30.44	29.21
Depreciation	1.22	1.12	.98	.83	.73	.66	.66	.63	.55	.50
Income Taxes	5.15	4.65	3.80	3.85	3.33	2.96	2.80	2.59	2.38	2.28
Common Earnings	5.26	4.73	4.39	4.31	3.77	3.23	2.96	2.68	2.51	2.48
Common Dividends	2.87	2.69	2.49	2.31	2.08	1.79	1.68	1.58	1.54	1.47
Price Index:										
High	165.05	139.63	136.87	108.79	106.68	82.95	75.16	79.44	80.66	69.57
Low	127.88	111.75	102.71	88.89	82.97	72.62	61.71	50.06	62.21	53.71
Average	146.52	125.69	119.79	98.84	94.83	79.29	68.44	64.75	71.44	61.64
Price/Earnings Ratio:										
High	31.4	29.5	31.2	25.2	28.3	25.7	25.4	29.6	32.1	28.0
Low	24.3	23.6	23.4	20.6	22.0	22.5	20.8	18.7	24.8	21.7
Average	27.8	26.5	27.3	22.9	25.1	24.1	23.1	24.1	28.4	24.8
Book Value Per Share	22.85	20.92	18.55	17.51	16.25	15.77	15.84	14.94	14.06	13.01
Book Value – % Return	23.02	22.61	23.67	24.61	23.20	20.48	18.69	17.94	17.85	19.06

Source: *S & P Analyst's Handbook.*

Case 12: Valuation of a Defense Oriented Firm

General Aviation Company

The point of all this is simply that, in this climate, one never knows what a Sunday night may bring. And the circumspect investor will keep all the alternatives in mind, his foot near the brake and his hand by the gear shift. (Wall Street Transcript.)

General Aviation (GA) was incorporated in California in 1937 to produce light aircraft for the U. S. Army. During the next 30 years the company experienced relatively steady growth through both internal expansion and mergers with other firms. In 19x7 one of the largest commercial aircraft producers in the world was merged into the company; the merger gave GA one of the best balanced product mixes in the aerospace industry. The sales breakdown for the company's various products is currently as follows: 30 percent commercial aircraft, 40.5 percent military aircraft, 23.3 percent spacecraft and missiles, and 6.2 percent automation, electronics, nucleonics, and optics.

GA's principal military aircraft in recent years has been the F-40 fighter plane, which has proven highly successful. The F-40 is still in production, but its future depends upon the speed of development and acceptance of improved attack aircraft now in the developmental stage.

The popular D-8 and D-9 jetliners have been the principal commercial aircraft produced by the company in recent years. Most of the orders for these two aircraft have been filled, but additional orders may be received if the development of more advanced planes is less rapid than expected.

The aerospace industry is closely tied to both commercial aviation and national defense. Aircraft sales in both markets have been depressed since 19x8. The return after taxes on sales in the two markets is expected to decline to 2.0 percent this year and even further next year. Most of the earnings of aerospace companies have come from sales to airline companies during this period since government business has generally resulted in losses. Industry officials are looking for an upturn in aircraft demand toward the end of next year because of an improved economics situation and higher procurement by the Federal Government. However, profits will probably not increase significantly until the following year because of relatively high costs normally associated with the early stages of increased production. Most contracts involving aircraft orders are accounted for on a percentage-of-completion basis.

Regardless of best estimates, the sales and earnings of aerospace companies are highly uncertain. Defense spending will depend upon a number of factors, but mainly upon international political and military developments, the growing emphasis on environmental improvements, and political elections. Furthermore, more time than expected may be required to arrest the growing sluggishness in the economy.

The U. S. is seeking to reduce its direct involvement in immediate war efforts. When and if this goal is reached, the Pentagon will probably turn most of its attention to strategic and tactical weaponry, an area in which the Soviet Union has made substantially greater progress than the U. S. has during the Vietnam War period. Increased government spending for strategic and tactical weapons will benefit aerospace companies because of their intimate relationship with modern warfare techniques. Budgeted expenditures for research and development in the area are expected to increase next year.

After a 2-year decline which resulted in the equities of many companies in the industry falling by as much as 70 percent, prices of aerospace common stocks have shown some strength in recent weeks. Future price trends, however, will depend primarily upon future industry performance as well as the movement of stock prices in general.

The Federal Government must put up much of the money for development and production of aerospace products used in the defense effort. Cost overruns have been a serious problem. A recent development which the government hopes will provide better control over costs is the "milestone" approach. This approach requires the aerospace contractor to meet specific price and performance criteria at a number of "tilt points" during the life of the contract.

Progress payments are made to aircraft producers on aircraft orders by airline companies. Because of poor current earnings, however, most airline companies now agree to make progress payments of only 35 percent of total costs to be made 6 months before delivery.

GA has been developing a new fighter plane, the F-51, which until recently had successfully met each milestone. A congressional committee has now found the plane to be substandard when compared with a new Russian fighter already in production. Consequently, the future of the F-51 is uncertain and depends essentially upon whether GA can make the necessary improvements at a cost the government is willing to accept. Billings applicable to the plane could amount to over $8 billion if development is completed successfully in the near future. The F-51 would compete with Lockheed's F-14, but development of that plane is also beset with serious difficulties.

The company's principal commercial aircraft for the future is the D-10 which will compete with the Boeing 747 and the Lockheed L-1011. Company officials believe that the D-10 will be more efficient and cost considerably less than the now operational 747. Production of the L-1011 is expected to be severely delayed, if not cancelled, because of Lockheed's problems associated with the insolvency of Rolls-Royce which was to produce the engines for the plane.

GA is the prime contractor for a long-range interceptor of the Safeguard missile system. Although this project is potentially very profitable, it is controversial and may not receive congressional funding.

The company's current funded backlog is approximately $3 billion (70 percent commercial), up from $2.5 billion at the same time last year.

As a result of a settlement of a renegotiation of profits for the period July 1, 19x4, through December 31, 19x6, GA will be required to refund $21.5 million to the U. S. Government over a 4-year period beginning in the middle of next year. Sales and earnings for the relevant years will be restated.

The company has over $400 million in a revolving credit agreement for the next 3 years, with only $20 million taken down to date.

The most recent price of GA's common stock was $29\frac{1}{2}$.

QUESTIONS

1. Why did earnings per share of GA's common stock increase in 19x9 despite a decline in the company's sales for the year?

2. (a) Explain the principal factors which will probably affect GA's earnings for the current year.
(b) Estimate the company's earnings per share for the current year and for next year.
(c) Estimate the rate of growth of the company's earnings per share over the next 5 years.

3. (a) Explain the principal risk factors with which GA is faced.
(b) Discuss the impact of these risk factors on the valuation of GA's common stock.

4. (a) Explain the factors that caused a decline in the company's average price-earnings ratio from 19x6 through 19x8.
(b) Why did the average price-earnings ratio decline in 19x9?

5. (a) Is a stock value model applicable to GA's common stock? Why or why not?
(b) What do you think should be the required return on GA's common? Explain your reasoning.
(c) Estimate the value of GA's common.

EXHIBIT 1

Balance Sheet Data (millions)*

GENERAL AVIATION COMPANY

	19x9	19x8	19x7	19x6	19x5	19x4	19x3	19x2	19x1
Assets:									
Current	792.9	777.0	892.1	808.0	610.1	447.3	422.4	402.9	352.3
Cash Items	36.2	5.4	51.9	97.9	40.5	41.7	21.9	35.1	56.2
Receivables	170.3	172.1	165.6	119.7	147.3	126.5	136.2	169.8	118.4
Inventory	586.4	599.5	674.6	590.4	422.3	279.1	264.3	198.0	177.7
Other	438.7	335.8	262.7	225.2	149.0	85.6	51.9	27.3	23.5
Fixed	276.7	221.0	211.1	193.9	145.2	137.2	130.9	93.4	83.8
Total Assets	1508.3	1333.8	1365.9	1227.1	904.3	670.1	605.2	523.6	459.6
Liabilities:									
Current	632.4	638.4	823.0	657.0	389.0	234.3	230.3	199.6	156.8
Bonds	145.3	164.5	161.4	171.4	128.5	121.4	109.4	91.9	96.2
Other	156.9	66.5	17.6	34.2	46.3	20.5	9.6	6.2	4.5
Common Stock	238.2	235.6	218.9	148.2	110.7	85.6	71.3	58.8	53.8
Surplus	335.5	228.8	145.0	216.3	229.8	208.3	184.6	167.1	148.3
Total Liabilities	1508.3	1333.8	1365.9	1227.1	904.3	670.1	605.2	523.6	459.6

*All data prior to 1966 are pro forma, reflecting the merger which took place in 1966.

EXHIBIT 2

Income Data (millions)

GENERAL AVIATION COMPANY

	19x9	19x8	19x7	19x6	19x5	19x4	19x3	19x2	19x1
Sales	3023.8	3609.3	2933.8	2239.4	1761.6	1576.2	1391.1	1226.6	1115.5
Cost of Goods Sold	2766.2	3379.7	2900.4	2182.8	1652.5	1473.5	1305.3	1160.7	1057.7
Depreciation	43.5	36.1	34.0	28.1	23.3	22.3	16.8	14.9	19.6
Operating Income	214.1	193.5	(.6)	28.5	85.8	80.4	69.0	51.0	38.2
Other Income	37.5	21.2	22.1	23.2	13.4	7.2	4.0	8.0	3.5
Earnings Before Interest & Taxes	251.6	214.7	21.5	51.7	99.2	87.6	73.0	59.0	41.7
Interest	10.5	21.1	30.1	17.9	8.8	8.1	5.3	6.1	6.9
Earnings Before Taxes	241.1	193.6	(8.6)	33.8	90.4	79.5	67.7	52.9	34.8
Taxes	123.4	98.9	(9.5)	15.5	41.7	38.6	34.9	26.5	17.2
Common Earnings	117.7	94.7	.9	18.3	48.7	40.9	32.8	26.4	17.6
Common Dividends	11.6	11.5	10.8	8.3	7.6	4.1	3.8	3.7	3.4
No. of Common Shares	29.0	28.7	27.0	26.9	26.2	25.9	25.8	25.7	25.5

EXHIBIT 3

Per Share Income Data

GENERAL AVIATION COMPANY

	19x9	19x8	19x7	19x6	19x5	19x4	19x3	19x2	19x1
Sales	104.27	125.76	108.78	83.25	67.24	60.86	53.92	47.73	43.75
Cost of Goods Sold	95.39	117.76	107.54	81.15	63.08	56.90	50.60	45.17	41.48
Depreciation	1.50	1.26	1.26	1.04	.89	.86	.65	.58	.77
Operating Income	7.38	6.74	(.02)	1.06	3.27	3.10	2.67	1.98	1.50
Other Income	1.30	.74	.82	.86	.52	.28	.16	.32	.14
Earnings Before Interest & Taxes	8.68	7.48	.80	1.92	3.79	3.38	2.83	2.30	1.64
Interest	.37	.73	1.12	.66	.34	.31	.21	.24	.28
Earnings Before Taxes	8.31	6.75	(.32)	1.26	3.45	3.07	2.62	2.06	1.36
Taxes	4.25	3.45	(.35)	.58	1.59	1.49	1.35	1.03	.67
Common Earnings	4.06	3.30	.03	.68	1.86	1.58	1.27	1.03	.69
Common Dividends	.40	.40	.40	.31	.29	.16	.15	.14	.13

EXHIBIT 4

Index Values per Share

GENERAL AVIATION COMPANY

	19x1	19x2	19x3	19x4	19x5	19x6	19x7	19x8	19x9
Total Assets	1.00	1.13	1.30	1.44	1.92	2.53	2.81	2.58	2.89
Sales	1.00	1.09	1.23	1.39	1.54	1.90	2.49	2.87	2.38
Cost of Goods Sold	1.00	1.09	1.22	1.37	1.52	1.96	2.59	2.84	2.30
Depreciation	1.00	.75	.85	1.12	1.16	1.36	1.64	1.64	1.95
Operating Income	1.00	1.32	1.79	2.07	2.19	.71	(.01)	4.50	4.93
Earnings Before Interest & Taxes	1.00	1.40	1.73	2.07	2.32	1.18	.49	4.57	5.31
Interest	1.00	.88	.76	1.16	1.24	2.46	4.12	2.72	1.34
Earnings Before Taxes	1.00	1.51	1.92	2.25	2.53	.92	(.23)	4.94	6.09
Taxes	1.00	1.53	2.01	2.21	2.36	.85	(.52)	5.11	6.31
Earnings After Taxes	1.00	1.49	1.84	2.29	2.69	.99	.05	4.78	5.88
Common Earnings	1.00	1.49	1.84	2.29	2.69	.99	.05	4.78	5.88
Common Dividends	1.00	1.08	1.10	1.19	2.18	2.31	3.00	3.01	3.00
No. of Common Shares	1.00	1.01	1.01	1.02	1.03	1.05	1.06	1.13	1.14

EXHIBIT 5

Selected Data

GENERAL AVIATION COMPANY

	19x9	19x8	19x7	19x6	19x5	19x4	19x3	19x2	19x1
Return on Sales (%)	3.9	2.6	-0-	.8	2.8	2.6	2.4	2.2	1.6
Return on Assets (%)	7.8	7.1	.1	1.5	5.4	6.1	5.4	5.0	3.8
Return on Equity (%)	20.5	20.4	.2	5.0	14.3	13.9	12.8	11.7	8.7
Capital Turnover	2.01	2.71	2.15	1.83	1.95	2.35	2.30	2.34	2.43
Inventory Turnover	4.72	5.64	4.30	3.70	3.91	5.28	4.94	5.86	5.95
Average Collection Period (Days)	20	17	20	19	30	29	35	50	38
Interest Coverage	23.96	10.18	.72	2.89	11.27	10.82	13.77	9.67	6.04
Total Debt to Equity	1.63	1.87	2.75	2.37	1.66	1.28	1.36	1.32	1.27
Tax Rate (%)	51.2	51.1	--	45.9	46.1	48.6	51.6	50.1	49.4
Book Value Per Share	19.78	16.18	13.49	13.55	13.00	11.35	9.92	8.79	7.93
Dividend Payout (%)	9.9	12.1	--	45.4	15.6	10.0	11.6	14.0	19.3
Debt Leverage, Dollars Per Share	2.45	2.03	--	.37	1.09	.82	.69	.53	.33
Relative Debt Leverage (%)	60	61	--	55	59	52	54	52	47

EXHIBIT 6

GENERAL AVIATION COMPANY

Per Share Data

	19x9	19x8	19x7	19x6	19x5	19x4	19x3	19x2	19x1
Price:									
High	49.75	59.63	59.00	30.13	29.63	16.75	11.75	11.50	5.38
Low	23.25	43.50	25.50	18.25	13.25	10.25	10.00	6.88	3.13
Average	36.50	51.56	42.25	24.19	21.44	13.50	10.88	9.19	4.25
Price-Earnings:									
High	12.3	18.1	--	44.3	15.9	10.6	9.2	11.2	7.8
Low	5.7	13.2	--	26.8	7.1	6.5	7.9	6.7	4.5
Average	9.0	15.6	--	35.6	11.5	8.5	8.5	8.9	6.2
Market-Book Value:									
High	2.52	3.69	4.37	2.22	2.28	1.48	1.19	1.31	.68
Low	1.18	2.69	1.89	1.35	1.02	.90	1.01	.78	.40
Average	1.85	3.19	3.13	1.79	1.65	1.19	1.10	1.05	.54

EXHIBIT 7

Selected Aerospace Industry Data per Share

GENERAL AVIATION COMPANY

	19x9	19x8	19x7	19x6	19x5	19x4	19x3	19x2	19x1
Sales	260.16	277.48	251.25	218.11	202.45	208.99	212.25	215.87	204.01
Depreciation	6.89	6.14	5.16	3.95	3.74	4.00	3.76	3.59	3.46
Income Taxes	3.12	6.89	4.20	4.59	5.58	4.46	4.13	4.13	2.98
Common Earnings	4.05	6.66	5.60	5.89	6.35	5.08	4.71	4.74	.24
Common Dividends	2.54	2.56	2.34	2.29	2.28	1.93	1.85	1.76	1.63
Price Index:									
High	96.01	106.10	125.02	108.45	102.21	58.01	53.57	61.36	61.87
Low	51.60	87.92	86.50	70.06	57.71	45.38	44.94	44.21	49.90
Average	73.81	97.01	105.76	89.26	79.96	51.70	49.26	52.79	55.89
Price/Earnings Ratio:									
High	23.7	15.9	22.3	18.4	16.1	11.4	11.4	12.9	257.8
Low	12.7	13.2	15.4	11.9	9.1	8.9	9.5	9.3	207.9
Average	18.2	14.5	18.8	15.1	12.6	10.1	10.4	11.1	232.8
Book Value Per Share	51.85	53.74	50.25	46.22	42.36	40.73	38.00	34.42	30.64
Book Value - % Return	7.81	12.39	11.14	12.74	14.99	12.47	12.39	13.77	.78

Source: *S & P Analyst's Handbook.*

Case 13:   Comprehensive Case

Imperial Industries

The time has come for the burden of proof to be shifted to the proponents of concentration and of mergers: They should begin to demonstrate empirically the benefits which they "assume" to exist. (Samuel Richardson Reid.)

Imperial Industries (IPL) was incorporated in New York in 1927 as Independent Broadcasters, Inc. The name Imperial Industries was adopted in 1937. In its early years, the company's growth was slow and was primarily internal. However, a recording company was acquired in 1938 and a radio and electronics firm in 1951, but the latter firm was sold a decade later. Then, beginning in 19x4, IPL embarked on an aggressive acquisition policy with the objective of becoming a leader in a broad area of operations perhaps best described as the amusement industry. Accordingly, IPL acquired firms in the following areas: sports, electronic music, film, cable television (later discarded to conform to government regulations), and recording. In addition, the company has recently added publishing and space technology firms to its conglomeration of enterprises.

The company's performance compared to similar type firms was well above average from 19x0 through 19x6. However, IPL's entrance into the publishing field was fraught with difficulties and resulted in a sharp decline in total company profits for 19x7. In spite of sharply increased tax rates, the company's profits rebounded slightly in 19x8 and more significantly in 19x9. The profit improvement was the result of very strict cost control measures.

One of the major reasons for improved efficiency was a new organizational structure in which the company was divided into four main operational groupings, with each group headed by its own president. The four groups were: (1) broadcasting—consisting of four divisions including television network, television stations, radio, and news; (2) recording—consisting of five divisions including marketing, musical, films, records, and international operations; (3) publishing—consisting of four divisions including textbook, creative, educational films, and medical materials; and (4) electronic laboratory—consisting of three divisions including research and development, electronic video, and television services. The company also established a sports group which consisted essentially of a major league baseball team. The effect of the reorganization was to segment IPL into separate business entities, with substantial authority delegated to the president of each group.

The Broadcasting Industry

Television, along with radio, has become an integral part of American life; some 95 percent of all households currently own television sets. Profits in the radio and television broadcasting industry are depressed this year due primarily to rising costs. Next year, however, profits of the television companies are expected to rise because of lower operating costs resulting from a greater use of (1) reruns relative to original shows, (2) tapes in place of films, and (3) studio facilities in place of outside facilities. In addition, savings are expected to result from a reduction in the number of special television programs. On the other hand, revenues will probably be under pressure in future years because of a number of factors. Cable television (CATV), although still in its infancy, is growing rapidly and may cut substantially into network revenues in the long run. Network companies are prohibited from owning CATV systems. Other adverse factors for broadcasting network earnings include the growth of local and regional programming, program syndication, increased restrictions imposed by regulatory authorities, and a more liberal interpretation of the fairness doctrine which is causing an increase in demand for free television time. Furthermore, advertising by proprietary drug firms could be reduced significantly in the future if current congressional investigations result in sharp restrictions on the production, advertising, and/or sale of drugs.

The Recording Industry

The recording industry is one of the more rapidly growing fields of entertainment. In the last 20 years the sales of records have grown from $220 million to $1.2 billion. Important reasons for this growth have been the emergence of a large youth population and numerous technological innovations such as stereophonic systems and cassette tapes. This industry should continue to grow at a rate in excess of 10 percent per year.

The Publishing Industry

The publishing industry has enjoyed good growth due partly to its continued cultivation of American reading habits. The growth of the college population and increased level of education have also been prime factors leading to an increase in reading. However, the formerly lucrative textbook market is beginning to feel the pressures of the intense competition caused by new entrants into the field and a declining rate of growth in college enrollments. Several leading publishing firms have suffered earnings declines recently.

Over the longer term a 5 percent rate of growth in demand is likely.

The fourth major grouping of IPL's product areas—the electronic laboratory group—includes a research and development division which engages in research in such diverse fields as space and underwater exploration, medicine, and photocomposition. Breakthroughs in any of these areas could have a major impact on profits, but if important new products are not discovered and developed, research and development expenditures may not even pay for themselves.

The electronic video division of the group develops and markets a video recording apparatus which makes possible the use of conventional television sets in showing, at low-cost, prerecorded programs. Although IPL intends to develop this field extensively both domestically and abroad, the profit potential is uncertain at this time.

The television services division of the electronic laboratory group manages all of the company's foreign investments in various television-related fields. Television in foreign countries is in its infancy compared with the U. S. However, as the market grows so also will the degree of competition, especially from Japanese producers.

The amusement industry's growth depends upon the amount of discretionary disposable income. As the Gross National Product increases, disposable income increases at a faster rate. Thus expenditures for the products and services of the amusement industry are expected to grow in the future at a more rapid rate than GNP.

IPL's sales for this year are expected to increase about 6 percent from their level in 19x9. Broadcasting revenues will fall but sales in the other areas of the company's operations should increase, with the recording group achieving substantial gains. Rapidly increasing costs, however, are expected to cause a decline in operating income of approximately 15 percent. A somewhat lower tax rate than last year's 50.4 percent should pare the decline in net income to around 11 percent, resulting in earnings per share of $2.29 compared with $2.59 for 19x9. The sales and earnings' breakdowns by group for this year are expected to be as follows: broadcasting and electronic laboratory, 55 and 68 percent; recording, 34 and 22 percent; and publishing, 11 and 10 percent, respectively. (No breakdown between the broadcasting and electronic laboratory groups is currently available.)

Next year, revenues from broadcasting and educational publishing are expected to fall further. However, since these declines are expected to be offset by improvements in the other areas of the company's operations, total revenues for next year should be virtually unchanged from this year's $1.23 billion.

Recently, IPL acquired for $10 million a 49 percent interest in a firm which is engaged in the development of residential communities. The sales last year of this firm were $30 million. IPL has an option to purchase all of the remaining stock of the firm.

IPL's current share price is in the mid 30s.

QUESTIONS

1. (a) Explain the factors that have been primarily responsible for IPL's earnings per share variance since 19x5.

   (b) Are these factors likely to persist? Why or why not?

   (c) Are other factors likely to affect IPL's future earnings variance? Explain.

2. Estimate IPL's earnings per share for next year and for 5 years hence. Justify your estimates.

3. (a) Explain the relationship between expected earnings variance and the discount rate used in stock valuation.

   (b) Are there any factors that may negate this relationship for IPL's stock? Explain.

4. (a) Enumerate the principal factors in addition to expected earnings and expected earnings variance that determine the value of a share of common stock.

   (b) Is the price of a share of common stock the same as its value? Explain.

5. Estimate the value of IPL's common. Justify your estimate.

IMPERIAL INDUSTRIES

EXHIBIT 1

Balance Sheet Data (millions)

	19x9	19x8	19x7	19x6	19x5	19x4	19x3	19x2	19x1	19x0
Assets:										
Current										
Cash Items	538.0	435.9	384.6	400.2	268.9	274.8	228.0	215.9	193.1	174.1
Receivables	202.7	168.5	154.6	199.1	122.9	155.8	122.1	107.9	98.5	65.7
Inventory	248.9	201.4	166.1	164.6	128.8	107.7	94.8	98.2	83.7	83.8
Other	86.4	66.0	63.9	36.5	17.2	11.3	11.1	9.8	10.9	24.6
Fixed	73.4	100.1	106.2	48.6	60.2	43.5	20.7	18.1	16.6	15.5
	206.5	196.1	189.8	155.6	140.3	121.7	87.7	72.3	66.2	75.7
Total Assets	817.9	732.1	680.6	604.4	469.4	440.0	336.4	306.3	275.9	265.3
Liabilities:										
Current	209.3	178.0	136.8	171.6	135.8	132.9	73.7	83.8	81.5	79.6
Bonds	183.6	153.2	169.0	131.9	58.9	61.5	57.7	53.5	49.5	46.4
Other	23.0	22.3	20.7	13.7	13.6	11.1	6.4	4.5	2.5	2.3
Preferred Stock	2.6	2.9	3.1	-0-	-0-	-0-	-0-	-0-	-0-	-0-
Common Stock	262.2	240.4	217.2	165.3	150.7	134.0	112.1	85.1	72.0	62.4
Surplus	137.2	135.3	133.8	121.9	110.4	100.5	86.5	79.4	70.4	74.6
Total Liabilities	817.9	732.1	680.6	604.4	469.4	440.0	336.4	306.3	275.9	265.3

EXHIBIT 2

Income Data (millions)

IMPERIAL INDUSTRIES

	19x9	19x8	19x7	19x6	19x5	19x4	19x3	19x2	19x1	19x0
Sales	1158.9	991.4	920.2	884.8	699.7	638.1	564.8	521.9	473.8	464.6
Cost of Goods Sold	764.8	661.7	622.0	576.2	462.4	416.9	356.9	348.5	325.2	315.9
Depreciation	28.8	24.7	20.9	16.0	10.8	8.7	8.7	9.1	8.9	9.6
Operating Expenses	223.0	188.3	180.7	165.1	132.1	118.1	115.5	101.6	95.0	90.3
Operating Income	142.3	116.7	96.6	127.5	94.4	94.4	83.7	62.7	44.7	48.8
Other Income	13.4	10.3	11.5	13.8	4.2	7.8	5.6	4.0	3.9	4.2
Earnings Before Interest & Taxes	155.7	127.0	108.1	141.3	98.6	102.2	89.3	66.7	48.6	53.0
Interest	10.8	8.2	9.6	6.8	1.5	2.3	1.8	1.7	1.5	1.7
Earnings Before Taxes	144.9	118.8	98.5	134.5	97.1	99.9	87.5	65.0	47.1	51.3
Taxes	73.0	60.6	43.6	63.8	48.0	50.2	45.7	35.3	25.1	28.1
Earnings After Taxes	71.9	58.2	54.9	70.7	49.1	49.7	41.8	29.7	22.0	23.2
Preferred Dividends	2.7	3.0	3.1	-0-	-0-	-0-	-0-	-0-	-0-	-0-
Common Earnings	69.2	55.2	51.8	70.7	49.1	49.7	41.8	29.7	22.0	23.2
Common Dividends	35.8	34.2	31.7	28.4	23.6	20.3	13.9	12.4	12.1	11.6
No. of Common Shares	26.7	25.9	24.6	25.1	22.1	21.9	21.7	21.7	21.6	20.0

EXHIBIT 3

Per Share Income Data (millions)

IMPERIAL INDUSTRIES

	19x9	19x8	19x7	19x6	19x5	19x4	19x3	19x2	19x1	19x0
Sales	43.40	38.28	37.41	35.25	31.66	29.14	26.03	24.05	21.94	23.23
Cost of Goods Sold	28.64	25.55	25.28	22.96	20.92	19.04	16.45	16.06	15.06	15.79
Depreciation	1.08	.95	.85	.64	.49	.40	.40	.42	.41	.48
Operating Expenses	8.35	7.27	7.35	6.57	5.98	5.39	5.32	4.68	4.40	4.51
Operating Income	5.33	4.51	3.93	5.08	4.27	4.31	3.86	2.89	2.07	2.44
Other Income	.50	.39	.46	.55	.19	.36	.26	.18	.18	.21
Earnings Before Interest & Taxes	5.83	4.90	4.39	5.63	4.46	4.67	4.12	3.07	2.25	2.65
Interest	.40	.31	.39	.27	.07	.11	.09	.07	.07	.09
Earnings Before Taxes	5.43	4.59	4.00	5.36	4.39	4.56	4.03	3.00	2.18	2.56
Taxes	2.74	2.34	1.77	2.54	2.17	2.29	2.10	1.63	1.16	1.40
Earnings After Taxes	2.69	2.25	2.23	2.82	2.22	2.27	1.93	1.37	1.02	1.16
Preferred Dividends	.10	.12	.12	-0-	-0-	-0-	-0-	-0-	-0-	-0-
Common Earnings	2.59	2.13	2.11	2.82	2.22	2.27	1.93	1.37	1.02	1.16
Common Dividends	1.34	1.32	1.29	1.13	1.07	.93	.64	.57	.56	.58

Index Values per Share

IMPERIAL INDUSTRIES

	19x0	19x1	19x2	19x3	19x4	19x5	19x6	19x7	19x8	19x9
Total Assets	1.00	.96	1.06	1.17	1.51	1.60	1.82	2.09	2.13	2.31
Sales	1.00	.94	1.04	1.12	1.25	1.36	1.52	1.61	1.65	1.87
Cost of Goods Sold	1.00	.95	1.02	1.04	1.21	1.32	1.45	1.60	1.62	1.81
Depreciation	1.00	.85	.88	.83	.83	1.02	1.33	1.77	1.98	2.25
Operating Expenses	1.00	.98	1.04	1.18	1.20	1.33	1.46	1.63	1.61	1.85
Operating Income	1.00	.85	1.18	1.58	1.77	1.75	2.08	1.61	1.85	2.18
Earnings Before Interest & Taxes	1.00	.85	1.16	1.55	1.76	1.68	2.12	1.66	1.85	2.20
Interest	1.00	.82	.92	.98	1.24	.80	3.19	4.59	3.72	4.76
Earnings Before Taxes	1.00	.85	1.17	1.57	1.78	1.71	2.09	1.56	1.79	2.12
Taxes	1.00	.83	1.16	1.50	1.63	1.55	1.81	1.26	1.67	1.95
Earnings After Taxes	1.00	.88	1.18	1.66	1.96	1.92	2.43	1.92	1.94	2.32
Common Earnings	1.00	.88	1.18	1.66	1.96	1.92	2.43	1.82	1.84	2.23
Common Dividends	1.00	.97	.99	1.10	1.60	1.84	1.95	2.22	2.28	2.31
No. of Common Shares	1.00	1.08	1.08	1.08	1.09	1.10	1.25	1.23	1.29	1.33

EXHIBIT 5
Selected Data

IMPERIAL INDUSTRIES

	19x9	19x8	19x7	19x6	19x5	19x4	19x3	19x2	19x1	19x0
Return on Sales (%)	6.0	5.6	5.6	8.0	7.0	7.8	7.4	5.7	4.6	5.0
Return on Assets (%)	8.8	7.9	8.1	11.7	10.5	11.3	12.4	9.7	8.0	8.7
Return on Equity (%)	17.3	14.7	14.8	24.6	18.8	21.2	21.0	18.1	15.4	16.9
Capital Turnover	1.42	1.35	1.35	1.46	1.49	1.45	1.68	1.70	1.72	1.75
Inventory Turnover	8.85	10.03	9.73	15.79	26.88	36.89	32.15	35.56	29.84	12.84
Average Collection Period (Days)	77	73	65	67	66	61	60	68	64	65
Interest Coverage	14.42	15.49	11.26	20.78	65.73	44.44	49.61	39.24	32.40	31.18
Total Debt to Equity	1.04	.94	.93	1.10	.80	.88	.69	.86	.94	.94
Tax Rate (%)	50.4	51.0	44.3	47.4	49.4	50.3	52.2	54.3	53.3	54.8
Book Value Per Share	14.96	14.51	14.27	11.44	11.81	10.71	9.15	7.58	6.59	6.85
Dividend Payout (%)	51.7	62.0	61.2	40.2	48.1	40.8	33.3	41.8	55.0	50.0
Debt Leverage, Dollars Per Share	1.27	1.01	.96	1.41	.97	1.03	.77	.61	.48	.54
Preferred Leverage, Dollars Per Share	(.09)	(.11)	(.11)	-0-	-0-	-0-	-0-	-0-	-0-	-0-
Relative Debt Leverage (%)	49	47	45	50	43	45	40	45	47	47
Relative Preferred Leverage (%)	(4)	(6)	(6)	-0-	-0-	-0-	-0-	-0-	-0-	-0-

EXHIBIT 6

Per Share Data

IMPERIAL INDUSTRIES

	19x9	19x8	19x7	19x6	19x5	19x4	19x3	19x2	19x1	19x0
Price:										
High	57.25	57.38	70.63	59.13	42.50	42.25	35.75	18.50	16.63	17.38
Low	40.13	41.25	43.50	38.13	29.75	31.00	17.88	12.88	12.13	12.88
Average	48.69	49.31	57.06	48.63	36.13	36.63	26.81	15.69	14.38	15.13
Price-Earnings:										
High	22.1	26.9	33.5	20.9	19.1	18.6	18.6	13.5	16.3	14.9
Low	15.5	19.4	20.7	13.5	13.4	13.7	9.3	9.4	11.9	11.1
Average	18.8	23.1	27.1	17.2	16.2	16.1	13.9	11.4	14.1	13.0
Market-Book Value:										
High	3.83	3.96	4.95	5.17	3.60	3.95	3.91	2.44	2.52	2.54
Low	2.68	2.84	3.05	3.33	2.52	2.90	1.95	1.70	1.84	1.88
Average	3.25	3.40	4.00	4.25	3.06	3.42	2.93	2.07	2.18	2.21

IMPERIAL INDUSTRIES

EXHIBIT 7

Selected Radio-TV Broadcasters Industry Data per Share

	19x9	19x8	19x7	19x6	19x5	19x4	19x3	19x2	19x1	19x0
Sales	279.32	193.27	179.27	181.52	158.04	145.34	125.91	110.99	105.98	103.66
Depreciation	7.81	6.03	5.16	4.17	3.50	2.91	2.62	2.21	2.23	2.33
Income Taxes	15.93	14.55	10.42	13.78	11.81	12.08	10.94	8.61	6.39	6.96
Common Earnings	14.35	12.84	11.89	15.20	12.53	12.15	10.11	7.29	5.57	5.92
Common Dividends	6.09	6.00	5.85	5.39	5.54	4.81	3.66	3.48	3.47	3.39
Price Index:										
High	317.79	343.79	362.90	303.39	233.77	207.06	177.40	101.01	93.17	93.99
Low	229.17	241.85	253.97	221.40	163.65	165.77	100.34	76.68	74.58	77.26
Average	273.48	292.82	308.44	262.40	198.71	186.42	138.87	88.85	83.88	85.63
Price/Earnings Ratio:										
High	22.2	26.8	30.5	20.0	18.7	17.0	17.6	13.9	16.7	15.9
Low	6.0	18.8	21.4	14.6	13.1	13.6	9.9	10.5	13.4	13.1
Average	19.1	22.8	6.0	17.3	15.9	15.3	13.8	12.2	15.1	14.5
Book Value Per Share	63.93	39.85	32.85	53.09	46.36	43.44	38.76	35.85	34.11	32.71
Book Value – % Return	22.45	32.22	36.19	28.63	27.83	27.97	26.08	20.33	16.33	18.10

Source: *S & P Analyst's Handbook.*

Case 14:   Comprehensive Case

Interchemco Corporation

We bought most of our Bessie at or around 21, which is close to the 10 year low. . . . If Bessie merely moves to the multiple of 10 times the next year's earnings, we'll make more than 40 per cent on our money. (Barron's.)

Interchemco Corporation (IC) was incorporated in New York in 1905. The company has become one of the largest producers of chemical fertilizer and fertilizer materials in the world and is a leading producer of industrial minerals and chemicals. The company currently has plants in over 300 locations with operations in 30 countries.

Potash and phosphates are the primary fertilizer materials produced by IC. In addition, the company manufactures several varieties of fertilizer mixes, plant growth regulators, and a microbiological insecticide. Industrial products include fluorspar for the chemical, aluminum, and steel industries; resins, oils, and esters for the paint and printing ink industries; and basic refractories for the steel industry. When all divisions are operating at the level considered normal, i.e., 90 percent of capacity, sales to the agricultural and industrial markets comprise approximately 55 and 45 percent respectively of the company's total sales. International operations account for 40 percent of total sales.

IC has undertaken diversification moves recently with the acquisition of several firms in the steel, food, and minerals industries. These firms were acquired on a pooling of interest basis through the exchange of both common and convertible preferred shares.

The company's earnings, which have been declining since 19x6, dropped to a 10-year low of $1.2 million last year. The decline in earnings reflects the generally depressed business conditions within the chemical industry as a whole and particularly the over capacity in the fertilizer sector.

Profit margins declined in the chemical industry in 19x9 from a year earlier in spite of an increase in sales. The primary reasons for the decline in profits were higher production costs and heavy pressures on prices resulting from the imbalance between supply and demand. The imbalance was caused by large increases in productive capacity in recent years. Much of the increase in capacity and a concomitant increase in competition was the result of the entrance of oil companies into the production of petrochemicals. In addition, the growth of the chemical industry in Japan and Western Europe has reduced U. S. companies' share of world trade. Chemical imports have been rising in recent years, but so have exports; the favorable balance of trade in chemicals has been maintained at about $5 billion. Despite the lowering of tariff barriers emanating from the "Kennedy Round," protection from imports still exists for domestic companies because duties on imports are based upon U. S. selling prices which are typically higher than foreign prices.

Irrespective of current excess capacity, construction outlays are expected to increase 20 percent this year. Since construction costs are rising faster than sales, average capital turnover in the industry is expected to decrease to .7:1 from 1:1 last year.

Chemical companies have been taking steps to improve profits by cutting costs whenever possible and eliminating unprofitable lines. New construction has generally led to larger and more efficient plants which should lower unit costs when volume is high. However, the added capacity will lead to continued pressure on prices unless demand improves.

Traditionally the chemical industry has been able to maintain demand for its output at high levels by the introduction of many new and improved products. Thus the profitability of the industry has been heavily dependent upon research and development. In recent months, however, many chemical firms have been reducing expenditures on research and development in order to report higher profits. If this policy is continued long run profits will be adversely affected.

The position of chemical companies in the petrochemical area has improved because of recent quotas granted by the Oil Import Administration; this action now allows some access to "low-cost" foreign crude oil. In addition, the lower oil depletion allowance will tend to improve the competitive position of chemical firms relative to that of oil producers.

Over the next 3 years, sales and earnings in the chemical industry are expected to increase at annual rates of 7 and 5.5 percent respectively. The growth rates after 3 years should increase if the improved conditions which are expected in the fertilizer sector materialize. Chemical industry sales and earnings are expected to remain cyclical, however, with earnings declines averaging as much as 10 percent in depressed years.

Major problems that will have to be overcome during the next decade include increased expenditures on pollution control and unfavorable government actions on pesticides. Chemical firms may benefit from the ecology issue in the long run because they have the technical knowledge with which to develop control products.

Fertilizer producers have been the most depressed sector of the chemical industry during the past few years. Nitrogen, phosphorus, and potassium are the basic fertilizer components, and the domestic capacity of each exceeds current requirements by a considerable margin. Overcapacity has resulted in heavy pressure on prices and profit margins; losses have been widespread. Although potash prices have recently shown some strength, generally depressed conditions caused by the imbalance between supply and demand are expected to continue for at least 3 years. Thereafter profits should benefit from improved prices.

Interchemco's sales are expected to increase by 5 percent this year, and earnings per share of common are estimated at approximately $.22, up from $.11 in 19x9. Much of this improvement is expected to result from higher potash selling prices. Sales next year are projected to increase 8-10 percent, and earnings per share are expected to fall in the range $.80-.85. These estimates assume that economic conditions will improve and that weather conditions for crop planting will be good. Management believes that if conditions are right, per share earnings should reach the $1.50 level within 3 years, and thereafter, earnings growth should approximate 10 percent per year.

The most recent share price of common stock was $20. The company's current capitalization consists of the following convertible securities:

$50 million of 4 percent subordinated debentures, convertible into common at $53.20 per share.

260,000 shares of $5 Series A cumulative preferred stock, convertible into common at $46.50 per share.

40,000 shares of $5 Series B cumulative preferred stock, convertible into common at $38.30 per share.

200,000 shares of $1 Series C cumulative preferred, convertible into common at $50 per share.

All preferred issues are redeemable at 105.

QUESTIONS

1. Are there any irregularities in IC's income statement? Explain.

2. (a) Compute the variance in IC's earnings per share during the past 10 years.
   (b) Explain the effect of the more significant factors that have contributed to the variance in the company's earnings.
   (c) Is there any relationship between the variance in IC's past earnings and the risks associated with IC's earnings expectations? Explain.

3. Determine the expected range in IC's common earnings per share for each of the next 5 years. Calculate the expected values for each year.

4. Will IC's future risk situation be changed from that of the past decade? Why or why not?

5. Estimate the return required by investors on IC's common stock. Explain the factors relevant to your estimate.

6. Explain in detail how you would determine whether investors have correctly valued IC's common.

EXHIBIT 1

Balance Sheet Data (millions)

INTERCHEMCO CORPORATION

	19x9	19x8	19x7	19x6	19x5	19x4	19x3	19x2	19x1	19x0
Assets:										
Current	254.9	277.9	192.5	157.7	118.7	101.7	80.6	61.9	52.2	42.1
Cash Items	27.9	36.1	16.1	32.3	11.7	14.3	5.8	7.7	5.3	3.8
Receivables	142.4	142.8	94.5	77.7	66.0	52.2	41.3	28.8	22.2	18.2
Inventory	84.6	99.0	81.9	47.7	41.0	35.2	33.5	25.4	24.7	20.1
Other	33.6	30.0	26.3	24.1	21.3	15.5	10.8	8.7	6.1	5.0
Fixed	249.0	296.1	283.5	236.9	184.3	138.1	124.3	113.0	93.5	91.9
Total Assets	537.5	604.0	502.3	418.7	324.3	255.3	215.7	183.6	151.8	139.0
Liabilities:										
Current	111.9	102.8	103.4	50.7	36.5	25.4	28.0	14.0	11.5	11.4
Bonds	210.5	260.2	181.7	181.9	122.9	80.5	64.6	54.9	31.8	29.2
Other	16.4	11.5	9.7	8.4	4.8	4.7	3.7	4.4	3.2	4.0
Preferred Stock	60.7	59.6	35.6	9.7	9.8	9.8	9.8	9.8	9.8	9.9
Common Stock	54.2	54.2	48.0	31.6	31.3	15.5	14.0	13.2	13.0	11.8
Surplus	83.8	115.7	123.9	136.4	119.0	119.4	95.6	87.3	82.5	72.7
Total Liabilities	537.5	604.0	502.3	418.7	324.3	255.3	215.7	183.6	151.8	139.0

EXHIBIT 2

Income Data (millions)

INTERCHEMCO CORPORATION

	19x9	19x8	19x7	19x6	19x5	19x4	19x3	19x2	19x1	19x0
Sales	500.8	501.8	329.5	299.3	263.0	225.7	184.2	149.0	131.8	123.9
Cost of Goods Sold	400.2	382.4	228.2	197.5	175.2	155.3	131.1	107.1	94.1	89.4
Depreciation	23.3	25.7	19.5	14.8	13.1	11.5	8.8	7.3	7.3	6.9
Operating Expenses	63.1	64.1	51.9	49.2	45.9	36.7	30.1	22.9	19.0	16.8
Operating Income	14.2	29.6	29.9	37.8	28.8	22.2	14.2	11.7	11.4	10.8
Other Income	2.7	1.3	.1	-0-	-0-	-0-	-0-	.1	.1	-0-
Earnings Before Interest & Taxes	16.9	30.9	30.0	37.8	28.8	22.2	14.2	11.8	11.5	10.8
Interest	16.6	16.5	10.8	8.2	5.6	4.5	4.0	2.5	1.7	1.4
Earnings Before Taxes	.3	14.4	19.2	29.6	23.2	17.7	10.2	9.3	9.8	9.4
Taxes	(3.0)	1.4	5.0	5.7	3.2	2.2	.1	1.0	1.9	2.0
Earnings After Taxes	3.3	13.0	14.2	23.9	20.0	15.5	10.1	8.3	7.9	7.4
Preferred Dividends	2.1	1.7	1.0	.4	.4	.4	.4	.4	.4	.4
Common Earnings	1.2	11.3	13.2	23.5	19.6	15.1	9.7	7.9	7.5	7.0
Common Dividends	4.6	9.7	9.5	7.5	6.2	5.9	4.4	4.2	4.0	3.8
No. of Common Shares	10.8	10.8	9.6	9.5	9.4	9.3	8.4	7.8	7.8	7.2

EXHIBIT 3

Per Share Income Data

INTERCHEMCO CORPORATION

	19x9	19x8	19x7	19x6	19x5	19x4	19x3	19x2	19x1	19x0
Sales	46.37	46.46	34.32	31.51	27.98	24.27	21.93	19.10	16.90	17.21
Cost of Goods Sold	37.06	35.41	23.77	20.79	18.64	16.70	15.61	13.73	12.06	12.42
Depreciation	2.16	2.38	2.03	1.56	1.39	1.24	1.05	.94	.94	.96
Operating Expenses	5.84	5.93	5.41	5.18	4.89	3.94	3.58	2.93	2.44	2.33
Operating Income	1.31	2.74	3.11	3.98	3.06	2.39	1.69	1.50	1.46	1.50
Other Income	.25	.12	.02	-0-	-0-	-0-	-0-	.01	.01	-0-
Earnings Before Interest & Taxes	1.56	2.86	3.13	3.98	3.06	2.39	1.69	1.51	1.47	1.50
Interest	1.53	1.53	1.13	.86	.59	.49	.48	.32	.21	.19
Earnings Before Taxes	.03	1.33	2.00	3.12	2.47	1.90	1.21	1.19	1.26	1.31
Taxes	(.28)	.13	.52	.60	.34	.23	.01	.13	.25	.28
Earnings After Taxes	.31	1.20	1.48	2.52	2.13	1.67	1.20	1.06	1.01	1.03
Preferred Dividends	.20	.15	.10	.05	.04	.05	.05	.05	.05	.06
Common Earnings	.11	1.05	1.38	2.47	2.09	1.62	1.15	1.01	.96	.97
Common Dividends	.43	.90	.99	.79	.66	.63	.52	.54	.51	.53

EXHIBIT 4

Index Values per Share

INTERCHEMCO CORPORATION

	19x9	19x8	19x7	19x6	19x5	19x4	19x3	19x2	19x1	19x0
Total Assets	2.58	2.90	2.71	2.28	1.79	1.42	1.33	1.22	1.01	1.00
Sales	2.69	2.70	1.99	1.83	1.63	1.41	1.27	1.11	.98	1.00
Cost of Goods Sold	2.98	1.85	1.91	1.67	1.50	1.34	1.26	1.11	.97	1.00
Depreciation	2.25	2.48	2.12	1.63	1.45	1.29	1.09	.98	.98	1.00
Operating Expenses	2.50	2.54	2.32	2.22	2.09	1.69	1.54	1.26	1.04	1.00
Operating Income	.88	1.83	2.08	2.65	2.04	1.59	1.13	1.00	.97	1.00
Earnings Before Interest & Taxes	1.04	1.91	2.08	2.65	2.04	1.59	1.13	1.01	.98	1.00
Interest	7.90	7.86	5.79	4.44	3.06	2.49	2.45	1.65	1.12	1.00
Earnings Before Taxes	.02	1.02	1.53	2.39	1.89	1.46	.93	.91	.96	1.00
Taxes	(1.00)	.47	1.88	2.16	1.23	.85	.04	.46	.88	1.00
Earnings After Taxes	.30	1.17	1.44	2.45	2.07	1.62	1.17	1.04	.99	1.00
Common Earnings	.11	1.08	1.41	2.54	2.14	1.67	1.19	1.04	.99	1.00
Common Dividends	.81	1.70	1.88	1.50	1.25	1.20	.99	1.02	.97	1.00
No. of Common Shares	1.50	1.50	1.33	1.32	1.31	1.29	1.17	1.08	1.08	1.00

EXHIBIT 5

Selected Data

INTERCHEMCO CORPORATION

	19x9	19x8	19x7	19x6	19x5	19x4	19x3	19x2	19x1	19x0
Return on Sales (%)	.2	2.3	4.0	7.9	7.5	6.7	5.3	5.3	5.7	5.6
Return on Assets (%)	.6	2.2	2.8	5.7	6.2	6.1	4.7	4.5	5.2	5.3
Return on Equity (%)	.9	6.7	7.7	14.0	13.0	11.2	8.9	7.9	7.9	8.3
Capital Turnover	.93	.83	.66	.72	.81	.88	.85	.81	.87	.89
Inventory Turnover	4.73	3.86	2.79	4.14	4.27	4.41	3.91	4.22	3.81	4.45
Average Collection Period (Days)	102	102	103	93	90	83	81	70	61	53
Interest Coverage	1.02	1.87	2.78	4.61	5.14	4.93	3.55	4.72	6.77	7.71
Prior Charge Coverage	.82	1.56	2.36	4.21	4.52	4.21	2.98	3.61	4.66	4.98
Total Debt to Equity	2.45	2.20	1.71	1.43	1.09	.82	.88	.73	.49	.53
Preferred to Equity	.44	.35	.21	.06	.06	.07	.09	.10	.10	.12
Tax Rate (%)	--	9.7	26.0	19.3	13.8	12.4	1.0	10.8	19.4	21.3
Book Value Per Share	12.78	15.73	17.91	17.68	15.99	14.51	13.05	12.89	12.24	11.74
Dividend Payout (%)	391	86	72	32	32	39	45	53	53	54
Debt Leverage, Dollars Per Share	--	.22	.52	1.15	.82	.48	.28	.25	.19	.23
Preferred Leverage, Dollars Per Share	--	.10	.06	.03	.04	.04	.03	.02	.03	.03
Relative Debt Leverage (%)	--	21	38	47	40	30	24	25	20	23
Relative Preferred Leverage (%)	-	9	4	1	2	2	3	2	3	3

EXHIBIT 6

Per Share Data INTERCHEMCO CORPORATION

	19x9	19x8	19x7	19x6	19x5	19x4	19x3	19x2	19x1	19x0
Price:										
High	24.38	30.13	47.50	57.50	49.38	27.25	22.00	19.00	18.13	12.13
Low	11.13	18.50	24.50	31.13	25.63	25.50	13.63	11.38	11.38	9.63
Average	17.75	24.31	36.00	44.31	37.50	26.38	17.82	15.19	14.75	10.88
Price-Earnings:										
High	--	28.7	34.4	23.3	23.6	16.8	19.1	18.8	18.9	12.5
Low	--	17.6	17.7	12.6	12.3	15.7	11.8	11.3	11.8	9.9
Average	--	23.1	26.0	17.9	18.0	16.2	15.4	15.0	15.3	11.2
Market-Book Value:										
High	1.91	1.92	2.65	3.25	3.09	1.88	1.69	1.48	1.48	1.03
Low	.87	1.18	1.37	1.76	1.60	1.76	1.05	.88	.93	.82
Average	1.39	1.55	2.01	2.51	2.34	1.82	1.37	1.18	1.20	.93

EXHIBIT 7

Selected Chemicals Industry Data per Share

INTERCHEMCO CORPORATION

	19x9	19x8	19x7	19x6	19x5	19x4	19x3	19x2	19x1	19x0
Sales	47.18	43.96	38.63	38.18	34.52	31.88	26.69	23.55	20.67	19.97
Depreciation	3.70	3.51	3.15	2.88	2.64	2.41	2.10	1.88	1.66	1.50
Income Taxes	2.52	2.56	1.99	2.58	2.55	2.58	2.22	2.01	1.64	1.65
Common Earnings	3.17	3.16	2.84	3.50	3.41	3.34	2.75	2.42	2.08	2.08
Common Dividends	1.94	2.00	1.87	1.94	1.89	1.99	1.83	1.67	1.55	1.46
Price Index:										
High	57.95	61.43	60.53	75.38	76.78	72.87	62.36	54.31	56.69	60.80
Low	40.08	50.20	50.87	49.82	68.78	62.96	52.50	39.16	47.55	44.15
Average	49.02	55.82	55.70	62.60	72.78	67.92	57.43	46.74	52.12	52.48
Price/Earnings Ratio:										
High	18.3	19.4	21.3	21.5	22.5	21.8	22.7	22.4	27.3	29.2
Low	12.6	15.9	17.9	14.2	20.0	18.9	19.1	16.2	22.9	21.2
Average	15.5	17.7	19.6	17.9	21.0	20.4	20.9	19.3	25.1	25.1
Book Value Per Share	27.17	26.25	24.40	23.51	21.94	20.09	18.61	17.34	16.66	15.79
Book Value – % Return	11.67	12.04	11.64	14.89	15.54	16.63	14.78	13.96	12.48	13.17

Source: *S & P Analyst's Handbook.*

PORTFOLIO INPUTS

3 Efficient Capital Markets

Case 15: Insider Accumulation and Listing on NYSE

Industrial Electronics

The volume of trading on the right shoulder was lower than on the left—which was true to type. In addition to this, the shoulder just formed is a soft shoulder, which causes the whole formation to sag badly to the right, and this is generally considered to be the weakest type of pattern. (The Value Line.)

Industrial Electronics (IE) is a leading producer of electronic and electrical circuit components. In the 1950s and early 1960s, the company was essentially a producer of capacitors, but in recent years the product line has been broadened considerably. Even though capacitors still accounted for approximately two-thirds of IE's sales in 19x9, new products were growing in importance. The new products included transistors, resistors, complex networks, special purpose subassemblies and microcircuits. IE's sales were primarily to computer manu-facturers, commercial and aerospace electronics firms, the Department of De-fense, and the home entertainment electronics industry.

The company has grown through a combination of internal and external means. Most of the external growth has occurred recently with acquisitions in 6 of the last 10 years. Foreign competition, combined with softness in U. S. durable goods sales, brought about severe price competition in the electronics industry both in 19x9 and in the current year. Because of high wage rates in the U. S., the company has had to look elsewhere for labor and just recently teamed with a Japanese firm to produce a complete line of capacitors in Japan. During recent years, the company has been increasing its productive capacity in foreign countries and at the same time reducing its domestic operations. Foreign countries in which plants are now located include Taiwan, Japan, Italy, Puerto Rico, Mexico, France, Belgium, Canada, Spain, and Germany.

The company has introduced stringent cost reduction programs during the past 2 years with the expressed objective of increasing productivity. These programs include employment cutbacks and plant consolidations. Common stock earnings for the current year are expected to be a record deficit of $6.07 million which will amount to a loss of approximately $1.78 per share. However, management expects the company to either break even or make a slight profit next year. Incoming orders have been increasing lately, reversing a 2-year declining trend. Cash dividends have been paid since 1937 but will be omitted this year due to a serious cash flow problem.

Since the management of the company believes the importance of microelectronics (integrated circuits) will grow very rapidly in the future, IE has made large research and facility commitments to this product area. While microelectronics currently account for only about 12 percent of IE's sales, management expects the area to account for one-half of sales within 5 years.

Most of the significant pronouncements affecting IE's stock price since 19x5 are indicated below. The specific dates refer to when the information was released to the public.

19x5

10-25   IE announces estimated operating profits for 19x5 of $4.25 million versus $3.75 million for 19x4.

19x6

3-4   Reports net income of $4.94 million for 19x5.

3-17   Senior vice-president acquires 2,600 shares of common through a stock option, thereby increasing his holdings to 4,100 shares.

5-23   Reports net income of $1.91 million for first quarter.

8-8   Chairman of the board estimates that first-half earnings exceeded $4 million with sales in excess of $70 million, the latter an increase of about 40 percent over 19x5.

8-9   Reports second-quarter net income of $2.43 million and first-half earnings of $4.34 million.

9-14   Company announces application for listing on the New York Stock Exchange; reports that sales are running at the annual rate of $145 million.

11-2   Reports net income of $2.13 million for third quarter and $6.47 million for last 9 months.

11-8   Chairman announces that the company will be listed as of November 21.

12-21   President reports to the New York Society of Security Analysts that he expects earnings to rise to a record $8.8 million or more for 19x6.

19x7

2-7   IE announces plans to split stock 2 for 1.

2-13   Reports net income of $8.83 million for 19x6.

4-3   President reports that first-quarter earnings will be slightly below last year's $1.91 million.

5-9   Reports first-quarter earnings of $1.53 million.

8-10   Announces net income of $835 thousand for second quarter and $2.36 million for last 6 months.

9-1   Reports registration of $25 million of convertible debenture bonds with SEC.

9-23 Company sells at par $25 million of $4\frac{1}{4}$ percent debentures, convertible into common at $45.50.

11-7 Reports net income of $765 thousand for third quarter and $2.89 million for last 9 months.

19x8

2-23 Announces net income of $3.33 million for 19x7.

5-7 Announces net income of $855 thousand for first quarter.

7-31 Announces net income of $255 thousand for second quarter and $1.06 million for last 6 months.

10-7 Reports that third-quarter operating loss will offset most of first-half profits, resulting in only a slight profit for the 9-month period.

10-10 President sells 350 shares of common. He and his family own over 500,000 shares.

10-25 A director with holdings of 74,000 shares sells 700 shares.

11-6 Reports third-quarter operating loss of $1.0 million.

11-13 New president elected; company cuts quarterly dividend to $.10 from $.15.

11-27 Announces a realignment of the executive organization.

19x9

1-14 Two officers acquire 300 shares of common.

2-20 Reports net loss of $2.87 million for fourth quarter of 19x8 and loss of $2.83 million for the year.

2-26 One officer acquires 200 shares of common; another sells 800 shares.

3-31 New president expects a small loss in the first quarter.

5-7 Company reports net loss of $360 thousand for the first quarter.

8-5 Reports net income of $813 thousand for second quarter and $417 thousand for last 6 months.

10-31 Officer sells 400 shares.

11-6 Reports net income of $670 thousand for third quarter and $1.09 million for last 9 months.

11-7 Director sells 1,000 shares.

11-12 Officer sells 500 shares.

12-3 Director sells 500 shares; officer purchases 100 shares.

12-12 Chairman sells 200 shares.

Current Year

2-19 Reports income of $1.46 million for 19x9.

4-13 President expects first-quarter results will exceed both the net income of $394 thousand and sales of $36.4 million of fourth quarter of 19x9.

5-12 Reports net income of $456 thousand for first quarter.

2-26 Announces an expansion in foreign operations.

7-14 Chairman of board reports that he expects a modest loss for the first half of the current year.

8-5   Reports net loss of $2.40 million for second quarter and $1.95 million for last 6 months.

8-11   Omits $.10 quarterly dividend.

9-2   Confirms rumors that the pay of its salaried employees was cut.

11-9   Reports net loss of $1.74 million for third quarter and loss of $3.69 million for last 9 months.

11-10   Board of directors votes to omit the $.10 fourth-quarter dividend.

11-20   Expects modest sales decline of current year to be reversed next year.

QUESTIONS

1. (a) Have the announcements of earnings by IE's management since 19x6 resulted in price increases (decreases) corresponding to the favorableness (unfavorableness) of the event? Base your answer upon a comparison of price changes from the week preceding to the week following the week of the announcement.

   (b) From 1(a) can you conclude that the market reacts quickly and fully to reported earnings? Discuss.

   (c) What difficulties arise in attempting to draw "cause and effect" conclusions suggested by 2(a)?

2. (a) Have the preliminary earnings reports by the president and the chairman of the board been accurate? Explain.

   (b) Would your answer to 2(a) affect your answer to 1(b)? Discuss.

3. Were the insider transactions timely in the sense that IE's executives were better off after a 6-month period? Assume all transactions at average weekly prices.

4. Which of the following would have been of value to an investor desiring short-term trading gains? Assume purchases were made in the week preceding the announcement of the event, and sales were made in the week following the announcement, at average weekly prices.

   (a) Advance knowledge that IE was going to list its stock on the NYSE.

   (b) Advance knowledge that IE was going to split its stock.

   (c) Advance knowledge that IE was going to decrease its dividend.

   (d) Advance knowledge that IE was going to omit its dividend.

5. (a) What is an efficient capital market?

   (b) From your answers to questions 1 through 4, would you conclude that the capital markets were efficient in pricing IE's common? Discuss.

6. (a) Is IE faced with any special business risk factors? Explain.

   (b) Are traders in IE's stock faced with any special trading risks? Explain.

   (c) Assess IE's earnings prospects for next year and estimate the range and expected value of the *HPR* of the company's common stock.

EXHIBIT 1

Balance Sheet Data (millions)

INDUSTRIAL ELECTRONICS

	19x9	19x8	19x7	19x6	19x5	19x4	19x3	19x2	19x1	19x0
Assets:										
Current	88.08	83.45	77.61	67.06	55.95	49.16	43.23	40.91	34.79	28.23
Cash Items	17.31	17.79	15.78	11.43	7.96	5.86	7.14	4.63	7.17	3.53
Receivables	19.41	18.40	15.50	15.58	12.90	10.92	9.11	9.75	9.35	8.95
Inventory	51.36	47.26	46.33	40.05	35.90	32.38	26.98	26.53	21.27	15.75
Other	4.54	5.56	4.85	4.42	3.24	5.14	5.53	4.63	4.34	4.53
Fixed	39.20	38.54	39.89	35.09	26.94	23.42	22.10	20.90	12.24	15.64
Total Assets	131.82	127.55	122.35	106.57	86.13	77.72	70.86	66.44	58.37	48.40
Liabilities:										
Current	25.23	17.95	7.73	19.35	9.55	11.14	6.56	16.36	12.44	10.76
Bonds	46.47	48.59	50.08	25.13	21.97	15.25	15.36	4.59	4.68	.80
Other	1.78	1.25	.48	-0-	.07	.11	.08	.06	.14	.54
Common Stock	31.98	31.82	31.43	30.76	24.41	25.52	24.33	22.79	20.16	17.43
Surplus	26.36	27.94	32.63	31.33	27.13	25.70	24.53	22.64	20.95	18.87
Total Liabilities	131.82	127.55	122.35	106.57	86.13	77.72	70.86	66.44	58.37	48.40

EXHIBIT 2

Income Data (millions)

INDUSTRIAL ELECTRONICS

	19x9	19x8	19x7	19x6	19x5	19x4	19x3	19x2	19x1	19x0
Sales	147.06	132.75	127.44	141.47	107.08	85.70	83.26	86.95	77.25	64.52
Cost of Goods Sold	137.60	130.28	117.85	124.28	97.22	77.25	73.52	73.04	64.27	55.00
Depreciation	5.82	5.65	5.13	4.28	3.54	3.16	2.88	2.67	2.42	1.94
Operating Income	3.64	(3.18)	4.46	12.91	6.32	5.29	6.86	11.24	10.56	7.58
Other Income	(.02)*	-0-	-0-	1.10	1.19	.91	.59	.45	.40	.34
Earnings Before Interest & Taxes	3.62	(3.18)	4.46	14.01	7.51	6.20	7.45	11.69	10.96	7.92
Interest	1.02	.61	.56	.84	.93	.78	.62	.44	.21	.09
Earnings Before Taxes	2.60	(3.79)	3.90	13.17	6.58	5.42	6.83	11.25	10.75	7.83
Taxes	1.14	(.96)	.57	4.34	1.64	1.67	2.20	4.82	4.66	3.74
Common Earnings	1.46	(2.83)	3.33	8.83	4.94	3.75	4.63	6.43	6.09	4.09
Common Dividends	1.36	1.86	2.02	1.96	1.90	1.86	1.82	1.77	1.73	1.67
No. of Common Shares	3.4	3.4	3.4	3.3	3.3	3.3	3.3	3.3	3.3	3.2

*Expense

EXHIBIT 3

Per Share Income Data

INDUSTRIAL ELECTRONICS

	19x9	19x8	19x7	19x6	19x5	19x4	19x3	19x2	19x1	19x0
Sales	43.38	38.93	37.48	42.36	32.35	25.81	25.15	26.67	23.70	20.04
Cost of Goods Sold	40.59	38.20	34.66	37.21	29.37	23.27	22.21	22.40	19.72	17.09
Depreciation	1.72	1.66	1.51	1.28	1.07	.95	.87	.82	.74	.60
Operating Income	1.07	(.93)	1.31	3.87	1.91	1.59	2.07	3.45	3.24	2.35
Other Income	-0-	-0-	-0-	.32	.36	.27	.18	.14	.12	.11
Earnings Before Interest & Taxes	1.07	(.93)	1.31	4.19	2.27	1.86	2.25	3.59	3.36	2.46
Interest	.30	.18	.16	.25	.28	.23	.19	.14	.06	.03
Earnings Before Taxes	.77	(1.11)	1.15	3.94	1.99	1.63	2.06	3.45	3.30	2.43
Taxes	.34	(.28)	.17	1.30	.50	.50	.66	1.48	1.43	1.16
Common Earnings	.43	(.83)	.98	2.64	1.49	1.13	1.40	1.97	1.87	1.27
Common Dividends	.40	.55	.60	.59	.58	.56	.55	.54	.53	.52

EXHIBIT 4

Selected Data

INDUSTRIAL ELECTRONICS

	19x9	19x8	19x7	19x6	19x5	19x4	19x3	19x2	19x1	19x0
Return on Sales (%)	1.0	(2.1)	2.6	6.2	4.6	4.4	5.6	7.4	7.9	6.3
Return on Assets (%)	1.1	(2.2)	2.7	8.3	5.7	4.8	6.5	9.7	10.4	8.5
Return on Equity (%)	2.5	(4.7)	5.2	14.2	9.1	7.3	9.5	14.2	14.8	11.3
Capital Turnover	1.12	1.04	1.04	1.33	1.24	1.10	1.18	1.31	1.32	1.33
Inventory Turnover	2.68	2.76	2.54	3.10	2.77	2.39	2.73	2.75	3.02	3.49
Average Collection Period (days)	47	50	44	40	43	46	39	40	43	50
Interest Coverage	3.55	(5.21)	7.96	16.68	8.08	7.95	12.02	26.57	52.19	88.00
Total Debt to Equity (%)	126	113	91	72	58	52	45	46	42	33
Tax Rate (%)	43.8	25.3	14.6	33.0	24.9	30.8	32.2	42.8	43.3	47.8
Book Value Per Share	17.21	17.53	18.41	18.59	16.48	15.43	14.76	13.94	12.61	11.27
Dividend Payout (%)	93	def	61	22	38	50	39	27	28	41
Debt Leverage (dollars per share)	.17	(.50)	.39	1.01	.41	.28	.35	.57	.53	.31
Relative Debt Leverage (%)	38	(61)	40	38	28	25	25	29	28	24

EXHIBIT 5
Per Share Price Data

INDUSTRIAL ELECTRONICS

	19x9	19x8	19x7	19x6	19x5	19x4	19x3	19x2	19x1	19x0
Price:										
High	34.88	37.88	58.38	52.38	26.88	22.50	35.38	43.88	40.50	30.13
Low	16.50	23.25	32.13	25.13	14.38	15.50	18.63	26.00	23.63	18.50
Average	25.69	30.56	45.25	43.75	20.63	19.00	27.00	34.94	32.06	24.31
Price-Earnings:										
High	81.0	--	59.6	19.8	18.0	19.9	25.3	22.2	21.7	23.7
Low	38.3	--	33.4	9.5	9.6	13.7	13.3	13.2	12.6	14.6
Average	59.6	--	46.5	14.6	13.8	16.8	19.3	17.7	17.1	19.1
Market-Book Value:										
High	2.03	2.16	3.10	2.82	1.63	1.46	2.40	3.15	3.21	2.67
Low	.96	1.33	1.74	1.35	.87	1.01	1.26	1.87	1.87	1.64
Average	1.49	1.75	2.42	2.37	1.25	1.23	1.83	2.51	2.54	2.16

EXHIBIT 6

Selected Industry Data per Share

INDUSTRIAL ELECTRONICS

	19x9	19x8	19x7	19x6	19x5	19x4	19x3	19x2	19x1	19x0
Sales	581.56	529.35	496.69	597.27	289.37	272.04	253.92	227.27	195.76	206.03
Depreciation	14.63	13.27	11.16	11.80	9.06	8.15	6.89	6.06	5.55	5.13
Income Taxes	20.88	17.84	17.40	17.67	5.31	4.84	4.19	3.22	3.03	4.23
Common Earnings	22.29	20.05	20.75	19.45	12.00	10.17	8.05	6.94	6.01	7.02
Common Dividends	3.97	3.42	3.22	2.95	2.35	2.18	1.80	1.72	1.48	1.83
Price Index:										
High	648.49	622.21	669.19	454.21	362.41	228.48	214.16	250.00	282.91	263.26
Low	522.16	472.86	410.04	352.22	229.03	190.98	171.31	135.53	223.93	189.78
Average	585.33	547.54	539.62	403.22	295.72	209.73	192.74	192.77	253.42	226.52
Price/Earnings Ratio:										
High	29.1	31.0	32.2	23.3	30.2	22.5	26.6	36.0	47.1	37.5
Low	23.4	23.6	19.8	18.1	19.1	18.8	21.3	19.5	37.3	27.0
Average	26.2	27.3	26.0	20.7	24.6	20.6	23.9	27.7	42.2	32.2
Book Value Per Share	186.03	169.44	153.73	177.20	82.21	82.94	78.15	75.59	67.38	71.50
Book Value - % Return	11.98	11.83	13.50	10.98	14.60	12.26	10.30	9.18	8.92	9.82

Source: *S & P Analyst's Handbook.*

EXHIBIT 7

Weekly Volume and Price Data*   INDUSTRIAL ELECTRONICS

Year 19x6		Volume (Sales in 100's)	Price Weekly Avg.	Year 19x7		Volume (Sales in 100's)	Price Weekly Avg.
January	3		54 1/8	January	2	716	101 3/8
	10		54 5/8		9	873	99 3/8
	17		60 1/2		16	1166	108 5/8
	24		60 1/4		23	575	113 1/4
	31		65		30	849	112 1/8
February	7		69 1/2	February	6	548	111 3/4
	14		66 5/8		13	526	112 3/8
	21		67		20	1412	102 7/8
	28		67 1/2		27	1331	93
March	7		63 1/8	March	6	598	93 7/8
	14		67 3/4		13	426	91 7/8
	21		75		20	547	84 7/8
	28		78 7/8		27	383	84 7/8
April	4		83 1/2	April	3	402	80 1/4
	11		84 7/8		10	429	78 3/4
	18		81		17	448	86
	25		76 3/4		24	280	84 1/4
May	2		71	May	1	49	84
	9		68 1/8		8‡	883	43 3/4
	16		76 1/2		15	608	42
	23		75 1/8		22	733	39 1/2
	30		75 3/4		29	703	37 1/8
June	6		80 3/4	June	5	642	36 1/8
	13		83		12	1150	38 3/4
	20		77 7/8		19	471	39 1/4
	27		79 3/4		26	529	36 3/8
July	4		81 3/8	July	3	319	37 1/8
	11		83		10	469	37 7/8
	18		81 3/4		17	474	37 7/8
	25		80 1/8		24	732	36 3/8
August	1		87 5/8		31	810	36 5/8
	8		88 3/8	August	7	595	37 1/2
	15		82 7/8		14	359	36 7/8
	22		77 7/8		21	257	36 3/8
	29		76 1/4		28	350	36 1/4
September	5		83 5/8	September	4	506	34 1/8
	12		83 1/2		11	687	35 5/8
	19		84 7/8		18	1339	38 7/8
	26		75		25	1091	41
October	3		78 1/2	October	2	826	42 7/8
	10		77 3/4		9	604	43 1/4
	17		75 1/8		16	473	41 5/8
	24		78		23	534	41 3/8
	31		79 7/8		30	909	39 1/8
November	7		83	November	6	378	36 1/2
	14		82		13	382	37 1/8
	21†	286	81 1/4		20	311	36 7/8
	28	420	82 1/8		27	558	39 1/4
December	5	395	86 3/8	December	4	561	40 7/8
	12	326	90 5/8		11	728	38 1/8
	19	868	93 3/4		18	611	36 3/4
	26	602	100 3/4		25	842	37 3/8

* Dates are beginning of the week in which average price occurs.
† Listed on New York Stock Exchange.
‡ Two-for-one split.

EXHIBIT 7 (continued)

Weekly Volume and Price Data   INDUSTRIAL ELECTRONICS

Year 19x8		Volume (Sales in 100's)	Price Weekly Avg.	Year 19x9		Volume (Sales in 100's)	Price Weekly Avg.
January	1	843	36 3/4	January	6	302	26 1/2
	8	443	36 3/4		13	198	26
	15	404	36		20	197	26 1/8
	22	376	34 3/4		27	260	25 1/2
	29	334	33 1/8	February	3	344	25 3/4
February	5	227	31 1/2		10	257	25 5/8
	12	262	30 1/4		17	253	25
	19	157	30 3/4		24	349	23
	26	274	29 1/4	March	3	232	22 3/4
March	4	324	28 1/4		10	297	21 1/2
	11	283	30 1/4		17	227	22
	18	227	29 5/8		24	148	22 1/2
	25	273	30 7/8		31	92	21 3/4
April	1	497	33 3/8	April	7	163	21 1/8
	8	221	33 1/4		14	209	21 3/4
	15	255	33		21	145	21 1/4
	22	401	33 3/4		28	439	22 7/8
	29	378	36 1/2	May	5	308	23 1/8
May	6	543	35 1/8		12	249	23 1/2
	13	320	34 3/8		19	257	23 1/8
	20	339	33 5/8		26	243	23 7/8
	27	368	34 3/8	June	2	385	24 1/8
June	3	562	35 3/4		9	246	23
	10	252	35 1/2		16	182	21 1/8
	17	230	33 1/2		23	173	20 3/8
	24	193	32 3/4		30	91	20 5/8
July	1	178	32 1/8	July	7	141	19 1/2
	8	286	32 1/4		14	178	18 3/8
	15	280	30 1/2		21	94	17 3/4
	22	353	28 1/2		28	233	17 3/4
	29	512	27 1/4	August	4	488	19 5/8
August	5	269	26 1/8		11	251	21 1/4
	12	195	26		18	316	22 1/4
	19	221	25 7/8		25	238	23 1/2
	26	230	25 1/8	September	1	135	22 3/4
September	2	519	25		8	211	22 1/8
	9	322	25 5/8		15	142	22 3/4
	16	364	25 1/2		22	442	24 7/8
	23	432	24 3/4		29	268	24 5/8
	30	491	25 3/4				
October	7	837	24 5/8	October	6	279	25
	14	498	25 1/4		13	695	26 3/4
	21	850	25 3/4		20	1599	30 1/8
	28	755	27 1/8		27	1726	31 1/4
November	4	513	25 1/2	November	3	1020	32 1/8
	11	559	26 1/4		10	786	33 1/8
	18	497	26 1/4		17	739	29 3/4
	25	706	27 1/4		24	462	27 7/8
December	2	448	27 3/4	December	1	352	27 3/4
	9	627	27 3/8		8	466	26 1/2
	16	631	27 3/8		15	496	25
	23	407	27 1/8		22	291	24 7/8
	30	631	26 5/8		29	535	25 5/8

EXHIBIT 7 (continued)

Weekly Volume and Price Data

INDUSTRIAL ELECTRONICS

Current Year		Volume (Sales in 100's)	Price Weekly Avg.	Current Year		Volume (Sales in 100's)	Price Weekly Avg.
January	5	836	23 3/8	August	3	165	11 7/8
	12	602	20 3/4		10	101	11
	19	661	20		17	87	10 3/8
	26	522	19 3/8		24	151	11 3/8
February	2	299	20 3/4		31	153	11 5/8
	9	213	20 3/4	September	7	132	11 1/2
	16	214	20 5/8		14	250	11 5/8
	23	125	21 1/2		21	286	12 5/8
March	2	258	20 7/8		28	164	13 1/8
	9	131	19 1/4	October	5	379	13 3/4
	16	84	18 5/8		12	168	12 1/8
	23	86	18 7/8		19	125	11 3/8
	30	97	18 7/8		26	130	10 1/2
April	6	421	17 5/8	November	2	243	9 7/8
	13	245	16 3/4		9	226	9 1/4
	20	199	16 1/2		16	134	8 7/8
	27	220	15 7/8		23	135	8 3/4
May	4	195	15 3/4		30	240	9 1/2
	11	192	15 3/4	December	7	247	10 3/8
	18	483	14 3/4		14	167	9 3/4
	25	1050	12 1/2		21	224	9 5/8
June	1	236	14 1/4				
	8	98	13 1/8				
	15	84	13 1/4				
	22	151	12				
	29	170	10 3/4				
July	6	100	10 7/8				
	13	114	10 1/2				
	20	67	11 1/8				
	27	189	11 3/4				

Case 16:   Insider Distribution and Stock Split

Scientific Instruments, Inc.

In theory at least, no one knows better than insiders about corporate prospects. The fact that these moves are effectively a species of selffulfilling prophecy over the short run detracts nothing from their efficiency. (The Value Line.)

Scientific Instruments, Inc. (SI), is a leading manufacturer of specialized analytical instruments and electrooptics. Primary customers for SI's specialized instruments are commercial and industrial firms, whereas the Federal Government is the firm's main customer for electrooptics. Sales to the government amounted to 58 percent of total company sales in 19x9 and are expected to be 56 percent in the current year. These sales are for space and defense but are not related directly to the immediate war effort.

The overall market for electronic testing and measuring equipment has doubled over the past decade. The past rate of growth is expected to continue in the future; demand will be particularly heavy for special purpose equipment and semi- and fully-automated measuring instruments. The sales growth of industrial electronic equipment averaged 10.5 percent annually during the past decade with sales reaching a record total of $421 million in 19x9. Demand for industrial instruments is cyclical because of the influence of the general level of business capital spending. However, the accelerating trend towards automation should contribute to a continued high rate of future growth in the demand for precision instruments. Although there are 15 firms presently competing in this market, SI is the only one with both a compound rate of growth in earnings of over 15 percent per year and consistent year-to-year earnings increases.

One of SI's major product groups includes analytical instruments used to measure the composition and molecular structure of matter. Another broad line of instruments is produced for the clinical, educational, and industrial markets, primarily comprised of firms in the chemical and petroleum industries. The products of the company, however, are used by firms in many industries as well as universities, hospitals, and research foundations. SI also ranks among the leaders in laser technology, and its laser systems are currently in use in setting up machine tool operations and in the production of semiconductors. The company spent $8.5 million of its own funds for research and development last year. Additional expenditures for research and development were made with funds from government contracts.

The company has expanded its operations in other countries to such an extent that foreign sales now comprise approximately 25 percent of total sales. Most instruments sold in foreign markets are produced by foreign subsidiaries which are located in West Germany, Great Britain, Mexico, and Japan.

SI's sales for the current year are expected to be off about 15 percent from last year, due primarily to sharp decreases in government orders. An improvement in operating margins has resulted this year from a product mix which includes a larger proportion of commercial sales and from improved performances on government contracts. Thus, the expected decline in operating income for the current year will be only about 2.5 percent from the 19x9 level. After lower depreciation and interest charges and a substantial increase in nonoperating income, earnings before taxes are expected to increase about 1.4 percent. Due to a lower overall tax rate, net income should increase approximately 8.2 percent and share earnings approximately 7.2 percent. Sales for next year are expected to be in the $170-$175 million range, substantially below the $203 million which is expected to be reported for this year. Management expects that the company's cost reduction efforts will result in an earnings increase next year greater than that for the current year.

The company is expected to complete arrangements during the next few months for the acquisition of a manufacturer of spray equipment for applying ceramics on metals. An offer of 980,000 shares of SI's common stock has been extended for the common stock of the spray equipment firm. Sales of the spray firm are estimated at somewhat over $23 million for the current year.

SI's common is presently selling in the mid 50s.

QUESTIONS

1. (a) What factors have been primarily responsible for SI's relatively high average price-earnings ratios over the past decade?
   (b) What factors have been primarily responsible for the variability in SI's price-earnings ratios?

2. (a) Is there any evidence that investors have "anticipated" the quarterly earnings pronouncements of SI since 19x7? Explain.
   (b) Can an investor reliably predict the (1) *day* and/or (2) *week* when the quarterly earnings pronouncements will be made by the company? Explain.

3. (a) Could knowledge a week in advance of the announcement of each of the following events or decisions have resulted in short-term (e.g., within a week after the event) trading profits in SI's common? Assume no brokerage fees and all trades at average weekly prices.
   (1) Registration of the stock offering with the SEC

(2) The receipt and winning of contracts and the receipts of installments on contracts

(3) SI's stock to be split, subject to stockholder approval

(4) Sales of the company's stock by mutual funds

(b) Answer 3(a) allowing for round-lot brokerage fees.

4. (a) Assume the president's insider transactions were made at average weekly market prices during the week of the transactions. Did he make above average profits from his purchase and subsequent sale decisions? Show calculations and explain.

(b) The senior vice-president?

5. Estimate the *HPR* for SI's common stock for next year. Justify your answer.

EXHIBIT 1

Balance Sheet Data (millions)

SCIENTIFIC INSTRUMENTS, INC.

	19x9	19x8	19x7	19x6	19x5	19x4	19x3	19x2	19x1	19x0
Assets:										
Current	77.33	67.60	55.62	44.93	36.43	30.13	21.26	20.57	18.76	11.61
Cash Items	8.41	10.47	5.68	2.79	3.90	2.04	1.72	2.70	6.12	1.32
Receivables	38.38	30.42	25.18	19.65	13.10	12.31	8.79	7.40	4.87	4.91
Inventory	30.54	26.71	24.76	22.49	19.43	15.78	10.73	10.47	7.77	5.38
Other	4.28	3.98	3.65	3.01	3.79	4.01	.73	.38	.31	1.10
Fixed	29.64	29.19	23.36	19.18	15.18	13.53	11.48	9.06	5.88	3.78
Total Assets	111.25	100.77	82.63	67.12	55.40	47.67	33.47	30.01	24.95	16.49
Liabilities:										
Current	30.02	28.59	23.01	19.54	12.87	9.33	7.29	7.70	5.00	2.82
Bonds	17.47	17.69	11.93	8.27	8.52	12.01	4.82	3.24	3.16	3.00
Other	.70	.67	.97	.86	.55	.50	.39	.30	.22	.13
Common Stock	21.54	19.87	18.72	15.59	15.19	11.51	9.24	9.15	9.05	4.82
Surplus	41.52	33.95	28.00	22.86	18.27	14.32	11.73	9.62	7.52	5.72
Total Liabilities	111.25	100.77	82.63	67.12	55.40	47.67	33.47	30.01	24.95	16.49

EXHIBIT 2

Income Data (millions)

SCIENTIFIC INSTRUMENTS, INC.

	19x9	19x8	19x7	19x6	19x5	19x4	19x3	19x2	19x1	19x0
Sales	199.45	151.16	111.60	88.39	66.70	56.91	49.06	39.60	31.77	22.12
Cost of Goods Sold	140.58	101.85	69.61	55.53	39.09	35.60	32.25	23.93	21.30	12.95
Depreciation	3.49	2.95	2.24	1.98	1.50	1.29	1.08	.81	.54	.35
Operating Expenses	39.48	33.47	29.61	22.17	18.97	15.08	12.05	11.21	7.34	6.38
Operating Income	15.90	12.89	10.14	8.71	7.14	4.94	3.68	3.65	2.59	2.44
Other Income	.45	.46	.37	.48	.54	.54	.45	.36	.55	.25
Earnings Before Interest & Taxes	16.35	13.35	10.51	9.19	7.68	5.48	4.13	4.01	3.14	2.69
Interest	1.43	1.42	1.04	.86	.75	.51	.33	.29	.17	.16
Earnings Before Taxes	14.92	11.93	9.47	8.33	6.93	4.97	3.80	3.72	2.97	2.53
Taxes	7.35	5.98	4.32	3.93	3.39	2.32	1.68	1.79	1.40	1.32
Common Earnings	7.57	5.95	5.15	4.40	3.54	2.65	2.12	1.93	1.57	1.21
No. of Common Shares	6.6	6.3	6.1	6.0	5.7	5.3	5.2	5.1	5.1	4.5

EXHIBIT 3

Per Share Income Data

SCIENTIFIC INSTRUMENTS, INC.

	19x9	19x8	19x7	19x6	19x5	19x4	19x3	19x2	19x1	19x0
Sales	30.31	23.88	18.21	14.66	11.68	10.74	9.49	7.80	6.28	4.94
Cost of Goods Sold	21.36	16.09	11.36	9.21	6.85	6.72	6.24	4.71	4.21	2.89
Depreciation	.53	.47	.37	.33	.26	.24	.21	.16	.11	.08
Operating Expenses	6.00	5.28	4.83	3.68	3.32	2.85	2.33	2.21	1.45	1.43
Operating Income	2.42	2.04	1.65	1.44	1.25	.93	.71	.72	.51	.54
Other Income	.06	.07	.06	.08	.10	.10	.09	.07	.11	.06
Earnings Before Interest & Taxes	2.48	2.11	1.71	1.52	1.35	1.03	.80	.79	.62	.60
Interest	.21	.23	.17	.14	.14	.09	.06	.06	.03	.04
Earnings Before Taxes	2.27	1.88	1.54	1.38	1.21	.94	.74	.73	.59	.56
Taxes	1.12	.94	.70	.65	.59	.44	.33	.35	.28	.29
Common Earnings	1.15	.94	.84	.73	.62	.50	.41	.38	.31	.27

EXHIBIT 4

Index Values per Share

SCIENTIFIC INSTRUMENTS, INC.

	19x9	19x8	19x7	19x6	19x5	19x4	19x3	19x2	19x1	19x0
Return on Sales (%)	3.8	3.9	4.6	5.0	5.3	4.7	4.3	4.9	4.9	5.5
Return on Assets (%)	6.8	5.9	6.2	6.6	6.4	5.6	6.3	6.4	6.3	7.3
Return on Equity (%)	12.0	11.1	11.0	11.4	10.6	10.3	10.1	10.3	9.5	11.5
Capital Turnover	1.79	1.50	1.35	1.32	1.20	1.19	1.47	1.32	1.27	1.34
Inventory Turnover	4.60	3.81	2.81	2.47	2.01	2.26	3.01	2.29	2.74	2.41
Average Collection Period (Days)	69	72	81	80	71	78	64	67	55	80
Interest Coverage	11.43	9.40	10.11	10.69	10.24	10.75	12.52	13.83	18.47	16.81
Total Debt to Equity(%)	76.4	87.2	76.9	74.6	65.6	84.6	59.6	59.9	50.6	56.5
Tax Rate (%)	49.3	50.1	45.6	47.2	48.9	46.7	44.2	48.1	47.1	52.2
Book Value Per Share	9.58	8.50	7.62	6.38	5.86	4.87	4.06	3.70	3.28	2.35
Debt Leverage, Dollars Per Share	.44	.38	.31	.27	.21	.20	.13	.12	.09	.09
Relative Debt Leverage (%)	37.9	40.2	37.2	36.8	33.1	40.3	31.9	32.6	29.8	32.0

EXHIBIT 5

Selected Data

SCIENTIFIC INSTRUMENTS, INC.

	19x9	19x8	19x7	19x6	19x5	19x4	19x3	19x2	19x1	19x0
Total Assets	4.59	4.32	3.66	3.02	2.64	2.44	1.76	1.60	1.34	1.00
Sales	6.14	4.84	3.69	2.97	2.37	2.17	1.92	1.58	1.27	1.00
Cost of Goods Sold	7.39	5.57	3.93	3.19	2.37	2.32	2.16	1.63	1.46	1.00
Depreciation	6.79	5.97	4.68	4.20	3.36	3.12	2.67	2.04	1.37	1.00
Operating Expenses	4.21	3.71	3.39	2.58	2.33	2.00	1.64	1.55	1.02	1.00
Operating Income	4.44	3.74	3.04	2.65	2.30	1.71	1.31	1.32	.94	1.00
Earnings Before Interest & Taxes	4.14	3.51	2.86	2.54	2.24	1.72	1.33	1.31	1.03	1.00
Interest	6.09	6.28	4.75	3.99	3.68	2.69	1.79	1.60	.94	1.00
Earnings Before Taxes	4.02	3.34	2.74	2.45	2.15	1.66	1.30	1.30	1.04	1.00
Taxes	3.79	3.21	2.39	2.21	2.01	1.49	1.10	1.20	.94	1.00
Common Earnings	4.26	3.48	3.11	2.70	2.30	1.85	1.52	1.41	1.15	1.00
No. of Common Shares	1.47	1.41	1.37	1.35	1.27	1.18	1.15	1.13	1.13	1.00

SCIENTIFIC INSTRUMENTS, INC.

EXHIBIT 6
Per Share Price Data

	19x9	19x8	19x7	19x6	19x5	19x4	19x3	19x2	19x1	19x0
Price:										
High	55.38	58.75	47.50	26.75	20.25	13.38	13.75	14.50	20.88	13.25
Low	39.75	32.00	23.38	19.13	11.75	9.00	9.50	6.25	10.88	10.88
Average	47.56	45.37	35.44	22.94	16.00	11.19	11.63	10.38	15.88	12.07
Price-Earnings:										
High	48.1	62.5	56.5	36.7	32.7	26.8	33.5	38.2	67.3	49.1
Low	34.5	34.0	27.8	26.2	18.9	18.0	23.2	16.4	35.1	40.3
Average	41.3	48.2	42.1	31.4	25.8	22.4	28.3	27.3	51.2	44.7
Market-Book Value:										
High	5.78	6.91	6.23	4.20	3.46	2.75	3.39	3.92	6.38	5.62
Low	4.15	3.76	3.07	3.00	2.01	1.85	2.34	1.69	3.32	4.65
Average	4.96	5.34	4.65	3.60	2.73	2.30	2.87	2.81	4.85	5.14

EXHIBIT 7

Selected Electronic Companies Industry Data per Share

SCIENTIFIC INSTRUMENTS, INC.

	19x9	19x8	19x7	19x6	19x5	19x4	19x3	19x2	19x1	19x0
Sales	581.56	529.35	496.69	579.27	289.37	272.04	253.92	227.27	195.76	206.83
Depreciation	14.63	13.27	11.16	11.80	9.06	8.15	6.89	6.06	5.55	5.13
Income Taxes	20.88	17.84	17.40	17.67	5.31	4.84	4.19	3.22	3.03	4.23
Common Earnings	22.29	20.05	20.75	19.45	12.00	10.17	8.05	6.94	6.01	7.02
Common Dividends	3.97	3.42	3.22	2.95	2.35	2.18	1.80	1.72	1.48	1.83
Price Index:										
High	648.49	622.21	669.19	454.21	362.41	228.48	214.16	250.00	282.91	263.26
Low	522.16	472.86	410.04	352.22	229.03	190.98	171.31	135.53	223.93	189.78
Average	585.33	547.54	539.62	403.22	295.72	209.73	192.74	192.77	253.42	226.52
Price/Earnings Ratio:										
High	29.1	31.0	32.2	23.3	30.2	22.5	26.6	36.0	47.1	37.5
Low	23.4	23.6	19.8	18.1	19.1	18.8	21.3	19.5	37.3	27.0
Average	26.2	27.3	26.0	20.7	24.6	20.6	23.9	27.7	42.2	32.2
Book Value Per Share	186.03	169.44	153.73	177.20	82.21	82.94	78.15	75.59	67.38	71.50
Book Value – % Return	11.98	11.83	13.50	10.98	14.60	12.26	10.30	9.18	8.92	9.82

Source: *S & P Analyst's Handbook.*

EXHIBIT 8

Selected Events, 19x5 to Current Year   SCIENTIFIC INSTRUMENTS, INC.

Date Announced	Event
Calendar 19x5	
4-5	Registered primary and secondary offerings of 100,000 shares each with SEC.
4-21	Sold the 200,000 shares at $55 per share.
5-12	Received first installment of $3.0 million on a $9.0 million Air Force Contract to make camera systems.
11-19	Announced 2 for 1 stock split subject to stockholder approval.
19x6	
1-13	Stock split was effective January 12.
3-31	Received $5 million Navy contract for camera systems.
10-13	Won $30 million optical development contract.
19x7	
11-17	Received $2.0 million of a $4.2 million Air Force contract for laser sets. Requested stockholder approval of 2 for 1 stock split to take effect December 7.
19x9	
8-22	A mutual fund reported sales of 45,300 shares of SI's common while another fund reported purchases of 10,000 shares of the stock during the second quarter of 19x9.
11-21	Two mutual funds sold 280,000 shares worth nearly $12 million during the third quarter of 19x9.

EXHIBIT 9

Quarterly Earnings   SCIENTIFIC INSTRUMENTS, INC.

Date Reported		Quarter Ending	Per Share	Year*
Calendar 19x5	2-26	Jan. 31	n.a.	
	5-21	Apr. 30	.65	
	9-8	July 31	.75	2.46
	11-19	Oct. 31	.56	
19x6	2-17	Jan. 31[†]	n.a.	
	5-19	Apr. 30	.33	
	9-8	July 31	.52	1.47
	11-18	Oct. 31	.25	
19x7	2-24	Jan. 31	.25	
	5-23	Apr. 30	.36	
	9-7	July 31	.69	1.68
	11-17	Oct. 31	.23	
19x8	2-16	Jan. 31[‡]	.19	
	5-21	Apr. 30	.22	
	9-18	July 31	.42	.94
	11-22	Oct. 31	.22	
19x9	2-21	Jan. 31	.26	
	5-22	Apr. 30	.26	
	9-4	July 31	.41	1.15
	11-21	Oct. 31	.23	
Current Year	2-20	Jan. 31	.30	
	5-21	Apr. 30	.30	
		July 31	est. .40	est. 1.23

* Fiscal year ends July 31.
† Stock split two for one, effective Jan. 12, 19x6.
‡ Stock split two for one, effective Dec. 7, 19x7.
Note: Earnings figures are those stated by the company on the date reported.

EXHIBIT 10

Insider Transactions   SCIENTIFIC INSTRUMENTS, INC.

	Executive	Purchased	Sold	Remaining Holdings
19x8				
9-24	President & Chairman of Board		3,800	6,000
10-3	Senior Vice President	12,333*		16,789
11-25	Executive Vice President		600	400
12-2	1st Vice President		400	0
12-2	2nd Vice President	476		4,692
19x9				
1-22	3rd Vice President		260	5,100
2-17	4th Vice President	800		1,600
3-3	5th Vice President	8,000*		17,397
3-25	President & Chairman of of the Board	16,000*		22,000
3-27	Director	249		10,000
4-10	3rd Vice President		100	5,000
5-9	Chairman, Executive Committee		1,000	25,000
5-9	Senior Vice President		5,000	11,789
6-6	1st Vice President	2,400		2,400
6-20	2nd Vice President	2,000*		6,692
6-30	3rd Vice President		300	4,700
7-1	Chairman, Executive Committee		5,000	20,000
7-22	3rd Vice President		4,000	700
7-31	6th Vice President	8,000*		8,770
9-4	1st Vice President	2,100*		4,500
9-10	7th Vice President	667		4,813
9-29	President and Chairman of the Board		4,200	17,800
9-30	President and Chairman of the Board		1,800	16,000
10-8	1st Vice President	700*		5,200
10-17	8th Vice President		1,000	2,100
19x9				
10-21	Senior Vice President		6,000	5,789
12-1	5th Vice President		100	17,297
Current Year				
1-6	7th Vice President	1,335		6,148
1-16	Executive Vice President	2,000		2,400
1-27	Chairman, Executive Committee		3,000	17,000
2-2	1st Vice President	2,800		8,000

*Purchased via option.

EXHIBIT 11

Weekly Volume and Price Data*   SCIENTIFIC INSTRUMENTS, INC.

Year 19x5		Volume (Sales in 100's)	Price Weekly Avg.	Year 19x5		Volume (Sales in 100's)	Price Weekly Avg.
January	4	136	53 7/8	December	6	88	74 7/8
	11	137	56 5/8		13	217	77 1/2
	18	79	56		20	60	77 3/4
	25	86	56		27	77	78 1/8
February	1	45	55 3/4				
	8	68	54 1/4	19x6			
	15	57	53 5/8				
	22	72	56	January	3	127	79 5/8
March	1	94	55		10	127	82 5/8
	8	202	57		17	107	85 1/2
	15	83	58 3/8		24	35	84 1/2
	22	107	58 5/8		31	458	45
	29	132	55 1/2	February	7	168	47 3/8
April	5	138	53 1/8		14	124	45 1/2
	12	75	54 1/4		21	112	43 3/4
	19	196	55 3/8		28	161	44 1/8
	26	161	54 1/8	March	7	166	43 1/8
May	3	118	53 3/8		14	190	40 7/8
	10	79	54 1/4		21	214	44
	17	166	55 1/4		28	194	47
	24	159	53 3/8	April	4	91	46
	31	117	52 5/8		11	290	50 3/4
June	7	161	50 1/2		18	149	49
	14	465	49 5/8		25	114	47 3/4
	21	140	50 1/4	May	2	183	44 7/8
	28	189	49 1/8		9	253	44 1/2
July	5	76	52 1/2		16	360	41 1/8
	12	139	54 7/8		23	206	42 1/2
	19	130	54 1/2		30	85	42 1/4
	26	98	55 3/8	June	6	86	43 3/4
August	2	193	57 1/8		13	165	46 1/2
	9	226	60 3/4		20	103	45 1/2
	16	220	62 7/8		27	134	44 5/8
	23	121	62 1/4	July	4	108	45 1/4
	30	115	63 3/4		11	80	45 5/8
September	6	185	65 5/8		18	136	43 7/8
	13	201	67 3/4		25	163	42 1/2
	20	140	68 3/4	August	1	240	45 1/2
	27	106	66 3/8		8	330	45 5/8
October	4	141	67 1/4		15	260	47
	11	112	70 1/4		22	232	45 1/2
	18	181	74		29	269	43 1/8
	25	133	72 1/2	September	5	159	42 1/4
November	1	49	74 3/8		12	111	43 1/2
	8	66	72 5/8		19	181	41 1/8
	15	211	76 3/4		26	163	40 3/8
	22	69	77 7/8				
	29	60	76 3/4				

*Dates are beginning of the week.

EXHIBIT 11 (continued)

Weekly Volume and Price Data

SCIENTIFIC INSTRUMENTS, INC.

Year 19x6		Volume (Sales in 100's)	Price Weekly Avg.	Year 19x7		Volume (Sales in 100's)	Price Weekly Avg.
October	3	210	36 7/8	September	4	251	72 1/4
	10	714	37 5/8		11	381	76 1/4
	17	279	36 7/8		18	296	78 7/8
	24	206	36 7/8		25	269	78 7/8
	31	307	38 1/4	October	2	154	79 3/8
November	7	238	38 7/8		9	191	80 7/8
	14	498	41 1/2		16	340	86 3/4
	21	227	43 3/4		23	413	89 1/8
	28	310	47		30	288	83 1/8
December	5	188	48 3/8	November	6	179	81 3/8
	12	431	51 7/8		13	225	85 1/8
	19	192	52 1/4		20	185	87 1/8
	26	150	50		27	188	88 3/8
				December	4	226	92
19x7					11	261	86 5/8
					18	488	80 3/4
January	2	266	48 1/4		25	408	77 3/8
	9	588	51				
	16	486	53 7/8	**19x8**			
	23	587	56				
	30	650	55 3/4	January	1	60	82 1/4
February	6	417	55 3/8		8	528	38 3/4
	13	517	56 3/4		15	316	39 7/8
	20	362	60		22	560	38 1/8
	27	262	59 3/8		29	336	36 1/2
March	6	478	61 1/4	February	5	387	34 3/4
	13	308	60 7/8		12	550	35 3/8
	20	162	61 3/8		19	794	35 3/8
	27	308	65 5/8		26	545	35 1/8
April	3	241	66 3/8	March	4	687	34 3/4
	10	198	66 1/4		11	443	37 1/8
	17	366	72 7/8		18	404	37 5/8
	24	136	74 1/8		25	449	37 7/8
May	1	263	72	April	1	672	41 1/8
	8	562	71 1/4		8	287	40 1/2
	15	391	71 5/8		15	338	41 7/8
	22	256	70 3/8		22	360	42 3/4
	29	151	70 1/8		29	255	42 7/8
June	5	349	70 5/8	May	6	215	44 3/8
	12	243	75 1/4		13	190	42 7/8
	19	184	77 3/8		20	397	44 3/8
	26	274	71 3/4		27	178	48 5/8
July	3	192	69 1/2	June	3	228	49
	10	229	73 1/8		10	255	50 3/4
	17	169	72 3/8		17	187	49 5/8
	24	429	67 3/4		24	336	45 7/8
	31	196	67 1/8	July	1	182	45 7/8
August	7	267	64 7/8		8	324	46 5/8
	14	232	64 5/8		15	264	45 1/8
	21	108	64 1/2		22	317	44 1/4
	28	264	66 3/4		29	191	43 5/8

EXHIBIT 11 (continued)

Weekly Volume and Price Data   SCIENTIFIC INSTRUMENTS, INC.

Year 19x8		Volume (Sales in 100's)	Price Weekly Avg.	Year 19x9		Volume (Sales in 100's)	Price Weekly Avg.
August	5	142	44	July	7	1603	45 3/4
	12	322	42 3/4		14	1002	45 1/2
	19	150	41 7/8		21	1062	43 7/8
	26	270	42 5/8		28	589	45
September	2	136	44 5/8	August	4	148	46 1/8
	9	177	48 1/8		11	168	46 3/8
	16	375	49 7/8		18	165	46 1/2
	23	259	50 1/2		25	220	46
	30	214	50	September	1	138	45 1/2
October	7	339	50 1/8		8	518	44 1/4
	14	125	49 7/8		15	282	46 1/4
	21	248	49		22	598	46 3/4
	28	275	48 5/8		29	554	42
November	4	241	47 3/8	October	6	366	43
	11	298	50 1/4		13	427	43 7/8
	18	409	54 1/8		20	476	45 3/8
	25	165	56 3/8		27	323	47 1/4
December	2	177	57 3/8	November	3	417	46 1/8
	9	170	56 3/8		10	299	45 1/2
	16	209	56		17	409	44
	23	102	54 3/8		24	185	44 3/8
				December	1	262	43 1/2
19x9					8	221	44 5/8
					15	196	45 7/8
January	6	273	52 5/8		22	210	45 5/8
	13	160	52				
	20	166	53 3/8	**Current Year**			
	27	141	54 5/8				
February	3	189	52 3/4	January	5	218	45 3/4
	10	133	52 3/8		12	242	45 5/8
	17	234	50 3/8		19	242	43 3/4
	24	468	50 1/8		26	393	41
March	3	351	49 1/8	February	2	371	36 3/4
	10	389	48 3/4		9	546	40 1/2
	17	271	49 3/8		16	249	40 1/2
	24	189	51 1/8		23	409	39 3/4
	31	93	51 1/8	March	2	548	43 3/8
April	7	353	50 3/8		9	377	37
	14	296	50		16	374	37 1/2
	21	364	48 1/4		23	263	37 3/8
	28	342	50 1/4		30	282	37 1/8
May	5	467	51	April	6	341	35 1/4
	12	235	49 1/2		13	497	32 1/8
	19	803	50 1/4		20	355	31 1/8
	26	208	48 5/8		27	602	30 1/2
June	2	438	49 5/8	May	4	331	29 5/8
	9	183	48 1/2		11	324	25 3/4
	16	300	47 1/8		18	451	24 1/2
	23	816	47		25	836	21 7/8
	30	481	48 1/8	June	1	299	24 5/8
					8	469	23 1/2
					15	283	25 5/8
					22	520	26 3/4

Case 17: Comprehensive Case—Coverage of Fama's Efficient Capital Market Hypothesis

Hercules Minerals

*The actual, private object of the most skilled investment today is "beat the gun," as the Americans so well express it, to outwit the crowd, and to pass the bad, or depreciating, half-crown to the other fellow. (*J. M. Keynes.*)*

Business and Prospects

Since its incorporation in 1909, Hercules Minerals (HM) has concentrated its activities in mining and especially in the exploration of sulphur. HM has grown mainly through acquisitions and agreements with other firms and is now one of the leading sulphur producers in the world, with operations in Canada, Mexico, and Australia as well as the United States. The company's sulphur is used in the sulphite pulp and rubber industries; the major portion is sold to sulphuric acid producers. HM is also engaged in the production of phosphate, potash, silver, copper, zinc, and lead. In 19x9, the company produced 2.9 million tons of sulphur, 13.0 million ounces of silver, 470,000 tons of 25 percent copper concentrates, 432,000 tons of 52 percent zinc concentrates, and 430,000 tons of potash. HM has recently diversified its operations to include exploration and production of oil and natural gas.

Widespread price cutting in the sulphur industry has occurred since 19x8 because world supply of sulphur has increased faster than consumption. The price cutting was initiated by Mexican and Polish producers who were more concerned with increasing exports than earning large profits. HM was forced to cut prices also, and the result has been a sharp decline in profits for the past 2 years. A sales decline of approximately 8.3 percent this year is expected to result in an earnings per share decline to $1.51 from $2.02 in 19x9. The declines reflect primarily the erosion of sulphur prices since HM's sales of phosphate fertilizers and potash are higher. Sales of metals are also up due mainly to price increases.

Preliminary forecasts indicate that sales for the first quarter of the coming year will decline by more than 20 percent from their level for the corresponding period of this year. The sales decline coupled with the effects of operating and financial leverages could reduce net income by more than 50 percent. Earnings for the remainder of next year are highly uncertain since the imbalance of supply and demand for sulphur is expected to continue whereas metals' prices should stabilize. The company's past policy of tax deferrals will accentuate any profit declines. The net effect of all of the above factors may be so adverse that dividends to shareholders will be reduced.

On the positive side, HM's Australian venture in high-grade iron ore development is well underway. Initial drilling has indicated a deposit of more than one billion tons of 60 percent or higher iron-ore concentrate. The venture has a total sales potential of $1.4 billion. HM is also planning to expand its oil and gas explorations. The company has already recovered its initial investment in this area, and explorations in Mexico and Africa are well underway.

The current price of HM's common stock is $15 per share.

Insider Dealings

The company discovered a large body of rich zinc, copper, and silver ore in late 19x3. Management denied the find in a press release dated April 12, 19x4, but admitted to the find four days later. The Securities and Exchange Commission found that between November 12, 19x3, when the engineers' mineral reports were being received and April 16, 19x4, HM's officers and directors purchased 12,100 shares of the company's common stock. In addition, directors and officers purchased call options for 5,200 shares and obtained executive stock options for another 31,200 shares. Officials of the company were also accused of giving tips to friends and associates who then purchased a total 14,100 common shares and 14,000 call options during the period.

After a series of lengthy legal battles between HM and its stockholders, the SEC, and adjacent mining companies, the conclusions of the highest court which has heard the case to date are that the firm, its executives and their associates were guilty of violating disclosure laws. The penalty assessed by the court was a forfeiture of all profits acquired by those involved as the result of "inside" information. Five executives and several of their associates returned profits amounting to over $150,000 on February 9, of the current year. As a result of the court decision, the rules on insider trading have been revised so that not only corporate executives but anyone in possession of "material" inside information, including an outside investor who receives a "tip," are "insiders" and as such they must return to the company any profits made as a result of having the information. The court stated that "insiders" have two choices: (1) they must disclose the information before trading in the stock, or (2) they must not trade in the stock.

Historical Events

HM's sales declined from $85 to $62 million during the 8 years preceding 19x4. Earnings per share of common declined from $.94 to $.31, and dividends per share from $.67 to $.13 during the same period. But in 19x4, when HM reported the huge sulphur find, the company was thrust into the international limelight for several years. The following is a detailed chronological listing of the most pertinent events that might have affected the price of HM's common shares. The dates refer to when the information was made public.

19x4

2-21	HM reports net income of $9.4 million for 19x3.
4-1	Announces a $2 per ton increase in the price of sulphur.
4-12	Refutes as premature and possibly misleading a rumor of a huge discovery of copper ore in Canada.
4-16	The president of HM reports a major discovery of zinc, copper, and silver in Canada. He states that preliminary data reveal a reserve of over 25 million tons of ore.
4-21	Reports net income of $2.8 million for first quarter.
5-14	Officers and directors of HM purchase 3,700 shares of common.
5-15	A director of HM purchases 2,000 shares of common.
5-21	Short interest of HM's common rises to 305,000 shares on the NYSE.
6-8	Court action for trespass is brought against HM by adjacent mining company.
7-17	Company reports income of $3.0 million for second quarter, an increase of 20 percent over the corresponding quarter in 19x3.
10-16	Reports net income of $2.9 million for third quarter and income of $8.6 million for 9 months.

19x5

2-19	Reports net income of $11.6 million for 19x4.
3-19	Announces ore deposit appears to be larger than 55 million tons.
3-30	Announces an increase in the price of sulphur of $4 per ton.
4-20	SEC accuses 13 officers, directors, and employees of HM of improperly using inside information for profit.
4-21	Two stockholder suits brought against HM.
4-23	HM reports net income of $3.3 million for first quarter.
4-26	Additional stockholder suits are announced.
7-9	Company denies SEC charge of 4-20.
7-20	Reports net income of $4.9 million for second quarter and income of $8.2 million for 6 months.
7-22	Several officers of company return, at cost, shares and call options purchased in early 19x4.
8-4	Six officers and directors deny SEC charges of improperly using inside information for private gain.
10-22	HM reports net income of $4.6 million for third quarter and income of $12.8 million for 9 months.
10-27	HM purchases additional mineral properties for $24 million.

<u>19x6</u>

1-21   Announces precious metals production capacity of company is expanded by 50 percent.

2-18   Reports net income of $18.2 million for 19x5.

4-27   President reports at the company's annual meeting a doubling of earnings during the first quarter of 19x6 over earnings of 19x5.

5-9   Court trial brought by SEC begins.

5-10   An officer testifies that he purchased 600 shares of the company's stock before the ore discovery was disclosed.

5-12   SEC contends that HM knew of substantial ore body long before the press release of April 12, 19x4.

6-7   Witnesses testify that they feel that securities dealers and analysts as well as the public were informed of the ore strike before the company release.

7-22   HM reports net income of $8.0 million for second quarter and earnings of $14.7 million for 6 months.

7-25   Construction at the ore site is halted by strike of machine operators.

8-10   Ironworkers strike.

8-22   HM is exonerated of charges of inadequate inside disclosure of corporate news and improper trading of the stock by lower court; however, two officials are charged with having used inside information unfairly.

9-8   SEC appeals ruling of 8-22.

10-21   HM announces company will explore for sulphur in Mexico in conjunction with the Mexican Government.

10-25   Reports net income of $5.9 million for third quarter and income of $20.5 million for 9 months.

11-17   Announces first processing of ore from the discovery site.

12-13   Announces sulphur price increase of $2.50 per ton.

<u>19x7</u>

2-17   Reports net income of $28.1 million for 19x6.

3-28   HM increases price of sulphur $4 per ton.

4-28   At annual meeting, the president of HM reports first-quarter net income of $10.1 million, up 50 percent from first quarter of 19x6.

7-31   Reports net income of $16.8 million in second quarter versus $8.0 million in second quarter of 19x6.

9-12   HM announces a shortage of sulphur necessitating a decrease in customer deliveries.

10-2   HM increases sulphur prices by $5.50 per ton to $39.

11-3   Reports that third-quarter earnings nearly tripled from same period in 19x6.

12-5   Sulphur allocation to customer of HM is reduced to 65 percent of 19x5 deliveries due to sulphur shortages.

12-8	Proposes a 3-for-1 stock split and a dividend increase to $1.20 from the $.40 current annual rate. Reports third-quarter net income of $17.3 million.

19x8

2-23	Reports net income of $62.1 million for 19x7.
4-26	Reports first-quarter net income of $17.2 million; increases quarterly dividend to $.30 payable June 15.
5-3	Announcement that SEC case against the firm is to be considered by a panel of 9 judges.
6-10	HM's stock is split 3 for 1.
6-16	Quarterly dividend of $.10 on new shares declared.
7-16	Current president becomes chairman of the board and a director becomes president.
7-30	Reports net income of $18.9 million for second quarter and net income of $36.1 million for 6 months.
8-1	Brokerage analysts cite several areas of potential profit deterioration for HM.
8-14	Nine Federal judges rule that HM's top officers violated disclosure laws.
8-16	HM to appeal decision of 8-14.
9-3	HM's exploration work in Australia produces mixed results.
11-4	Reports net income of $17.7 million for third quarter and net income of $53.8 million for 9 months.
12-2	Court suit by adjacent mining firm for trespass is dismissed by Supreme Court.
12-9	Mining company announces it will not appeal decision of 12-2.

19x9

1-21	Price of sulphur cut $2 per ton.
2-18	HM reports net income for 19x8 of $70.5 million.
2-21	Mutual funds, on balance, purchased 160,800 shares of HM's common during the fourth quarter of 19x8.
3-19	Company announces that earnings from metals operations, which were primarily responsible for the 19x8s profits increase, should continue to improve for several years.
4-22	Supreme Court concurs with SEC's original suit against company in 19x5.
4-23	Mutual funds sold on balance 472,600 of HM's shares during the first quarter of 19x9.
4-25	President of HM reports first quarter net income of $16.3 million at annual meeting; proposes a 60 percent increase in the quarterly dividend.
7-2	Director sells 500 shares of HM's common.
7-3	Director sells 500 shares of HM's common.

7-7   Quarterly dividend of $.15 per share paid to stockholders of record 9-15.

7-8   Director sells 500 shares of common.

7-22   Officer purchases 500 shares of common, increasing holdings to 5,000 shares.

7-25   Reports net income of $18.3 million for first quarter and net income of $34.6 million for 6 months.

8-22   Mutual funds sold 58,300 shares of HM's common during the second quarter of 19x9.

11-5   Company reports net income of $12.1 million for third quarter and net income of $46.7 million for 9 months.

11-21   Mutual funds sold 309,300 shares on balance during the third quarter of 19x9.

<u>Current Year</u>

2-9   HM reaches agreement for exploratory work in Australia.

2-9   Federal judge rules that HM and its executives failed to exercise "due diligence" in issuing press release of April 12, 19x4.

2-16   Company announces plans to appeal ruling of 2-9.

2-20   Reports net income for 19x9 as $61.5 million.

4-17   HM announces plans for $30 million investment in Australia.

4-24   Reports net income for first quarter of $13.9 million.

7-10   Purchases adjacent mine interest for $27 million to settle a long standing court suit.

7-29   Reports net income of $12.2 million for second quarter and net income of $26.1 million for 6 months.

9-2   Rumors of active trading in HM's stock.

9-17   Company discontinues sulphur operations at one of its older, local mines.

10-26   Reduces price of copper to 57.3 cents per pound from 59 cents.

10-27   Reports net income of $11.5 million for third quarter and net income of $37.7 million for 9 months.

QUESTIONS

1. (a) Discuss the meaning of each of the following terms which have been applied to the "efficient capital markets" hypothesis: (1) weak form test, (2) semistrong form test, and (3) strong form test.

   (b) Which events presented in the case could be used in one or more of the above tests?

   (c) Which of the events presented in the case for 19x4 and 19x9 would have produced profits and which would have produced losses from a trading policy of buying on good news and selling short on bad news, and then reversing the transaction 1 week later. Use average weekly price, and assume a purchase or short sale of one hundred shares is made at closing prices the week during the announcement, and assume further that the reverse trade is made at closing prices the week following the announcement.

(d) How could the overall market effects be taken into consideration separately in your answers to 1(c)? Explain.

2. Based upon your answer to 1(c), has the market been (a) efficient or (b) inefficient in the pricing of HM's stock since January 19x4? Discuss.

3. (a) Do you agree with the testimony of the witnesses on June 7, 19x6? Why?
   (b) Do you agree with the final disposition of the case as rendered by the judges on August 14, 19x8? Explain.

4. (a) How can you explain the sulphur allocation policy of December 5, 19x7 and the subsequent price reduction only 14 months later?
   (b) What justification did HM's management have for the dividend increase of July 7, 19x9?

5. (a) Appraise HM's overall performance since 19x4.
   (b) Estimate the $\overline{HPR}$ and the expected variance in the HPR of the company's common stock for the coming year.

EXHIBIT 1

Balance Sheet Data (millions)

HERCULES MINERALS

	19x9	19x8	19x7	19x6	19x5	19x4	19x3	19x2	19x1	19x0
Assets:										
Current	226.17	199.49	92.70	57.25	64.50	97.20	64.77	55.83	75.20	82.18
Cash Items	122.97	102.69	17.60	8.05	20.70	42.10	19.27	10.33	26.90	32.42
Receivables	45.90	51.90	39.10	25.80	21.50	29.00	15.80	13.30	17.60	21.11
Inventory	57.30	44.90	36.00	23.40	22.30	26.10	29.70	32.20	30.70	28.65
Other	56.23	30.65	31.19	30.41	30.97	36.86	49.78	23.66	16.81	8.20
Fixed	293.79	293.42	288.69	275.38	145.41	86.38	72.73	62.11	41.86	35.02
Total Assets:	576.19	523.56	412.58	363.04	240.88	220.44	187.28	141.60	133.87	125.40
Liabilities:										
Current	50.70	46.22	22.99	23.72	11.87	9.88	17.79	4.40	6.37	3.54
Bonds	117.35	125.50	115.00	135.00	55.00	55.00	0.0	0.0	0.0	0.0
Other	63.69	54.96	39.06	27.90	22.01	18.17	39.77	12.68	9.61	6.53
Common Stock	27.08	27.05	26.68	26.43	26.35	26.21	26.18	26.18	26.18	26.18
Surplus	317.37	269.83	208.85	149.99	125.65	111.18	103.54	93.34	91.71	89.15
Total Liabilities:	576.19	523.56	412.58	363.04	240.88	220.44	187.28	141.60	133.87	125.40

EXHIBIT 2

Income Data (millions)

HERCULES MINERALS

	19x9	19x8	19x7	19x6	19x5	19x4	19x3	19x2	19x1	19x0
Sales	301.77	309.92	253.10	132.72	98.98	70.37	62.25	58.97	58.95	58.94
Cost of Goods Sold	191.73	177.52	141.75	79.75	65.88	48.12	44.62	36.69	35.79	36.17
Depreciation	18.31	22.37	16.07	6.62	4.88	4.06	3.01	2.94	2.98	2.96
Operating Expense	11.80	10.39	10.27	9.76	7.36	6.04	5.05	5.33	4.85	4.63
Operating Income	79.93	99.64	85.01	36.59	20.86	12.15	9.57	14.01	15.33	15.18
Other Income	10.76	7.95	3.78	3.34	3.30	2.91	1.33	1.88	2.00	3.29
Earnings Before Interest & Taxes	90.69	107.59	88.79	39.93	24.16	15.06	10.90	15.89	17.33	18.47
Interest	6.87	6.60	6.84	4.73	2.60	2.30	-0-	-0-	-0-	-0-
Earnings Before Taxes	83.82	100.99	81.95	35.20	21.56	12.76	10.90	15.89	17.33	18.47
Taxes	22.35	29.51	19.85	7.10	3.40	1.20	1.55	3.75	4.75	4.75
Common Earnings	61.47	71.48	62.10	28.10	18.16	11.56	9.35	12.14	12.58	13.72
Common Dividends	16.74	10.00	3.94	4.01	4.01	4.01	4.01	5.51	10.02	9.84
No. of Common Shares	30.4	30.3	30.3	30.2	30.3	30.4	30.2	30.3	30.0	30.0

EXHIBIT 3

Per Share Income Data

HERCULES MINERALS

	19x9	19x8	19x7	19x6	19x5	19x4	19x3	19x2	19x1	19x0
Sales	9.92	10.23	8.36	4.39	3.27	2.31	2.06	1.94	1.97	1.98
Cost of Goods Sold	6.30	5.86	4.68	2.64	2.18	1.58	1.48	1.21	1.19	1.21
Depreciation	.60	.74	.53	.22	.16	.13	.10	.10	.10	.10
Operating Expense	.39	.34	.34	.32	.24	.20	.16	.17	.17	.16
Operating Income	2.63	3.29	2.81	1.21	.69	.40	.32	.46	.51	.51
Other Income	.35	.26	.12	.11	.11	.10	.04	.06	.07	.11
Earnings Before Interest & Taxes	2.98	3.55	2.93	1.32	.80	.50	.36	.52	.58	.62
Interest	.23	.22	.22	.16	.09	.08	-0-	-0-	-0-	-0-
Earnings Before Taxes	2.75	3.33	2.71	1.16	.71	.42	.36	.52	.58	.62
Taxes	.73	.97	.66	.23	.11	.04	.05	.12	.16	.16
Common Earnings	2.02	2.36	2.05	.93	.60	.38	.31	.40	.42	.46
Common Dividends	.55	.33	.13	.13	.13	.13	.13	.18	.33	.33

EXHIBIT 4

Index Values per Share

HERCULES MINERALS

	19x9	19x8	19x7	19x6	19x5	19x4	19x3	19x2	19x1	19x0
Total Assets	4.50	4.11	3.24	2.86	1.89	1.72	1.48	1.11	1.06	1.00
Sales	5.02	5.18	4.23	2.22	1.65	1.17	1.04	.98	1.00	1.00
Cost of Goods Sold	5.19	4.83	3.86	2.18	1.79	1.30	1.22	1.00	.99	1.00
Depreciation	6.06	7.44	5.34	2.21	1.62	1.34	1.01	.98	1.00	1.00
Operating Expenses	2.50	2.21	2.18	2.08	1.57	1.28	1.08	1.13	1.04	1.00
Operating Income	5.16	6.46	5.51	2.38	1.35	.78	.62	.91	1.01	1.00
Earnings Before Interest & Taxes	4.81	5.73	4.73	2.13	1.29	.80	.58	.85	.93	1.00
Earnings Before Taxes	4.45	5.38	4.37	1.88	1.15	.68	.58	.85	.93	1.00
Taxes	4.61	6.12	4.11	1.47	.71	.25	.32	.78	1.00	1.00
Common Earnings	4.39	5.13	4.46	2.02	1.30	.83	.67	.87	.91	1.00
Common Dividends	1.67	1.00	.40	.40	.40	.40	.40	.55	1.01	1.00
No. of Common Shares	1.02	1.02	1.02	1.01	1.02	1.02	1.01	1.02	1.00	1.00

EXHIBIT 5

Selected Data

HERCULES MINERALS

	19x9	19x8	19x7	19x6	19x5	19x4	19x3	19x2	19x1	19x0
Return on Sales (%)	20.4	23.1	24.5	21.2	18.3	16.4	15.0	20.6	21.3	23.3
Return on Assets (%)	10.7	13.7	15.1	7.7	7.5	5.2	5.0	8.6	9.4	10.9
Return on Equity (%)	17.8	24.1	26.4	15.9	11.9	8.4	7.2	9.7	10.7	11.9
Capital Turnover	.52	.59	.61	.37	.41	.32	.33	.42	.44	.47
Inventory Turnover	3.35	3.95	3.94	3.41	2.95	1.84	1.50	1.14	1.17	1.26
Average Collection Period (days)	55	60	56	70	78	148	91	81	107	129
Interest Coverage	13.20	16.30	12.98	8.44	9.29	6.55	–	–	–	–
Total Debt to Equity (%)	67	76	75	106	58	60	44	14	14	9
Tax Rate (%)	26.7	29.2	24.2	20.2	15.8	9.4	14.2	23.6	27.4	25.7
Book Value Per Share	11.32	9.80	7.78	5.84	5.02	4.52	4.30	4.10	3.94	3.87
Dividend Payout (%)	27	14	6	14	22	35	43	45	80	72
Debt Leverage (dollars per share)	.71	.93	.78	.42	.18	.10	.09	.05	.05	.04
Relative Debt Leverage (%)	35	40	38	45	29	26	31	12	12	8

EXHIBIT 6
Per Share Data

HERCULES MINERALS

	19x9	19x8	19x7	19x6	19x5	19x4	19x3	19x2	19x1	19x0
Price:										
High	39.88	49.88	53.38	43.88	31.38	21.38	7.88	7.75	9.00	6.63
Low	19.13	29.00	32.25	22.75	16.25	7.00	4.50	3.75	6.25	5.13
Average	29.50	39.44	42.81	33.31	23.81	14.19	6.19	5.75	7.63	5.88
Price-Earnings:										
High	19.7	21.1	26.0	47.2	52.2	56.2	25.4	19.4	21.4	14.4
Low	9.5	12.3	15.7	24.5	27.1	18.4	14.5	9.1	14.9	11.2
Average	14.6	16.7	20.8	35.8	39.6	37.3	19.9	14.2	18.1	12.7
Market-Book Value:										
High	3.5	5.1	6.9	7.5	6.2	4.7	1.8	1.9	2.3	1.7
Low	1.7	3.0	4.2	3.9	3.2	1.6	1.1	.9	1.6	1.3
Average	2.6	4.0	5.5	5.7	4.7	3.1	1.4	1.4	1.9	1.5

EXHIBIT 7

Selected Sulphur Producers Industry Data per Share

HERCULES MINERALS

	19x9	19x8	19x7	19x6	19x5	19x4	19x3	19x2	19x1	19x0
Sales	28.75	30.17	25.70	18.93	14.18	10.99	9.36	8.74	8.37	7.82
Depreciation	1.96	2.03	1.57	.99	.80	.58	.57	.56	.60	.55
Income Taxes	1.45	2.52	1.32	1.32	.70	.53	.42	.46	.49	.38
Common Earnings	5.37	6.92	6.10	4.09	2.64	1.91	1.54	1.69	1.70	1.66
Common Dividends	2.74	2.31	1.69	1.39	1.17	.95	.93	.99	1.26	1.22
Price Index:										
High	113.14	149.59	168.36	117.78	89.94	63.94	33.10	28.78	33.97	28.01
Low	57.72	96.95	100.69	76.96	57.76	32.18	20.88	18.17	27.57	21.85
Average	85.43	123.27	134.52	97.37	73.85	48.06	26.99	23.48	30.77	29.49
Price-Earnings Ratio:										
High	21.1	21.6	27.6	28.8	34.1	33.5	21.5	17.0	20.0	16.9
Low	10.8	14.0	16.5	18.8	21.9	16.9	13.6	10.8	16.2	13.2
Average	16.0	17.8	22.1	23.8	28.0	25.2	17.6	13.9	18.1	15.1
Book Value Per Share	38.80	35.93	31.28	24.12	21.35	19.67	18.58	17.72	17.08	16.84
Book Value – % Return	13.84	19.26	19.50	16.96	12.37	9.71	8.29	9.54	9.95	9.86

Source: S & P Analyst's Handbook.

EXHIBIT 8

Weekly Volume and Price Data*   HERCULES MINERALS

Year 19x4		Volume (Sales in 100's)	Price Weekly Avg.	Year 19x5		Volume (Sales in 100's	Price Weekly Avg.
January	6	1533	22 3/4	January	4	1740	53 1/8
	13	902	21 3/4		11	3762	56 7/8
	20	763	22 1/4		18	4111	58 3/4
	27	659	22 1/4		25	3655	61 3/8
February	3	516	22 1/8	February	1	3286	63 5/8
	10	1036	22 1/4		8	4908	63 1/4
	17	1436	23 5/8		15	3146	65 5/8
	24	1016	23 1/4		22	1777	66 1/8
March	2	540	22 3/8	March	1	2544	67
	9	512	22 1/2		8	1850	68 1/8
	16	1009	23 3/8		15	1791	68 1/8
	23	1548	24 5/8		22	2484	64 3/4
	30	2103	26 1/8		29	1476	65 1/8
April	6	3397	28 3/4	April	5	1854	67 5/8
	13	11906	35 1/2		12	2646	69 5/8
	20	17405	43 3/4		19	6603	68
	27	26967	51 7/8		26	4842	63 3/8
May	4	15915	50 1/2	May	3	1583	64 1/8
	11	16378	55 3/8		10	861	65 1/8
	18	14143	57		17	1068	65 5/8
	25	6431	56 1/8		24	789	63 1/8
June	1	10529	51 7/8		31	1512	60 3/8
	8	15046	45 7/8	June	7	1595	57 3/4
	15	9946	51 1/8		14	2085	56 3/4
	22	3530	50 3/4		21	1432	54 1/8
	29	2056	47 1/2		28	2542	51 7/8
July	6	1941	48 1/8	July	5	753	55 5/8
	13	1616	49 1/2		12	512	55 3/4
	20	966	49 1/8		19	572	54 1/2
	27	3195	50 1/2		26	1599	58 3/8
August	3	2625	51 3/8	August	2	1119	60 1/2
	10	2776	53 3/8		9	1125	62 5/8
	17	2593	53 7/8		16	966	63 1/4
	24	1988	53 3/4		23	778	62
	31	2660	52 1/8		30	770	63 3/4
September	7	1812	52 1/2	September	6	662	62 7/8
	14	1684	52 3/4		13	3053	65 1/4
	21	12070	57 5/8		20	2975	69 5/8
	28	5030	62 1/2		27	1676	68 7/8
October	5	4386	63	October	4	1372	70 1/8
	12	4711	61 3/4		11	2981	68 1/4
	19	2677	60 3/8		18	1779	66 3/4
	26	3178	58 1/8		25	2818	69 3/8
November	2	1316	57	November	1	1826	71 3/4
	9	2363	56 1/8		8	2393	73 3/4
	16	1210	57 3/4		15	1345	73 1/2
	23	1730	54 3/4		22	1068	71 5/8
	30	2634	52 1/2		29	1821	71 1/8
December	7	2377	51	December	6	3403	75 3/8
	14	3106	50		13	2971	82 5/8
	21	867	52 3/8		20	2076	85 5/8
	28	1380	52 3/4		27	3934	91 1/4

*Dates are beginning of the week in which average price occurs.

EXHIBIT 8 (continued)

Weekly Volume and Price Data   HERCULES MINERALS

Year 19x6		Volume (Sales in 100's)	Price Weekly Avg.	Year 19x7		Volume (Sales in 100's)	Price Weekly Avg.
January	3	2873	89 3/8	January	2	1315	103 1/8
	10	2146	89 1/4		9	3341	112 7/8
	17	2305	94 1/8		16	1812	116 7/8
	24	3142	101 1/2		23	2913	113 3/8
	31	2311	99 7/8		30	1935	120 3/4
February	7	4136	107 7/8	February	6	2096	118 3/4
	14	4622	121 3/8		13	2219	112 5/8
	21	2558	119 3/8		20	1136	108 1/2
	28	4374	124 7/8		27	1217	109 1/8
March	7	5188	114 1/4	March	6	2115	105 5/8
	14	4014	108 1/2		13	2051	100 5/8
	21	2839	114 1/8		20	1272	105 3/8
	28	3022	118 1/4		27	1267	108 3/8
April	4	1872	119 1/4	April	3	712	104 3/4
	11	2756	113 1/2		10	683	104 3/4
	18	1867	112 1/8		17	1355	108 1/4
	25	1963	112 3/4		24	1950	114 1/2
May	2	4127	101 3/4	May	1	1051	115 5/8
	9	3083	92 7/8		8	1038	113 1/8
	16	3988	83 5/8		15	1770	116 1/4
	23	2164	89 1/4		22	2675	120 1/2
	30	1288	91 3/4		29	1383	117 1/2
June	6	2236	96	June	5	3825	122
	13	2328	105		12	1491	130 1/2
	20	2032	110 1/8		19	866	127 1/2
	27	1903	102 3/4		26	1300	124 1/2
July	4	1030	106 3/8	July	3	427	124 1/2
	11	1325	104 3/4		10	1656	135 1/4
	18	963	102 1/8		17	1089	139 1/4
	25	1736	97 1/2		24	1373	144 3/4
August	1	1376	95		31	1141	148 7/8
	8	971	96 3/4	August	7	572	144 7/8
	15	1344	92 7/8		14	690	140 3/8
	22	1953	87 1/4		21	823	138
	29	1834	82 1/4		28	693	142 3/4
September	5	937	79	September	4	763	149
	12	1309	84 1/8		11	645	148 1/8
	19	708	83 7/8		18	1018	156
	26	796	83 1/8		25	1165	154 1/4
October	3	1664	77 1/4	October	2	987	151 7/8
	10	1543	73 3/8		9	1129	149 5/8
	17	804	77 7/8		16	940	144 3/8
	24	970	75 5/8		23	1117	144 3/8
	31	1243	80 1/4		30	3054	137
November	7	938	86 3/4	November	6	1095	133 1/2
	14	1500	89 1/4		13	1395	125 7/8
	21	1687	93 1/8		20	925	128 7/8
	28	2950	104		27	2672	127 1/4
December	5	2279	107 3/4	December	4	1885	126 1/4
	12	1289	108 5/8		11	1776	135 5/8
	19	1224	109 5/8		18	1219	131 3/4
	26	814	107 1/2		25	740	128 3/4

EXHIBIT 8 (continued)

Weekly Volume and Price Data   HERCULES MINERALS

Year 19x8		Volume (Sales in 100's)	Price Weekly Avg.	Year 19x9		Volume (Sales in 100's)	Price Weekly Avg.
January	1	776	122 1/4	January	6	3053	37
	8	728	121 7/8		13	2494	35 1/2
	15	1081	117 3/8		20	2399	34 3/4
	22	1293	113 1/8		27	1713	33 3/4
	29	638	111 5/8	February	3	1685	34 1/4
February	5	606	110 1/8		10	946	34 1/8
	12	430	110 5/8		17	1546	32 1/4
	19	348	113		24	1631	31 1/8
	26	540	114 5/8	March	3	1474	31 3/8
March	4	813	112 1/2		10	2437	30 3/8
	11	1535	118 1/2		17	5094	29 7/8
	18	1162	119 3/4		24	2023	30 3/4
	25	531	118 3/8		31	1008	30
April	1	1129	118	April	7	1572	30 3/8
	8	823	119 3/4		14	2347	28 7/8
	15	1265	125 7/8		21	1725	28 3/4
	22	1468	130 3/4		28	1803	28 7/8
	29	1168	136 3/4	May	5	180	28 5/8
May	6	629	132 1/2		12	4153	31 1/2
	13	827	127		19	2486	32 1/4
	20	775	122 7/8		26	939	31 1/4
	27	685	123 3/8	June	2	1082	29 7/8
June	3	251	130 1/4		9	1652	28 1/8
	10†	2679	44 3/8		16	1545	26 3/4
	17	4368	47 3/4		23	1614	26
	24	2982	44 7/8		30	875	26 1/4
July	1	1455	43 3/8	July	7	1065	25 7/8
	8	2050	43 1/4		14	1017	24 7/8
	15	2560	40 1/4		21	1243	23 1/8
	22	2600	37 5/8		28	1825	23
	29	4318	33 7/8	August	4	844	24 1/8
August	5	2694	33 1/4		11	4209	24 1/4
	12	3216	32 1/8		18	3384	25 5/8
	19	1866	32 7/8		25	1241	24 3/8
	26	1764	31 1/8	September	1	753	23 3/4
September	2	3398	30 1/2		8	2982	24 1/2
	9	1838	31 5/8		15	1442	25 1/2
	16	2131	30 5/8		22	2192	26 1/2
	23	1517	31		29	1999	25 3/4
	30	2499	32 1/8	October	6	1542	25 1/2
October	7	1207	31 3/8		13	2342	27 1/4
	14	1734	31		20	1881	26 5/8
	21	2137	31		27	3720	21 5/8
	28	2831	33 1/8	November	3	1991	25 3/8
November	4	1385	31 7/8		10	1402	24 3/8
	11	2159	31 1/2		17	1579	22 7/8
	18	1981	31 1/4		24	1338	22 3/4
	25	5691	33 7/8	December	1	1636	22 3/8
December	2	17811	39 3/8		8	2054	20 7/8
	9	4291	38 3/4		15	2223	20 1/4
	16	3042	37 7/8		22	2008	20 1/4
	23	1746	37 5/8				
	30	2569	38 1/8				

†Three-for-one stock split.

EXHIBIT 8 (continued)

Weekly Volume and Price Data   HERCULES MINERALS

Year Current		Volume (Sales in 100's)	Price Weekly Avg.	Year Current		Volume (Sales in 100's)	Price Weekly Avg.
January	5	1220	22 1/2	June	1	2537	17
	12	1178	21 3/4		8	763	16 3/4
	19	1140	21 5/8		15	1141	16 7/8
	26	1306	20		22	1138	15 7/8
February	2	1578	19 1/2		29	540	14 3/4
	9	2034	18 1/2	July	6	1359	14 1/8
	16	1621	18 5/8		13	1228	14 3/8
	23	857	19 1/2		20	1024	14
March	2	899	19 1/2		27	1242	14 1/8
	9	760	18 3/4	August	3	1365	13 5/8
	16	860	18 5/8		10	2673	14
	23	808	18 1/2		17	1163	13 7/8
	30	946	18 3/4		24	2680	14 7/8
April	6	830	17 7/8		31	6858	15 5/8
	13	1781	16 3/8	September	7	3805	17 1/2
	20	1748	15 5/8		14	2182	17 3/4
	27	2402	14 1/2		21	1656	17 1/4
May	4	1353	15 1/2		28	1738	17 1/2
	11	1892	15 1/8	October	5	2342	18 5/8
	18	1244	15 5/8		12	1242	17 3/8
	25	1886	15 1/4		19	787	16 5/8
					26	1897	25 5/8

4 Return/Risk Measures

Case 18:   Rate of Return

Richardson Chemicals, Inc.

There is only one intelligent approach to the employment or protection of capital, and that is to use it for profit. "Profit" is the net increase in the market value of invested capital at the current bid price, adding to it the dividends or interest received. (G. M. Loeb.)

Richardson Chemicals (RC) was incorporated in Delaware in 1930 as a specialty chemical company. For many years, the company relied solely upon internal growth as a basis for sales increases. At the beginning of 19x7, however, the company changed its past expansion policy and acquired four small chemical firms during the next 2 years.

The chemical industry is comprised of two types of firms: specialty (i.e., special order) chemical firms and commodity (i.e., regular order) chemical firms. Over the next several years specialty chemical firms are expected to have higher growth rates, higher average earnings, and fewer pricing problems than commodity chemical firms. During the past few years, commodity chemical producers have had to contend with competition from the major oil companies, which has resulted in severe price cutting in the face of rising production and financing costs. The commodity firms, however, are expected to benefit from the petroleum industry's current disenchantment with petrochemicals and from the recently reduced oil depletion allowance.

RC is now essentially a commodity chemical producer, with facilities located in 26 cities in the U. S. and 24 foreign countries. The company produces over 7,000 products which are sold by a technical sales force to over 10,000 customers; no single customer accounts for as much as 1 percent of total sales. Basic products of the company are polyester resins, polyurethane foam, epoxy and adhesive resins for the furniture, construction, auto, and boating industries; coating resins used in flooring, paints, and packaging; finished wall panels; and fiberglass. The company has also recently begun manufacturing a complete line of low-profile resin esters and hydrocarbon resins which are expected to eliminate the need for additives in molding applications. In terms of broad product groups, RC's sales in 19x9 were as follows: plastics, 33 percent; coatings,

28 percent; miscellaneous, 15 percent; adhesives, 13 percent; and chemicals, 11 percent. A recent major expansion program is expected to enhance the company's position in the plastics and coatings field.

Approximately one-fourth of the firm's pretax income this year will come from dividends and royalties. The royalties accrue from technical assistance to other firms.

The chemical industry has an important advantage over other major industries with respect to labor relations because four unions represent its workers. Thus, even though most chemical companies are engaged in labor negotiations in some of their plants every year, the companies are not subjected to the paralyzing work stoppages such as those that often occur in the auto industry and other basic industries.

The chemical industry is capital-intensive and highly competitive. An almost constant need exists to upgrade production facilities. Direct labor costs are relatively high in the industry in spite of highly mechanized operations; chemical workers have received larger wage increases since World War II than workers in most other industries. Wage increases and high interest rates have contributed heavily to the decline in industry profits in recent years. However, investment tax credits have substantially moderated the profit decline, particularly for those companies, such as RC, that have flowed the credits directly through to income. On the other hand, the earnings of those firms that have amortized the credits over the life of the investment will continue to benefit from the credits for several years.

RC's sales in the current year are expected to decline to $178 million from $181 million in 19x9. The decline is attributed to the "slow-down" in the economy, a 5-week strike at one of RC's plants, and disruptions due to strikes in other industries. Operating income is expected to fall about 38 percent this year. This decline, along with a decline in other income and higher interest charges, is expected to result in a decrease in net income of nearly 60 percent. Earnings per share of about $.47 are projected for the year, down from $1.09 in 19x9.

Sales next year should resume their upward trend, and earnings are expected to approach $.60 per share. The dividend rate for next year will probably be reduced from the $.12 quarterly rate paid in the current year. Dividends have been paid for 17 consecutive years, and only once has RC had to reduce its dividend due to a severe profit squeeze.

Rumors have been circulated on several occasions that RC might be taken over by outside interests, but the chairman-founder and current owner of 13 percent of the stock is still firmly in control.

The current share price of RC's common stock is $10.

QUESTIONS

1. (a) Briefly evaluate RC's overall performance over the past decade.
   (b) Identify any special risks with which RC is faced.

2. Has the market been efficient in the pricing of RC's common stock? Explain.

3. (a) Compute each of the following for both RC and the Standard and Poor's Industrial Stock Index for the period 19x0 through 19x9: (1) the growth in earnings per share, (2) the variance in earnings per share, (3) the *HPR*s and *HPR*s, (4) the variance in the *HPR*s, and (5) the coefficients of variation for the earnings per share and the *HPR*s.

   (b) Compute the slope value *(b)* between the *HPR*s of RC and the S & P Industrial Index. Consider RC's *HPR* the dependent variable.

4. Based upon your computations for question 3, compare and contrast RC's return/risk position with that of the S & P Industrial Index.

5. (a) Do the historical return and risk factors for RC portend the results an investor in the company's common can expect in the future? Why or why not?

   (b) Would RC be included in a portfolio emphasizing (1) high returns and/or (2) low risk? Why or why not in each case?

EXHIBIT 1

Balance Sheet Data (millions)

RICHARDSON CHEMICALS, INC.

	19x9	19x8	19x7	19x6	19x5	19x4	19x3	19x2	19x1	19x0
Assets:										
Current	59.8	55.1	50.3	46.6	41.8	38.8	40.0	37.9	36.5	35.8
Cash Items	5.9	6.8	6.7	7.0	7.3	4.9	7.0	6.7	5.3	6.4
Receivables	29.3	26.7	22.0	19.6	17.5	16.4	16.4	15.0	16.3	15.1
Inventory	24.6	21.6	21.6	20.0	17.0	17.5	16.6	16.2	14.9	14.3
Other	12.0	11.0	11.0	11.9	12.0	12.7	17.1	14.6	15.4	19.6
Fixed	73.8	49.2	45.5	43.1	42.6	44.9	39.3	37.9	38.8	33.0
Total Assets	145.6	115.3	106.8	101.6	96.4	96.4	96.4	90.4	90.7	88.4
Liabilities:										
Current	24.2	21.3	19.6	18.9	16.0	14.6	17.3	13.3	16.3	12.0
Bonds	35.7	12.9	13.1	15.0	17.2	19.0	18.8	19.8	21.1	22.5
Other	5.6	5.4	4.9	4.6	4.8	4.5	4.6	3.8	3.1	2.2
Preferred Stock	1.6	1.8	2.0	2.2	2.4	2.6	2.8	3.0	1.2	1.3
Common Stock	6.6	6.6	5.7	5.0	4.7	4.6	4.4	4.2	4.1	3.9
Surplus	71.9	67.3	61.5	55.9	51.3	51.1	48.5	46.3	44.9	46.5
Total Liabilities	145.6	115.3	106.8	101.6	96.4	96.4	96.4	90.4	90.7	88.4

EXHIBIT 2

Income Data (millions)

RICHARDSON CHEMICALS, INC.

	19x9	19x8	19x7	19x6	19x5	19x4	19x3	19x2	19x1	19x0
Sales	181.2	173.1	146.6	140.9	122.9	117.2	110.7	109.1	102.3	99.2
Cost of Goods Sold	132.1	127.5	110.1	105.9	95.2	89.8	86.1	83.7	80.2	74.7
Depreciation	4.9	4.7	4.7	4.0	3.7	3.7	3.6	3.4	3.1	2.6
Operating Expenses	30.0	26.4	23.6	21.2	18.4	18.3	16.7	16.4	17.8	17.2
Operating Income	14.2	14.5	8.2	9.8	5.6	5.4	4.3	5.6	1.2	4.7
Other Income	1.8	1.8	2.2	1.9	1.9	.9	.8	.6	.6	1.9
Earnings Before Interest & Taxes	16.0	16.3	10.4	11.7	7.5	6.3	5.1	6.2	1.8	6.6
Interest	.6	1.0	1.3	1.0	1.2	1.2	1.4	1.3	1.4	1.0
Earnings Before Taxes	15.4	15.3	9.1	10.7	6.3	5.1	3.7	4.9	.4	5.6
Taxes	8.1	7.9	4.3	4.7	2.7	1.5	1.5	2.4	.1	2.2
Earnings After Taxes	7.3	7.4	4.8	6.0	3.6	3.6	2.2	2.5	.3	3.4
Preferred Dividends	.1	.1	.1	.1	.1	.1	.1	.1	.1	.1
Common Earnings	7.2	7.3	4.7	5.9	3.5	3.5	2.1	2.4	.2	3.3
Common Dividends	3.1	2.1	1.9	1.9	1.2	.7	.4	.4	1.3	1.3
No. of Common Shares	6.6	6.6	5.8	5.2	4.9	4.9	4.9	4.9	4.9	4.9

EXHIBIT 3

Per Share Income Data

RICHARDSON CHEMICALS, INC.

	19x9	19x8	19x7	19x6	19x5	19x4	19x3	19x2	19x1	19x0
Sales	27.45	26.23	25.28	27.10	25.08	23.92	22.59	22.27	20.88	20.24
Cost of Goods Sold	20.02	19.32	18.98	20.37	29.43	18.33	17.57	17.08	16.37	15.24
Depreciation	.74	.71	.81	.77	.76	.76	.73	.69	.63	.53
Operating Expenses	4.54	4.00	4.08	4.08	3.75	3.73	3.41	3.36	3.64	3.51
Operating Income	2.15	2.20	1.41	1.88	1.14	1.10	.88	1.14	.24	.96
Other Income	.27	.27	.38	.37	.39	.19	.16	.13	.13	.39
Earnings Before Interest & Taxes	2.42	2.47	1.79	2.25	1.53	1.29	1.04	1.27	.37	1.35
Interest	.09	.15	.22	.19	.24	.25	.28	.27	.29	.21
Earnings Before Taxes	2.33	2.32	1.57	2.06	1.29	1.04	.76	1.00	.08	1.14
Taxes	1.22	1.19	.74	.91	.56	.31	.31	.49	.02	.45
Earnings After Taxes	1.11	1.13	.83	1.15	.73	.73	.45	.51	.06	.69
Preferred Dividends	.02	.02	.02	.02	.02	.02	.02	.02	.02	.02
Common Earnings	1.09	1.11	.81	1.13	.71	.71	.43	.49	.04	.67
Common Dividends	.47	.32	.33	.37	.24	.14	.08	.08	.27	.27

EXHIBIT 4

Index Values per Share

RICHARDSON CHEMICALS, INC.

	19x0	19x1	19x2	19x3	19x4	19x5	19x6	19x7	19x8	19x9
Total Assets	1.00	1.03	1.02	1.09	1.09	1.09	1.08	1.02	.97	1.22
Sales	1.00	1.03	1.10	1.12	1.18	1.24	1.34	1.25	1.30	1.36
Cost of Goods Sold	1.00	1.07	1.12	1.15	1.20	1.27	1.34	1.25	1.27	1.31
Depreciation	1.00	1.19	1.31	1.38	1.42	1.42	1.45	1.53	1.34	1.40
Operating Expenses	1.00	1.03	.95	.97	1.06	1.07	1.16	1.16	1.14	1.29
Operating Income	1.00	.26	1.19	.91	1.15	1.19	1.96	1.47	2.29	2.24
Earnings Before Interest & Taxes	1.00	.27	.94	.77	.95	1.14	1.67	1.33	1.83	1.80
Interest	1.00	1.40	1.30	1.40	1.20	1.20	.94	1.10	.74	.45
Earnings Before Taxes	1.00	.07	.88	.66	.91	1.13	1.80	1.37	2.03	2.04
Taxes	1.00	.05	1.09	.68	.68	1.23	2.01	1.65	2.67	2.73
Earnings After Taxes	1.00	.09	.74	.65	1.06	1.06	1.66	1.19	1.62	1.59
Common Earnings	1.00	.06	.73	.64	1.06	1.06	1.68	1.20	1.64	1.62
Common Dividends	1.00	1.00	.30	.30	.52	.89	1.37	1.22	1.19	1.74
No. of Common Shares	1.00	1.00	1.00	1.00	1.00	1.00	1.06	1.18	1.35	1.35

EXHIBIT 5

Selected Data

RICHARDSON CHEMICALS, INC.

	19x9	19x8	19x7	19x6	19x5	19x4	19x3	19x2	19x1	19x0
Return on Sales (%)	4.0	4.2	3.2	4.2	2.8	3.0	1.9	2.2	.2	3.3
Return on Assets (%)	5.0	6.4	4.5	5.9	3.7	3.7	2.3	2.8	.3	3.8
Return on Equity (%)	9.2	9.9	7.0	9.7	6.3	6.3	4.0	4.8	.4	6.5
Capital Turnover	1.25	1.50	1.37	1.39	1.28	1.22	1.15	1.21	1.13	1.12
Inventory Turnover	5.37	5.90	5.10	5.30	5.60	5.13	5.19	5.17	1.38	5.22
Average Collection Period (Days)	58	55	54	50	51	50	53	49	57	55
Interest Coverage	26.67	16.30	8.00	11.70	6.25	5.25	3.64	4.77	1.29	6.60
Fixed Charge Coverage	20.19	13.67	6.97	9.81	5.39	4.52	3.20	4.15	1.13	5.53
Total Debt to Equity (%)	83.4	53.6	56.0	63.2	67.9	68.4	76.9	73.1	82.7	72.8
Preferred to Equity (%)	2.0	2.4	3.0	3.6	4.3	4.7	5.3	5.9	2.4	2.6
Tax Rate (%)	52.6	51.6	47.3	43.9	42.9	29.4	40.5	49.0	25.0	39.3
Book Value Per Share	11.89	11.20	11.59	11.71	11.43	11.37	10.80	10.31	10.00	10.29
Dividend Payout (%)	43	29	40	32	34	20	19	17	50	39
Debt Leverage, Dollars Per Share	.47	.34	.21	.37	.20	.19	.09	.13	(.09)	.22
Relative Debt Leverage (%)	43	31	27	33	29	26	21	26	(225)	32

EXHIBIT 6

Per Share Data

RICHARDSON CHEMICALS, INC.

	19x9	19x8	19x7	19x6	19x5	19x4	19x3	19x2	19x1	19x0
Price:										
High	19.50	17.38	20.13	13.88	15.88	14.63	12.88	14.88	21.63	24.13
Low	11.38	11.38	10.38	9.50	9.13	9.38	8.75	8.13	12.88	14.63
Average	15.44	14.38	15.25	11.69	12.50	12.00	10.81	11.50	17.25	19.38
Price-Earnings:										
High	17.9	15.7	24.8	12.3	22.4	20.6	29.9	30.4	540.7	36.0
Low	10.4	10.3	12.8	8.4	12.8	13.2	20.3	16.6	322.0	21.8
Average	14.1	13.0	18.8	10.3	17.6	16.9	25.1	23.5	431.3	28.9
Market-Book Value:										
High	1.64	1.55	1.74	1.18	1.39	1.29	1.20	1.45	2.16	2.34
Low	.96	1.02	.89	.81	.80	.83	.81	.78	1.29	1.42
Average	1.30	1.29	1.31	1.00	1.10	1.06	1.00	1.12	1.72	1.88

EXHIBIT 7

RICHARDSON CHEMICALS, INC.

Selected Chemicals Industry Data per Share

	19x9	19x8	19x7	19x6	19x5	19x4	19x3	19x2	19x1	19x0
Sales	47.18	43.96	38.63	38.18	34.52	31.88	26.69	23.55	20.67	19.97
Depreciation	3.70	3.51	3.15	2.88	2.64	2.41	2.10	1.88	1.66	1.50
Income Taxes	2.52	2.56	1.99	2.58	2.55	2.58	2.22	2.01	1.64	1.65
Common Earnings	3.17	3.16	2.84	3.50	3.41	3.34	2.75	2.42	2.08	2.08
Common Dividends	1.94	2.00	1.87	1.94	1.89	1.99	1.83	1.67	1.55	1.46
Price Index:										
High	57.95	61.43	60.53	75.38	76.78	72.87	62.36	54.31	56.69	60.80
Low	40.08	50.20	50.87	49.82	68.78	62.96	52.50	39.16	47.55	44.15
Average	49.02	55.82	55.70	62.60	72.78	67.92	57.43	46.74	52.12	52.48
Price/Earnings Ratio:										
High	18.3	19.4	21.3	21.5	22.5	21.8	22.7	22.4	27.3	29.2
Low	12.6	15.9	17.9	14.2	20.0	18.9	19.1	16.2	22.9	21.2
Average	15.5	17.7	19.6	17.9	21.0	20.4	20.9	19.3	25.1	25.1
Book Value Per Share	27.17	26.25	24.40	23.51	21.94	20.09	18.61	17.34	16.66	15.79
Book Value - % Return	11.67	12.04	11.64	14.89	15.54	16.63	14.78	13.96	12.48	13.17

Source: *S & P Analyst's Handbook.*

Case 19:   Systematic Risk

Klimate Control Company

*We believe that the majority of investors will invariably be found to be bullish at market tops and bearish at market bottoms. (*Barron's.*)*

Klimate Control (KC) was established in New York in 1896 to manufacture home appliances. After growing primarily through internal means for approximately 50 years, the company began making acquisitions in the late 1940s. The company's most significant acquisition occurred in 19x8 when Frigid Air Company was acquired for over $45 million in common stock, notes, and cash. Frigid Air added $110 million to KC's sales for 19x9 and nearly $.50 in earnings per share of common stock. KC has continued its acquisition policy this year by acquiring a manufacturer of fractional-horsepower motors which are used in its household appliance line.

KC's product lines include air conditioners, heaters, environmental control systems, fractional-horsepower motors, and major household appliances. The company is one of six U. S. firms which concentrates its activities mainly in the production of air conditioning systems; a dozen other firms produce air conditioning systems but have their main lines of business in other products. KC is currently among the top five producers of air conditioning equipment in the country.

The company manufactures both window air conditioners and central air conditioning systems for homes and commercial establishments. Its air conditioning systems range up to 60 tons, capable of cooling buildings as large as supermarkets and bowling alleys. The latter units can also be installed in multiples, along with heating elements, to heat or cool even the largest structures. This "system packaging" has resulted in increased system reliability and flexibility, along with consequent operating economies.

The environmental control product line includes humidifiers, dehumidifiers, and a highly efficient electronic air cleaner which removes up to 95 percent of the air pollutants and 99 percent of hay fever pollens. This filtration system is adaptable to both window units and large air conditioning systems. A complete environmental control system for any size structure can be adapted from various combinations of separate components.

KC's line of appliances includes ranges, clothes dryers, washing machines, dishwashers, refrigerators, and freezers.

Since the company has a strong dealer organization, it is in a good position to increase its share of the air conditioning, heating, and major appliance markets. However, most of KC's recent sales and earnings increases have been the result of an aggressive acquisition policy. All of these acquisitions have complemented KC's existing product lines.

Air conditioning is being regarded increasingly as a necessity rather than a luxury. Industry sales have grown rapidly in recent years; during the period 19x0 through 19x9, the value of installed air conditioning equipment in the U. S. increased from $1.75 billion to $5.60 billion. Unitary systems for homes, apartments, and small commercial establishments currently account for 40 percent of industry dollar volume; commercial central systems account for 35 percent of the volume; and room air conditioners account for 25 percent. Total shipments increased from 1.2 million units in 19x8 to 1.6 million units in 19x9.

Less than 10 percent of U. S. residents currently have central air conditioning systems. Based upon new housing projections and the fact that one out of every three new homes constructed includes a central system, a large potential market exists. Sales of central systems are expected to grow at more than a 10 percent annual rate over the next decade. This growth should not cut into room air conditioner sales because most of those sales are to owners or renters of older homes which are not well suited for the installation of central systems. Unlike the central systems, room air conditioners have a highly seasonal demand pattern; sales surge during hot summer months but are sluggish in the cooler seasons.

Other areas of high potential growth are cooling systems for public buildings including hospitals, colleges, and schools. In addition, airplanes, autos, mobile homes, and government defense installations provide an important market.

Preliminary reports indicate that KC's sales for the current year will increase by $44 million from their 19x9 level. Much of this gain is due to the acquisition of two companies on a pooling of interest basis. Income before, and after, taxes is expected to advance 40 percent and 47 percent respectively. An increase in shares outstanding during the current year will pare the increase in earnings per share to about $1.57 versus the $1.28 of last year.

Sales for next year are expected to increase by at least $50 million from the approximately $296 million of the current year. Again, recent acquisitions are expected to play a big part in this increase. Common shares outstanding are expected to increase by over 1.2 million as the result of conversions and the planned sale of 800,000 new shares early next year. Nevertheless, earnings per share for next year are expected to be up significantly. Dividends are expected to be increased to about 12 cents quarterly.

In June of the current year, KC sold 880,000 new shares of common stock and $60 million of 5 percent debentures, convertible into common at $50 per share. The $19 million in stock proceeds were used to pay off short-term bank loans, whereas the bond proceeds were used for expansion. The company's capitalization currently consists of $82.0 million of long-term debt (which includes the $60.0 million convertible debentures); 227,000 shares of $4.25 preferred stock, par value $100; and 11.1 million shares of common stock. The preferred stock was issued in December of the current year for Tempco Corporation, an air conditioning manufacturer with sales of $54 million in 19x9.

The current share price of KC's common stock is in the mid 40s.

QUESTIONS

1. (a) Enumerate the factors that seem to be responsible for KC's success in recent years. Are these factors temporary or are they likely to persist for some time? Explain.

    (b) Can the rates of sales and earnings growth enjoyed by KC from 19x6 through 19x9 be maintained? Why or why not?

2. (a) Calculate each of the following for both the common stock of KC and the Standard and Poor's Industrial Stock Index for the period 19x9 through 19x9: (1) the $\overline{HRP}$s and HPRs, (2) the standard deviations of the HPRs, and (3) the geometric means of the HPRs.

    (b) Calculate the slope value (b) and correlation coefficient between the HPRs of KC's stock and the HPRs of the S & P stocks; consider KC's HPRs as the dependent variable.

3. Based upon your answers to question 2, appraise the return/risk situation of KC's common in relation to the return/risk situation of the S & P Index.

4. Assuming that the S & P Index HPR is expected to increase by 30 percent or decline by 10 percent, with each state of nature equally likely, estimate KC's:

    (a) Expected return

    (b) Systematic risk

5. Based upon your answers to questions 1 and 4, estimate the $\overline{HPR}$ for KC's common for next year. Explain the reasoning behind your estimate.

EXHIBIT 1

KLIMATE CONTROL

Balance Sheet Data (millions)

	19x9	19x8	19x7	19x6	19x5	19x4	19x3	19x2	19x1	19x0
Assets:										
Current	114.5	93.7	38.8	36.5	44.9	38.9	41.6	41.4	32.2	32.4
Cash Items	5.0	6.9	2.9	4.5	8.2	4.1	1.7	4.3	8.3	1.7
Receivables	67.8	44.5	18.2	20.3	24.7	26.2	29.7	25.1	11.1	16.2
Inventory	41.7	42.3	17.7	11.7	12.0	8.6	10.2	12.0	12.8	14.5
Other	6.6	5.8	4.9	4.7	9.5	4.2	4.1	3.8	2.7	2.7
Fixed	32.8	29.6	17.8	16.4	3.9	3.3	3.6	4.3	4.0	4.2
Total Assets	153.9	129.1	61.5	57.6	58.3	46.4	49.3	49.5	38.9	39.3
Liabilities:										
Current	35.8	28.4	10.4	8.8	9.0	6.8	9.7	9.7	8.2	9.9
Bonds	50.4	55.4	18.7	19.6	16.1	8.0	8.6	9.1	6.0	6.1
Other	2.2	1.3	.9	.8	4.3	3.8	4.2	3.5	-	-
Common Stock	9.6	4.5	2.1	2.1	2.1	2.1	2.1	2.1	2.0	1.9
Surplus	55.9	39.5	29.4	26.3	26.8	25.7	24.7	25.1	22.7	21.4
Total Liabilities	153.9	129.1	61.5	57.6	58.3	46.4	49.3	49.5	38.9	39.3

EXHIBIT 2

Income Data (millions)

KLIMATE CONTROL

	19x9	19x8	19x7	19x6	19x5	19x4	19x3	19x2	19x1	19x0
Sales	252.3	135.0	88.9	62.3	63.7	56.8	51.2	60.6	59.3	68.8
Cost of Goods Sold	202.7	107.4	69.6	52.5	50.7	44.2	41.2	48.0	45.5	51.7
Depreciation	3.3	1.9	1.4	.9	.8	.9	1.1	1.1	1.0	1.1
Operating Expense	16.3	10.0	8.0	6.0	4.9	4.6	4.3	5.5	5.1	5.8
Operating Income	30.0	15.7	9.7	2.9	7.3	7.1	4.6	6.0	7.7	10.2
Earnings Before Interest & Taxes	30.0	15.7	9.7	2.9	7.3	7.1	4.6	6.0	7.7	10.2
Interest	5.3	3.0	1.7	1.6	1.2	1.4	1.4	1.0	.9	.9
Earnings Before Taxes	24.7	12.7	8.0	1.3	6.1	5.7	3.2	5.0	6.8	9.3
Taxes	13.0	6.4	3.6	.1	2.7	2.6	1.6	2.4	3.3	4.8
Common Earnings	11.7	6.3	4.4	1.2	3.4	3.1	1.6	2.6	3.5	4.5
Common Dividends	3.0	2.2	1.4	1.7	2.1	2.1	2.1	2.1	2.0	1.9
No. of Common Shares	9.6	9.0	8.4	8.4	8.4	8.4	8.4	8.4	8.0	7.6

EXHIBIT 3

Per Share Income Data

KLIMATE CONTROL

	19x9	19x8	19x7	19x6	19x5	19x4	19x3	19x2	19x1	19x0
Sales	26.28	15.00	10.58	7.42	7.58	6.76	6.10	7.21	7.41	9.05
Cost of Goods Sold	21.11	11.93	8.29	6.25	6.04	5.26	4.90	5.71	5.69	6.80
Depreciation	.34	.21	.17	.11	.10	.11	.13	.13	.13	.14
Operating Expense	1.70	1.12	.95	.71	.57	.54	.52	.66	.63	.77
Operating Income	3.13	1.74	1.17	.35	.87	.85	.55	.71	.96	1.34
Earnings Before Interest & Taxes	3.13	1.74	1.15	.35	.87	.85	.55	.71	.96	1.34
Interest	.56	.33	.20	.20	.14	.17	.17	.11	.11	.12
Earnings Before Taxes	2.57	1.41	.95	.15	.73	.68	.38	.60	.85	1.22
Taxes	1.35	.71	.43	.01	.33	.31	.19	.29	.41	.63
Common Earnings	1.22	.70	.52	.14	.40	.37	.19	.31	.44	.59
Common Dividends	.31	.24	.17	.20	.25	.25	.25	.25	.25	.25

EXHIBIT 4

Index Values per Share

KLIMATE CONTROL

	19x9	19x8	19x7	19x6	19x5	19x4	19x3	19x2	19x1	19x0
Total Assets	3.10	2.77	1.42	1.33	1.34	1.07	1.13	1.14	.94	1.00
Sales	2.90	1.66	1.17	.82	.84	.75	.67	.80	.82	1.00
Cost of Goods Sold	3.10	1.75	1.22	.92	.89	.77	.72	.84	.84	1.00
Depreciation	2.38	1.46	1.15	.74	.66	.74	.90	.90	.86	1.00
Operating Expense	2.22	1.46	1.25	.94	.76	.72	.67	.86	.84	1.00
Operating Income	2.33	1.30	.88	.26	.65	.63	.41	.53	.72	1.00
Earnings Before Interest & Taxes	2.33	1.30	.86	.26	.65	.63	.41	.53	.72	1.00
Interest	4.66	2.81	1.71	1.61	1.21	1.41	1.41	1.01	.95	1.00
Earnings Before Taxes	2.10	1.15	.78	.13	.59	.55	.31	.49	.69	1.00
Taxes	2.14	1.13	.68	.02	.51	.49	.30	.45	.65	1.00
Common Earnings	2.06	1.18	.88	.24	.68	.62	.32	.52	.74	1.00
Common Dividends	1.25	.98	.67	.81	1.00	1.00	1.00	1.00	1.00	1.00
No. of Common Shares	1.26	1.18	1.11	1.11	1.11	1.11	1.11	1.11	1.05	1.00

EXHIBIT 5

KLIMATE CONTROL

Selected Data

	19x9	19x8	19x7	19x6	19x5	19x4	19x3	19x2	19x1	19x0
Return on Sales (%)	4.6	4.7	4.9	1.9	5.3	5.5	3.1	4.3	5.9	6.5
Return on Assets (%)	7.6	4.9	7.2	2.1	5.8	6.7	3.2	5.3	9.0	11.5
Return on Equity (%)	17.9	14.3	14.0	4.2	11.8	11.2	6.0	9.6	14.2	19.3
Capital Turnover	1.64	1.05	1.45	1.08	1.09	1.22	1.04	1.22	1.52	1.75
Inventory Turnover	4.86	2.54	3.93	4.49	4.22	5.14	4.04	4.00	3.55	3.57
Average Collection Period (days)	97	119	74	117	140	166	209	149	67	85
Interest Coverage	5.66	5.23	5.71	1.81	6.08	5.07	3.29	6.00	8.56	11.33
Total Debt to Equity	1.35	1.93	.95	1.03	1.02	.67	.84	.82	.57	.69
Tax Rate (%)	52.6	50.4	45.0	7.7	44.3	45.6	50.0	48.0	48.5	51.6
Book Value Per Share	6.82	4.89	3.75	3.38	3.44	3.31	3.19	3.24	3.09	3.07
Dividend Payout (%)	25.6	34.9	31.8	141.7	61.8	67.7	131.3	80.8	57.1	42.2
Debt Leverage (dollars per share)	.59	.40	.20	(.01)	.16	.09	.04	.10	.12	.21
Relative Debt Leverage (%)	48	58	38	(7)	41	25	22	34	28	35

EXHIBIT 6

Per Share Data

KLIMATE CONTROL

	19x9	19x8	19x7	19x6	19x5	19x4	19x3	19x2	19x1	19x0
Price:										
High	34.25	30.00	12.38	4.88	5.50	4.88	4.88	4.13	5.00	4.63
Low	22.25	14.63	3.25	2.75	4.38	4.00	3.88	2.13	3.88	3.25
Average	28.25	22.32	7.82	3.82	4.94	4.44	4.38	3.13	4.44	3.94
Price-Earnings:										
High	28.1	42.8	23.6	34.2	13.6	13.2	25.7	13.3	11.4	7.8
Low	18.2	20.9	6.2	19.2	10.9	10.8	20.4	6.9	8.8	5.5
Average	23.1	31.8	14.9	26.7	12.2	12.0	23.0	10.1	10.1	6.6
Market-Book Value:										
High	5.02	6.14	3.30	1.44	1.60	1.48	1.54	1.29	1.60	1.53
Low	3.26	2.99	.87	.81	1.28	1.20	1.19	.64	1.25	1.04
Average	4.14	4.56	2.09	1.13	1.44	1.34	1.36	.97	1.42	1.28

EXHIBIT 7

Industry Data per Share

KLIMATE CONTROL

	19x9	19x8	19x7	19x6	19x5	19x4	19x3	19x2	19x1	19x0
Sales	39.06	31.99	29.13	25.75	24.11	22.30	19.95	19.42	18.47	17.93
Depreciation	.83	.74	.66	.55	.52	.52	.51	.50	.50	.44
Income Taxes	1.97	1.56	1.41	1.31	1.27	1.05	.79	.90	.81	.79
Common Earnings	1.78	1.50	1.49	1.41	1.30	1.01	.73	.78	.69	.65
Common Dividends	.62	.56	.55	.46	.41	.36	.35	.35	.34	.30
Price-Index:										
High	47.19	44.24	34.45	24.48	23.72	15.41	13.72	15.35	16.92	11.94
Low	38.09	30.88	21.33	16.28	14.59	12.34	11.72	10.06	11.54	9.72
Average	42.64	37.56	27.89	20.38	19.16	13.88	12.72	12.71	14.23	10.83
Price-Earnings Ratio:										
High	26.5	29.5	23.1	17.4	18.3	15.3	18.8	19.7	24.5	18.4
Low	21.4	20.6	14.3	11.6	11.2	12.2	16.1	12.9	16.7	15.0
Average	24.0	25.0	18.7	14.5	14.7	13.7	17.4	16.3	20.6	16.7
Book Value Per Share	14.83	13.43	12.32	11.27	10.33	9.42	8.66	8.54	8.28	7.40
Book Value - % Return	12.00	11.17	12.09	12.51	12.58	10.72	8.43	9.13	8.33	8.78

Source: *S & P Analyst's Handbook.*

Case 20:   Random Risk

Central Processing

Both common stock investments and marriage are risky endeavors: stock risks, however, are diversifiable.

Central Processing (CP) is a medium-sized processor of food-product raw materials. CP was incorporated in Indiana in 1934 and soon thereafter established an aggressive program of acquiring other companies in related fields. Acquisitions have included businesses involved in grain processing and storage, milling, feed sales, poultry operations, and the manufacture of insecticides and animal health products. Recent acquisitions have expanded the company's operations to include egg marketing and frozen foods for institutional buyers. CP's growth has resulted in both vertical and horizontal integration of the company's activities.

The processing of soybeans along with the manufacture and distribution of derivative products is CP's main business. This business accounts for 38 percent of total sales, making the company the second largest domestic processor of soybeans in the U. S. Animal feeds and products also comprise 38 percent of total sales, making the company the third largest feed producer in the U. S.; the company is rapidly expanding this segment of its business both domestically and internationally. Grain operations account for 18 percent of total sales; approximately 30 percent of the grain is used in the company's poultry operations and about 70 percent is sold in the eastern half of the U. S. A variety of other products comprise the remainder of CP's sales which are primarily to industrial and institutional users. One of the fastest growing areas of the company's operations is the production and sale of frozen foods.

The retail food industry is relatively stable, and its growth tends to reflect population trends. Increased interest in human nutrition and convenience foods has caused a shift in the demand for many food items and new methods of packaging and preservation have increased the sales volume of convenience foods. New freezing techniques, which provide for longer preservation and better taste, are permitting a growing number of food products to be commercially frozen.

Since the price spread of soybeans and related products such as margarine and shortening can fluctuate widely, earnings in this segment of the food industry tend to be unstable. Numerous gluts have occurred in the raw materials and food processing markets, caused by producers shifting their resources to those product areas in which prices have been rising. Prices of food raw materials also fluctuate due to natural disasters such as droughts and diseases in plants and animals. CP has smoothed out some of its cost-price fluctuations through hedging on the commodity futures market.

While raw materials have not changed significantly, newer methods of production and distribution and faster transportation have tended to expand markets, and this trend is expected to continue in the future. Intense competition exists in CP's product areas due to the volatile nature of the raw materials production, the competitive nature of many products, and the consumer's ability to select from a wide variety of slightly differentiated products.

CP's sales and earnings per share for the current year are expected to increase to approximately $675 million and $2.75 respectively. These expected gains reflect increased animal feed volume, continued strong demand for soybean meal and oil, and increased profitability from grain distribution activities. Next year, management believes that margins will be reduced due to industry wide overproduction of poultry operations and increased competition from low-priced pork products.

CP's stock price is currently about $26.

QUESTIONS

1. Calculate the holding period returns and variances in the holding period returns for CP and the Standard and Poor's Industrial Stock Index.

2. Plot a scatter diagram of CP's holding period returns against the holding period returns of the S & P Index.

3. Calculate:
   (a) The slope of the regression line
   (b) The coefficient of correlation
   (c) The standard error of estimate

4. Assuming that the S & P Index *HPR* over the next year will either increase by 30 percent or decrease by 10 percent with each state of nature being equally probable, estimate CP's:
   (a) Expected return
   (b) Systematic risk
   (c) Diversifiable or random risk

5. Based upon your answers to the above questions, would you consider CP to be a desirable selection in a diversified portfolio? In a nondiversified portfolio? Explain in each case.

6. (a) What factors have been primarily responsible for CP's unusual price performance over the past decade?

   (b) Are these factors likely to persist? Why or why not?

CENTRAL PROCESSING

EXHIBIT 1

Balance Sheet Data (millions)

	19x9	19x8	19x7	19x6	19x5	19x4	19x3	19x2	19x1	19x0
Assets:										
Current	107.25	101.08	97.02	90.07	74.68	73.68	69.73	61.82	51.83	56.29
Cash Items	22.99	9.59	11.47	15.73	14.76	8.54	11.18	9.49	5.32	12.30
Receivables	46.56	41.24	39.32	26.74	28.43	24.72	22.42	20.11	17.68	15.65
Inventory	37.70	50.25	46.23	47.60	31.49	40.42	36.13	32.22	28.83	28.34
Other	5.09	5.29	3.85	3.30	3.31	2.78	1.04	.69	1.13	.65
Fixed	60.28	56.69	55.79	50.48	47.61	46.09	46.05	46.52	42.16	33.02
Total Assets	172.62	163.06	156.66	143.85	125.60	122.55	116.82	109.03	95.12	89.96
Liabilities:										
Current	20.97	16.53	33.12	24.68	17.72	19.48	21.46	20.73	11.28	7.87
Bonds	37.75	38.49	20.93	23.37	22.95	24.65	21.90	18.55	18.40	19.00
Other	3.16	3.08	2.79	2.47	3.10	2.72	2.53	2.03	1.47	1.20
Common Stock	45.72	45.65	44.48	43.56	42.54	42.08	42.06	40.44	38.48	36.76
Surplus	65.02	59.31	55.34	49.77	39.29	33.62	28.87	27.28	25.49	25.13
Total liabilities	172.62	163.06	156.66	143.85	125.60	122.55	116.82	109.03	95.12	89.96

EXHIBIT 2

Income Data (millions)

CENTRAL PROCESSING

	19x9	19x8	19x7	19x6	19x5	19x4	19x3	19x2	19x1	19x0
Sales	556.69	516.67	578.03	519.87	467.38	394.82	342.75	324.02	298.24	276.07
Cost of Goods Sold	506.19	474.97	537.12	469.85	428.29	360.40	312.09	294.73	271.55	252.34
Depreciation	6.33	5.86	5.40	5.54	4.36	4.16	4.03	3.67	2.81	2.56
Operating Expenses	19.79	17.99	16.40	16.41	13.99	12.43	11.56	10.87	9.57	9.42
Operating Income	24.38	17.85	19.11	28.07	20.74	17.83	15.07	14.75	14.31	11.75
Other Income	1.91	2.11	1.97	1.67	.54	.52	.47	.33	(1.83)	(1.30)
Earnings Before Interest & Taxes	26.29	19.97	21.08	29.75	21.28	18.35	15.54	15.08	12.48	10.45
Interest	4.66	5.53	4.22	3.22	3.56	3.13	2.45	2.10	2.10	2.10
Earnings Before Taxes	21.63	14.44	16.86	26.53	17.71	15.22	13.09	12.97	10.38	8.35
Taxes	10.57	6.80	7.62	12.05	8.24	7.30	6.39	6.83	5.35	4.17
Common Earnings	11.05	7.64	9.24	14.48	9.47	7.92	6.70	6.15	5.03	4.18
Common Dividends	5.13	5.09	4.99	4.29	3.92	3.60	3.24	3.16	3.08	3.01
No. of Common Shares	6.5	6.4	6.3	6.2	6.1	6.0	6.0	6.0	5.9	5.9

CENTRAL PROCESSING

EXHIBIT 3
Per Share Income Data

	19x9	19x8	19x7	19x6	19x5	19x4	19x3	19x2	19x1	19x0
Sales	85.78	80.35	92.04	84.39	77.13	65.80	57.13	54.00	50.12	46.63
Cost of Goods Sold	78.00	73.87	85.53	76.27	70.67	60.07	52.01	49.12	45.64	42.63
Depreciation	.98	.91	.86	.90	.72	.69	.67	.61	.47	.43
Operating Expenses	3.04	2.79	2.61	2.66	2.32	2.07	1.94	1.81	1.60	1.59
Operating Income	3.76	2.78	3.04	4.56	3.42	2.97	2.51	2.46	2.41	1.98
Other Income	.29	.33	.32	.27	.09	.09	.08	.05	(.31)	(.22)
Earnings Before Interest & Taxes	4.05	3.11	3.36	4.83	3.51	3.06	2.59	2.51	2.10	1.76
Interest	.72	.86	.67	.52	.59	.52	.41	.35	.35	.35
Earnings Before Taxes	3.33	2.25	2.69	4.31	2.92	2.54	2.18	2.16	1.75	1.41
Taxes	1.63	1.06	1.22	1.96	1.36	1.22	1.06	1.14	.90	.70
Common Earnings	1.70	1.19	1.47	2.35	1.56	1.32	1.12	1.02	.85	.71
Common Dividends	.79	.79	.79	.70	.65	.60	.54	.53	.52	.51

EXHIBIT 4

CENTRAL PROCESSING

Index Values per Share

	19x0	19x1	19x2	19x3	19x4	19x5	19x6	19x7	19x8	19x9
Total Assets	1.00	1.05	1.20	1.28	1.34	1.36	1.54	1.64	1.67	1.75
Sales	1.00	1.07	1.16	1.22	1.41	1.65	1.81	1.97	1.72	1.84
Cost of Goods Sold	1.00	1.07	1.15	1.22	1.41	1.66	1.79	2.01	1.73	1.83
Depreciation	1.00	1.09	1.41	1.56	1.60	1.67	2.08	1.99	2.11	2.26
Operating Expenses	1.00	1.01	1.14	1.21	1.30	1.45	1.67	1.64	1.76	1.92
Operating Income	1.00	1.21	1.24	1.27	1.50	1.72	2.30	1.53	1.40	1.89
Earnings Before Interest & Taxes	1.00	1.19	1.42	1.47	1.73	1.99	2.74	1.90	1.76	2.30
Interest	1.00	.99	.99	1.15	1.47	1.66	1.47	1.89	2.42	2.03
Earnings Before Taxes	1.00	1.24	1.53	1.55	1.80	2.07	3.05	1.90	1.59	2.36
Taxes	1.00	1.28	1.62	1.51	1.73	1.93	2.78	1.72	1.50	2.31
Common Earnings	1.00	1.20	1.45	1.58	1.87	2.21	3.33	2.08	1.68	2.41
Common Dividends	1.00	1.02	1.04	1.06	1.18	1.27	1.37	1.55	1.55	1.55
No. of Common Shares	1.00	1.01	1.01	1.01	1.01	1.02	1.04	1.06	1.09	1.10

EXHIBIT 5

Selected Data

CENTRAL PROCESSING

	19x9	19x8	19x7	19x6	19x5	19x4	19x3	19x2	19x1	19x0
Return on Sales (%)	2.0	1.5	1.6	2.8	2.0	2.0	2.0	1.9	1.7	1.5
Return on Assets (%)	6.4	4.7	5.9	10.1	7.5	6.5	5.7	5.6	5.3	4.6
Return on Equity (%)	10.0	7.3	9.3	15.5	11.6	10.5	9.4	9.1	7.9	6.8
Capital Turnover	3.22	3.17	3.69	3.61	3.72	3.22	2.93	2.97	3.13	3.07
Inventory Turnover	13.42	9.45	11.62	9.87	13.60	8.91	8.64	9.15	9.42	8.90
Average Collection Period (Days)	30	29	24	18	22	22	23	22	21	20
Interest Coverage	5.64	3.61	5.00	9.25	5.97	5.86	6.35	7.17	5.94	4.97
Total Debt to Equity(%)	55.9	55.4	56.9	54.1	53.5	61.9	64.7	61.0	48.7	45.4
Tax Rate (%)	48.9	47.1	45.2	45.4	46.5	48.0	48.8	52.6	51.5	50.0
Book Value Per Share	17.06	16.32	15.90	15.15	13.50	12.62	11.82	11.29	10.75	10.45
Dividend Payout (%)	46.4	66.6	54.0	29.6	41.4	45.5	48.4	51.4	61.2	72.0
Debt Leverage, Dollars Per Share	.37	.13	.30	.64	.34	.34	.31	.28	.16	.10
Relative Debt Leverage (%)	22.0	11.0	20.4	27.3	21.8	25.5	28.0	27.8	19.2	13.9

EXHIBIT 6

Per Share Data

CENTRAL PROCESSING

	19x9	19x8	19x7	19x6	19x5	19x4	19x3	19x2	19x1	19x0
Price:										
High	30.50	25.75	30.38	33.75	27.13	18.50	16.00	16.75	16.63	12.00
Low	21.00	19.00	22.75	22.00	17.13	13.00	13.00	11.88	12.50	10.13
Average	25.75	22.38	26.57	27.88	22.13	15.75	14.50	14.32	14.57	11.07
Price-Earnings:										
High	17.9	21.7	20.6	14.4	17.3	14.0	14.3	16.3	19.7	16.9
Low	12.3	16.0	15.5	9.4	10.9	9.8	11.6	11.6	14.8	14.4
Average	15.1	18.8	18.0	11.9	14.1	11.9	13.0	13.9	17.2	15.6
Market-Book Value:										
High	1.79	1.58	1.91	2.23	2.01	1.47	1.35	1.48	1.55	1.14
Low	1.23	1.16	1.43	1.45	1.27	1.03	1.10	1.05	1.16	.97
Average	1.51	1.37	1.67	1.84	1.64	1.25	1.22	1.26	1.35	1.05

Case 21:   Pure Risk Yield

Fashion Faire Cosmetics

*The main point to remember is that the worst time to sell and the best
time to buy selectively is when the background news is blackest, and the worst
and best time to buy and sell, respectively, is when the news is overwhelmingly
bullish and a "sky is the limit" attitude prevails. (*Wall Street Transcript.*)*

Fashion Faire (FF) was incorporated in New York in 1880 as Fashion
Manufacturing Company. The present name was adopted in 1955 at the time of
a merger with Princess Faire Co., a manufacturer of fragrances. FF then initiated
an acquisition policy, and some 18 firms have since been acquired in a planned
and orderly manner. Most of the firms acquired in the early stages of the
external expansion program complemented FF's line of cosmetic products.
However, in 19x6 the company formed its Hospital Supply Division with the
acquisition of a hospital supply company and since that time, several other firms
in that area have been acquired. In 19x9 FF added another dimension to its
cosmetics and hospital supply lines by acquiring a food packing firm for 885,000
shares of common stock. Although most of FF's acquisitions have been made
through an exchange of common stock, a few have been purchased with a lump
sum of cash plus stock. The company's domestic sales breakdown for the current
year is estimated as follows: cosmetics, 37 percent; proprietary products for
medicinal purposes, 34 percent; specialty food products, 12 percent; fragrances,
8 percent; and hospital supplies, 5 percent.

FF also has major investments in firms located in several foreign countries.
Foreign sales should comprise about 43 percent of the company's total expected
sales of $261 million for the current year. The foreign sales breakdown is
estimated to be: Europe, 17 percent; Canada and Latin America, 12 percent; the
Far East, 6 percent; Great Britain, 4 percent; and Africa, 4 percent. Earnings
from foreign operations will comprise approximately 40 percent of the current
year's total earnings which are estimated at $20.9 million.

The cosmetics industry has been growing at an 8 percent annual rate and is
expected to continue at this rate of growth in the future. This industry has
traditionally been one of the most profitable in the U. S. Recently however,
acceleration of costs have put pressure on profits and a number of cosmetics

companies have resorted to selective price increases to offset the higher costs. The foreign market continues to make strong gains, and U. S. firms will continue to expand their operations in foreign countries.

The high profits in the industry in the past have attracted many new entrants, including drug, food, tobacco, and liquor firms. There is also the threat of foreign competition, since Japanese producers are expected to enter the U. S. market soon. Currently, there are over 650 firms operating in the cosmetics and toiletries fields, with the top 25 companies accounting for over 80 percent of total industry shipments. Forecasts indicate that shipments this year will exceed $3.5 billion. FF was tenth in sales in the industry in 19x9.

The second main line of products produced by FF, proprietary medicines, is also expected to grow at about 8 percent per year. The demand for these products is relatively immune from changing economic conditions. The key to success in this field, as in the cosmetics field, is the continued introduction of new products. FF introduced more new products during the current year than it had introduced in the previous 5 years.

The executives of FF have a relatively unique incentive pay plan; they may purchase the company's common shares at 14 times the average earnings of the previous 5 years. No doubt this stock option plan has been responsible for the significant amount of insider trading in FF's common. Since 19x6, corporate officials of FF have been consistently selling the company's shares; net distributions were especially heavy in 19x8, 19x9, and the current year. During the current year, approximately 100,000 common shares have been sold but only 20,000 purchased by FF's executives.

Company sales for the coming year are expected to increase to the $290 million level from the $261 million estimated for the current year. Earnings per share expectations for next year are $1.90 versus the $1.76 estimated for this year.

The company's current capitalization consists of $70 million long-term debt and 12.0 million shares of common stock. The long-term debt includes $25 million of recently issued $6\frac{1}{4}$ percent debenture bonds, convertible into common at $53\frac{1}{2}$ per share, and $9.5 million of $4\frac{3}{4}$ percent debentures, convertible at $49 per common share.

The share price of common is currently in the mid 50s.

QUESTIONS

1. (a) Briefly summarize FF's overall performance record since the beginning of 19x0.
   (b) Can FF's growth trends be maintained indefinitely? Explain.
   (c) Compare FF's performance with that of the Standard and Poor's Industrial Stock Index.

2. Calculate each of the following for the period 19x0 to 19x9 inclusive:
   (a) *HPR*s for the common stock of FF and the S & P Industrial Index

(b) The slope value (*b*) between the *HPR*s for the common stock of FF and the *HPR*s for the S & P Industrial Index

(c) The standard error of estimate

3. Based upon your answers to question 2 and assuming that the S & P Index *HPR* over the next year will either increase by 30 percent or decline by 10 percent, with each state of nature assumed equally likely, calculate the following for FF's common stock:

(a) Expected return

(b) Systematic risk

(c) Diversifiable risk

4. (a) Based upon your answers to question 3, estimate next year's *HPR*s for FF's common for each of four states of nature. One state of nature will be a good market year represented by a 30 percent increase in the S & P Index *and* a good company year represented by a one-standard error of estimate increase in the firm's rate of return from the expected return derived from the index increase; another state of nature will be a good market year *and* a poor company year represented by a one-standard error of estimate decline in the firm's rate of return from that expected return derived from the index increase. *HPR*s should be determined in the same manner, given a poor market year represented by a 10 percent decline in the S & P Index.

(b) What is the likelihood of each of the above events occurring? Explain.

5. (a) Calculate the pure risk yield for FF's common stock (assume a 6 percent riskless rate).

(b) Assess FF's desirability for inclusion in a portfolio.

(c) What assumptions have to be made in order to justify your answer to 5(b)?

(d) How realistic are the assumptions of 5(c)? Explain.

6. Critically evaluate FF's expected *HPR* for next year on the basis of the evidence presented in the text of the case and the calculations you have already made.

EXHIBIT 1

Balance Sheet Data (millions)

FASHION FAIRE COSMETICS

	19x9	19x8	19x7	19x6	19x5	19x4	19x3	19x2	19x1	19x0
Assets:										
Current	111.9	97.2	75.6	68.0	63.5	58.2	54.1	51.6	43.2	39.4
Cash Items	17.7	22.0	14.0	10.3	16.5	14.9	13.4	12.4	9.9	9.0
Receivables	47.0	37.5	29.2	24.7	19.6	20.0	18.8	17.4	14.6	12.7
Inventory	47.2	37.7	32.4	33.0	27.4	23.3	21.9	21.8	18.7	17.7
Other	35.5	16.1	10.0	9.5	8.5	8.5	8.7	9.0	8.7	9.3
Fixed	38.5	28.6	24.0	24.0	21.9	16.3	15.4	14.8	13.4	13.6
Total Assets	185.9	141.9	109.6	101.5	93.9	83.0	78.2	75.4	65.3	62.3
Liabilities:										
Current	41.9	38.1	24.1	23.9	20.4	20.1	20.9	20.3	14.9	13.2
Bonds	50.0	20.8	14.4	15.4	16.0	10.5	10.4	12.4	13.4	16.0
Common Stock	11.7	11.7	10.6	10.5	10.2	10.1	6.8	6.7	6.1	6.0
Surplus	82.3	71.3	60.5	51.7	47.3	42.3	40.1	36.0	30.9	27.1
Total Liabilities	185.9	141.9	109.6	101.5	93.9	83.0	78.2	75.4	65.3	62.3

EXHIBIT 2

Income Data (millions)

FASHION FAIRE COSMETICS

	19x0	19x1	19x2	19x3	19x4	19x5	19x6	19x7	19x8	19x9
Sales	70.2	99.0	114.6	116.9	126.0	138.6	157.2	165.7	205.5	231.0
Cost of Goods Sold	25.9	39.7	43.7	44.4	47.8	51.7	60.8	66.0	86.4	99.3
Depreciation	.9	1.2	1.5	1.7	1.7	1.8	2.0	2.1	2.7	3.1
Operating Expense	35.1	47.6	55.5	54.8	60.2	66.5	72.7	72.2	83.5	91.9
Operating Income	8.3	10.5	13.9	16.0	16.3	18.6	21.7	25.4	32.9	36.7
Other Income	.6	1.7	1.8	2.0	2.6	2.5	1.8	1.8	2.4	3.5
Earnings Before Interest & Taxes	8.9	12.2	15.7	18.0	18.9	21.1	23.5	27.2	35.3	40.2
Interest	.4	.7	.7	.7	.6	.6	1.0	.8	1.2	2.7
Earnings Before Taxes	8.5	11.5	15.0	17.3	18.3	20.5	22.5	26.4	34.1	37.5
Taxes	4.0	5.7	7.7	9.2	8.5	9.5	10.0	11.5	16.5	17.5
Common Earnings	4.5	5.8	7.3	8.1	9.8	11.0	12.5	14.9	17.6	20.0
Common Dividends	2.6	2.8	3.5	4.2	5.0	6.3	7.2	8.1	9.1	10.1
No. of Common Shares	9.0	9.2	10.0	10.0	10.1	10.2	10.3	10.6	11.3	11.6

EXHIBIT 3

Per Share Income Data

FASHION FAIRE COSMETICS

	19x9	19x8	19x7	19x6	19x5	19x4	19x3	19x2	19x1	19x0
Sales	19.86	18.22	15.68	15.22	13.60	12.48	11.69	11.46	10.75	7.80
Cost of Goods Sold	8.54	7.66	6.24	5.89	5.07	4.73	4.44	4.37	4.31	2.88
Depreciation	.27	.24	.20	.19	.18	.17	.17	.15	.13	.10
Operating Expense	7.89	7.40	6.84	7.04	6.52	5.97	5.48	5.55	5.17	3.90
Operating Income	3.16	2.92	2.40	2.10	1.83	1.61	1.60	1.39	1.14	.92
Other Income	.30	.21	.17	.17	.24	.26	.20	.18	.18	.07
Earnings Before Interest & Taxes	3.46	3.13	2.57	2.27	2.07	1.87	1.80	1.57	1.32	.99
Interest	.24	.11	.07	.09	.06	.06	.07	.07	.07	.05
Earnings Before Taxes	3.22	3.02	2.50	2.18	2.01	1.81	1.73	1.50	1.25	.94
Taxes	1.50	1.46	1.09	.97	.93	.84	.92	.77	.62	.44
Common Earnings	1.72	1.56	1.41	1.21	1.08	.97	.81	.73	.63	.50
Common Dividends	.87	.81	.77	.70	.62	.50	.42	.35	.30	.29

EXHIBIT 4

Index Values per Share

FASHION FAIRE COSMETICS

	19x0	19x1	19x2	19x3	19x4	19x5	19x6	19x7	19x8	19x9
Total Assets	1.00	1.02	1.09	1.13	1.19	1.33	1.42	1.50	1.82	2.31
Sales	1.00	1.38	1.47	1.50	1.60	1.74	1.95	2.01	2.34	2.55
Cost of Goods Sold	1.00	1.50	1.52	1.54	1.64	1.76	2.05	2.17	2.66	2.97
Depreciation	1.00	1.30	1.50	1.70	1.68	1.77	1.94	1.99	2.39	2.67
Operating Expense	1.00	1.33	1.42	1.41	1.53	1.67	1.80	1.75	1.90	2.03
Operating Income	1.00	1.24	1.51	1.73	1.75	1.98	2.28	2.61	3.16	3.42
Earnings Before Interest & Taxes	1.00	1.34	1.59	1.82	1.89	2.09	2.30	2.60	3.16	3.50
Interest	1.00	1.71	1.57	1.57	1.34	1.32	2.18	1.70	2.39	5.22
Earnings Before Taxes	1.00	1.32	1.59	1.83	1.92	2.13	2.31	2.64	3.20	3.41
Taxes	1.00	1.39	1.73	2.07	1.89	2.10	2.18	2.45	3.29	3.39
Common Earnings	1.00	1.26	1.46	1.62	1.94	2.16	2.42	2.82	3.12	3.44
Common Dividends	1.00	1.05	1.21	1.45	1.71	2.14	2.41	2.65	2.79	3.01
No. of Common Shares	1.00	1.02	1.11	1.11	1.12	1.13	1.15	1.17	1.25	1.29

EXHIBIT 5

Selected Data

FASHION FAIRE COSMETICS

	19x9	19x8	19x7	19x6	19x5	19x4	19x3	19x2	19x1	19x0
Return on Sales (%)	8.7	8.6	9.0	8.0	7.9	7.8	6.9	6.4	5.9	6.4
Return on Assets (%)	10.8	12.4	13.6	12.3	11.7	11.8	10.4	9.7	8.9	7.2
Return on Equity (%)	21.3	21.2	21.0	20.1	19.1	18.7	17.3	17.1	15.7	13.6
Capital Turnover	1.24	1.45	1.51	1.55	1.48	1.52	1.50	1.52	1.52	1.13
Inventory Turnover	2.10	2.29	2.04	1.84	1.89	2.05	2.03	2.01	2.12	1.46
Average Collection Period (days)	73	66	63	56	51	57	58	55	53	65
Interest Coverage	14.89	29.42	34.00	23.50	35.17	31.50	25.71	22.43	17.43	22.25
Total Debt to Equity (%)	97.8	71.0	54.1	63.2	63.3	58.4	66.7	76.6	76.5	88.2
Tax Rate (%)	46.7	48.4	43.6	44.4	46.3	46.4	53.2	51.3	49.6	47.1
Book Value Per Share	8.08	7.36	6.73	6.02	5.64	5.19	4.69	4.27	4.02	3.68
Dividend Payout (%)	50.5	51.7	54.4	57.6	57.3	51.0	51.9	47.9	48.3	57.8
Debt Leverage (dollars per share)	.79	.62	.47	.44	.40	.34	.30	.30	.25	.22
Relative Debt Leverage (%)	45.8	39.4	33.2	36.0	37.0	34.8	37.6	40.7	39.9	44.4

FASHION FAIRE COSMETICS

EXHIBIT 6
Per Share Data

	19x9	19x8	19x7	19x6	19x5	19x4	19x3	19x2	19x1	19x0
Price:										
High	54.63	48.63	44.63	31.88	30.88	22.75	20.88	20.75	22.00	15.38
Low	37.13	34.25	27.63	19.88	21.50	20.25	17.25	12.38	14.13	9.50
Average	45.88	41.44	36.13	25.88	26.19	21.50	19.06	16.56	18.06	12.44
Price-Earnings:										
High	31.8	31.2	31.7	26.3	28.6	23.4	25.8	28.4	34.9	30.8
Low	21.6	21.9	19.6	16.4	19.9	20.9	21.3	17.0	22.4	19.0
Average	26.7	26.5	25.6	21.3	24.2	22.1	23.5	22.7	28.6	24.9
Market-Book Value:										
High	6.76	6.61	6.64	5.30	5.47	4.39	4.45	4.86	5.48	4.18
Low	4.59	4.66	4.11	3.30	3.81	3.90	3.68	2.90	3.52	2.58
Average	5.68	5.63	5.37	4.30	4.64	4.14	4.07	3.88	4.50	3.38

EXHIBIT 7

Selected Industry Data per Share

FASHION FAIRE COSMETICS

	19x9	19x8	19x7	19x6	19x5	19x4
Sales	21.09	18.90	16.87	14.19	12.96	11.48
Depreciation	.29	.24	.21	.18	.16	.13
Income Taxes	2.06	1.93	1.56	1.29	1.13	1.02
Common Earnings	2.09	1.86	1.74	1.38	1.27	1.06
Common Dividends	1.10	.99	.89	.76	.64	.54
Price Index:						
High	96.04	82.31	79.50	49.00	44.19	34.11
Low	72.08	66.40	45.95	40.26	32.81	29.56
Average	84.06	74.36	62.73	44.63	38.19	31.84
Price-Earnings Ratio:						
High	46.0	44.3	45.7	35.5	34.8	32.2
Low	34.5	35.7	26.4	29.2	25.8	27.9
Average	40.3	40.0	36.1	32.3	30.3	30.0
Book Value Per Share	8.51	7.50	6.52	5.28	4.84	4.13
Book Value – % Return	24.56	24.80	26.69	26.14	26.24	25.67

Source: *S & P Analyst's Handbook.*

Case 22:   Comprehensive Case

Air Cargo, Inc.

*As a result, we have conceived the idea of the chicken market—one whose future course is unknown. (*Barron's.)

Air Cargo, Inc. (AC), was incorporated as a holding company in 1945, and then immediately merged with Air Freight Corporation, an operating company. No additional acquisitions were made until December of this year when American Car, a lessor of railway cars, was acquired through an exchange of convertible preferred stock and warrants. This latest acquisition is expected to add about $.50 a share to next year's earnings and, in addition, is expected to add more stability to both sales and earnings in future years. AC is the fourth largest carrier of air freight in the U. S. Its major competition comes from Atlantic Airlines Company, also exclusively an air freight shipper, and several of the leading airline companies which carry air freight as an adjunct of their passenger business.

Currently, passenger airline companies are looking increasingly to their air freight operations to enhance revenues. The recent recession in air passenger travel resulted in the sharpest overall profit decline in the history of the airline industry, precipitating several of the leading companies to take a closer look at the air freight business even though this part of their operations has not been profitable heretofore. Forecasters have been predicting that the growth rate of air freight income will accelerate in the future and that by the end of the current decade, it will become more important than air passenger revenue.

AC struggled as a fledgling operation for many years and as recently as 19x8 the company's domestic routes covered only 4,000 miles. Then in 19x9, federal authorities awarded the company an intercontinental network system linking nine nations and spanning over 17,000 miles. As a result, sales increased over 30 percent in 19x9 and are expected to increase approximately 27 percent this year. Continued sales gains are expected for several years. Earnings per share for the current year are estimated at $2.20 compared with $.95 in 19x9. These results are exclusive of American Car's revenues of $52 million and profits of $7.1 million expected for the current year.

Beginning in 19x4, the investment tax credit became a significant factor in AC's reported earnings. In 19x9 alone, the tax credit amounted to $1.6 million or nearly $.36 per share of common. AC currently has $10 million in unused credits available which will be amortized over future operations. The company changed its accounting treatment of initial training and preoperating costs associated with fleet aircraft acquisitions. Rather than amortizing these costs over a 5-year period, the current policy is to flow them immediately through the income statement.

AC has updated its cargo fleet from C-44 turbo-props to DC-8 cargo jets exclusively. The $200 million aircraft fleet has long-range, high-speed, economy, and thus high profitability. The company provides daily service to most major cities in the U. S. and some service to most major cities in the free world. All parts of the globe are serviced through a series of interline agreements with 90 other airlines. Recently, AC contracted to carry 35 percent of all air traffic for the United Parcel Service.

Beginning in 19x9, AC adopted a new marketing approach. The approach is a terminal profit center plan which gives to each general manager broad authority and responsibility for the sales, service, and profit in his area. This decentralization plan has been working out well to date, primarily because a number of significant cost-saving measures have been introduced. In addition, several new terminals costing on the average of about $1 million each either have been completed or are in progress. Automated loading systems have been introduced which permit a "big jet" to be loaded or unloaded within 30 minutes. AC's data processing equipment is comprised of third-generation computers, which are utilized for flight scheduling operations, and the company trains its pilots with a recently purchased $1.5 million flight simulator. Many other innovations have also been made.

Sales for next year are expected to increase sharply, due mainly to the inclusion of American Car's results, but much of the increase in revenues from commercial operations will be offset by declines in military airlift operations. Nevertheless, preliminary estimates indicate increases in sales of 70 percent and in earnings per share of 30 percent.

After the inclusion of American Car's results, AC's capitalization consists of $319 million long-term debt; 200,000 shares of $3 cumulative preferred stocks, par value $50; 1.8 million shares of $1.20 convertible preferred stock, redeemable at $22.50 and convertible into .74 of a share of common; and 4.5 million shares of $1 par value common stock. In addition, warrants to purchase 622,000 shares of common at $29.50 are outstanding. The company recently called for redemption $25 million of its outstanding convertible debt. Since bondholders can gain by converting their bonds, the call will result in an increase of 848,000 in outstanding shares.

Current share price of common is approximately $40.

QUESTIONS

1. (a) Compute and plot on a scatter diagram the annual *HPR*s for AC's common stock and the Standard and Poor's Industrial Stock Index for the past decade.
   (b) Calculate the corresponding geometric mean returns of the *HPR*s in 1(a).
   (c) Calculate: (1) the slope coefficient between the *HPR*s of AC and the *HPR*s of the S & P Index, (2) the coefficient of correlation, and (3) the standard error of estimate.

2. (a) Based upon the above information, what especially desirable portfolio characteristics did AC exhibit over the past decade?
   (b) Identify the basic factors which were largely responsible for these characteristics.
   (c) Is the assumption of efficiency in the capital markets consistent with the continuation of AC's characteristic price performance? Explain.

3. (a) Given that the S & P Industrial Index *HPR* is expected to increase by 30 percent in the current year and that the basic relationships of question 1(c) are expected to apply, what is the expected mean *HPR* for AC's common?
   (b) Estimate the 68 percent probability range of including the mean *HPR* calculated in 3(a).
   (c) Re-answer questions 3(a) and 3(b) assuming that the Index *HPR* declines by 10 percent.

4. (a) Assess AC's degree of systematic risk relative to its random risk.
   (b) Based upon an analysis of the case data, estimate the expected *HPR* and *HPR* variability for AC's stock over the next year.

5. (a) Calculate AC's pure risk yield based upon historical data.
   (b) Estimate AC's pure risk yield based upon expected data.
   (c) Is AC desirable in a diversified portfolio? In a nondiversified portfolio? Explain.

EXHIBIT 1

Balance Sheet Data (millions)

AIR CARGO, INC.

	19x9	19x8	19x7	19x6	19x5	19x4	19x3	19x2	19x1	19x0
Assets:										
Current	53.48	42.08	37.20	38.25	21.56	20.51	16.72	18.56	9.59	7.07
Cash Items	26.75	19.34	17.49	20.66	9.27	11.13	10.60	12.09	5.13	3.21
Receivables	21.94	18.00	15.04	14.27	9.80	7.05	4.31	4.90	3.69	3.11
Inventory	4.79	4.74	4.67	3.32	2.49	2.33	1.81	1.57	.77	.75
Other	1.52	6.62	4.18	3.54	3.19	2.60	3.21	3.89	1.90	-0-
Fixed	142.74	139.27	122.41	68.60	64.54	40.91	46.16	50.21	49.33	31.46
Total Assets	197.74	187.97	163.79	110.39	89.29	64.02	66.09	72.66	60.82	38.53
Liabilities:										
Current	21.70	27.21	17.53	18.68	12.41	12.80	10.68	10.99	11.09	5.96
Bonds	118.13	102.54	79.97	34.87	48.15	29.28	36.02	42.79	31.93	15.27
Other	15.00	16.54	18.93	16.36	9.33	6.14	5.05	4.78	2.51	2.30
Preferred Stock	-0-	-0-	-0-	-0-	.99	.99	.99	.99	.99	.99
Common Stock	4.56	4.54	4.54	2.22	1.61	1.53	1.53	1.50	1.49	1.49
Surplus	38.35	37.14	42.82	38.26	16.80	13.28	11.82	11.61	12.81	12.52
Total Liabilities	197.74	187.97	163.79	110.39	89.29	64.02	66.09	72.66	60.82	38.53

EXHIBIT 2

Income Data (millions)

AIR CARGO, INC.

	19x9	19x8	19x7	19x6	19x5	19x4	19x3	19x2	19x1	19x0
Sales	96.89	76.70	87.03	86.02	56.16	45.47	42.21	52.26	27.97	25.99
Operating Expenses*	73.36	67.29	67.62	58.61	41.11	35.80	34.25	38.56	23.01	22.62
Depreciation	10.72	6.72	7.12	6.95	6.23	5.67	6.19	5.96	3.91	4.16
Operating Income	12.81	2.69	12.29	20.46	8.82	4.00	1.77	7.74	1.05	(.79)
Other Income	1.78	.50	.90	.24	.34	.36	.24	(.09)	(.06)	.15
Earnings Before Interest & Taxes	14.59	3.19	13.19	20.70	9.16	4.36	2.01	7.65	.99	(.64)
Interest	8.68	3.09	1.78	2.30	2.42	2.12	2.43	2.79	.67	.92
Earnings Before Taxes	5.91	.10	11.41	18.40	6.74	2.24	(.42)	4.86	.32	(1.56)
Taxes	1.60	.01	3.82	6.95	3.10	.94	(.22)	2.53	.15	(.39)
Earnings After Taxes	4.31	.09	7.59	11.45	3.64	1.30	(.20)	2.33	.17	(1.17)
Preferred Dividends	--	--	--	.03	.05	.05	.05	.05	.05	.05
Common Earnings	4.31	.09	7.59	11.42	3.59	1.25	(.25)	2.28	.12	(1.22)
Common Dividends	.45	.45	.45	-0-	-0-	-0-	-0-	-0-	-0-	.10
No. of Common Shares	4.5	4.5	4.5	4.2	3.2	2.8	2.7	2.5	1.7	1.2

*The following lease charges are included in operating expenses:

	19x9	19x8	19x7	19x6	19x5	19x4	19x3	19x2	19x1	19x0
	7.73	8.96	-0-	-0-	-0-	-0-	-0-	-0-	-0-	-0-

EXHIBIT 3

Per Share Income Data

AIR CARGO, INC.

	19x9	19x8	19x7	19x6	19x5	19x4	19x3	19x2	19x1	19x0
Sales	21.34	17.04	19.17	20.58	17.50	16.36	15.63	21.07	16.36	20.79
Operating Expenses	16.16	14.95	14.89	14.03	12.81	12.88	12.68	15.55	13.46	18.09
Depreciation	2.36	1.49	1.57	1.66	1.94	2.04	2.29	2.40	2.29	3.33
Operating Income	2.82	.60	2.71	4.89	2.75	1.44	.66	3.12	.61	(.63)
Other Income	.39	.11	.20	.06	.10	.13	.08	(.04)	(.03)	.12
Earnings Before Interest & Taxes	3.21	.71	2.91	4.95	2.85	1.57	.74	3.08	.58	(.51)
Interest	1.91	.69	.40	.55	.75	.76	.90	1.12	.39	.74
Earnings Before Taxes	1.30	.02	2.51	4.40	2.10	.81	(.16)	1.96	.19	(1.25)
Taxes	.35	-0-	.84	1.66	.97	.34	(.09)	1.02	.09	(.31)
Earnings After Taxes	.95	.02	1.67	2.74	1.13	.47	(.07)	.94	.10	(.94)
Preferred Dividends	-0-	-0-	-0-	.01	.01	.02	.02	.02	.03	.04
Common Earnings	.95	.02	1.67	2.73	1.12	.45	(.09)	.92	.07	(.98)
Common Dividends	.10	.10	.10	---	---	---	---	---	---	.08

EXHIBIT 4

Selected Data

AIR CARGO, INC.

	19x9	19x8	19x7	19x6	19x5	19x4	19x3	19x2	19x1	19x0
Return on Sales (%)	4.4	.1	8.7	13.3	6.4	2.7	(.6)	4.4	.4	(4.7)
Return on Assets (%)	2.2	-0-	4.6	10.4	4.1	2.0	(.3)	3.2	.3	(3.0)
Return on Equity (%)	10.0	.2	16.0	28.2	19.5	8.4	(1.9)	17.4	.8	(8.7)
Capital Turnover	.49	.41	.53	.78	.63	.71	.64	.72	.46	.69
Average Collection Period (Days)	81	84	62	60	63	56	37	34	47	43
Interest Coverage	1.68	1.03	7.41	9.00	3.79	2.06	.83	2.74	1.48	(.70)
Prior Charge Coverage	1.36	1.01	7.41	8.78	3.64	1.97	.80	2.65	1.29	(.63)
Total Debt to Equity (%)	3.61	3.51	2.46	1.73	3.80	3.26	3.88	4.47	3.18	1.68
Preferred to Equity (%)	-0-	-0-	-0-	-0-	.05	.07	.07	.08	.07	.07
Tax Rate (%)	27.1	10.0	33.5	37.8	46.0	42.0	52.4	52.1	46.9	25.0
Book Value Per Share	9.45	9.26	10.43	9.68	5.74	5.33	4.94	5.29	8.36	11.21
Dividend Payout (%)	10.4	500.0	5.9	-0-	-0-	-0-	-0-	-0-	-0-	-0-
Debt Leverage, Dollars Per Share	.44	(.12)	1.11	1.61	.80	.24	(.15)	.65	.02	(.79)
Relative Debt Leverage (%)	46	-	67	59	72	54	-	71	32	-

EXHIBIT 5

Per Share Data

AIR CARGO, INC.

	19x9	19x8	19x7	19x6	19x5	19x4	19x3	19x2	19x1	19x0
Price:										
High	33.25	31.25	48.50	25.50	16.38	5.38	7.75	8.00	10.00	6.63
Low	15.63	17.50	21.63	22.13	4.63	3.50	3.38	3.88	4.63	3.88
Average	24.44	24.38	35.07	23.82	10.51	4.44	5.57	5.94	7.32	5.26
Price-Earnings:										
High	35.0	--	29.0	9.3	14.6	12.0	--	8.7	142.5	--
Low	16.5	--	12.9	8.1	4.1	7.8	--	4.2	66.0	--
Average	25.7	--	20.9	8.7	9.3	9.9	--	6.4	104.2	--
Market-Book Value:										
High	3.52	3.37	4.65	2.63	2.86	1.01	1.57	1.51	1.20	.59
Low	1.65	1.89	2.07	2.29	.81	.66	.68	.73	.55	.35
Average	2.59	2.63	3.36	2.46	1.83	.83	1.13	1.12	.88	.47

EXHIBIT 6

Selected Industry Data per Share

AIR CARGO, INC.

	19x9	19x8	19x7	19x6	19x5	19x4	19x3	19x2	19x1	19x0
Revenues	141.64	127.21	124.32	111.36	109.57	106.12	96.51	89.20	81.29	77.56
Depreciation	13.46	11.57	10.87	9.76	9.76	9.72	10.26	10.99	10.32	8.55
Income Taxes	1.40	1.89	2.84	3.71	3.87	3.49	2.46	.71	(.53)	1.06
Common Earnings	2.62	4.03	6.95	6.38	7.14	4.83	2.52	.32	(.45)	1.25
Common Dividends	1.38	1.70	1.70	1.49	1.09	1.05	.64	.64	.68	.77
Price Index:										
High	98.16	97.24	143.23	145.43	108.97	68.29	47.28	28.08	32.29	29.39
Low	58.02	73.92	96.20	84.93	60.78	48.67	23.75	18.25	24.87	21.76
Average	78.09	85.58	119.72	115.18	84.88	58.48	35.52	23.17	28.58	25.58
Price/Earnings Ratio:										
High	37.5	24.1	20.6	22.8	15.3	14.1	18.8	87.8	–	23.5
Low	22.2	18.3	13.8	13.3	8.5	10.1	9.4	57.0	–	17.4
Average	29.9	21.2	17.2	18.1	11.9	12.1	14.1	72.4	–	20.5
Book Value Per Share	51.49	50.41	51.80	45.46	38.46	31.50	27.01	25.69	26.75	27.91
Book Value – % Return	5.09	7.99	13.42	14.03	18.56	15.33	9.33	1.25	–	4.48

Source: *S & P Analyst's Handbook.*

III PORTFOLIO SELECTION AND EVALUATION

5 Selection and Evaluation

Case 23:   Sharpe's Responsiveness Model

Investment Advisory Consultants I

*Our problem is how to remain properly venturesome and experimental
without making fools of ourselves. (*Bernard M. Baruch.*)*

Investment Advisory Consultants (IAC) was incorporated in Houston, Texas,
in 1959 as an advisory consultant firm. The company was organized by John
Tomson who was formerly a vice-president of a leading advisory service named
Technical Volume Indicators, Incorporated. Since Mr. Tomson felt that TVII, as
well as other advisory services, lacked "personal touch" with their customers, he
decided to form a new company which would manage accounts of investors with
$5,000 or more to invest in common stocks. The company was first organized as
a partnership with five partners, all of whom were registered representatives.
When the business was incorporated, Mr. Tomson assumed the presidency, and
his four partners became vice-presidents.

IAC's fee structure consists of three parts:

1. A $200 flat fee per account per year.
2. A basic advisory fee of $\frac{1}{2}$ of 1 percent per year of the first $100,000
invested in the account and $\frac{3}{8}$ of 1 percent per year of the funds over $100,000
invested in the account.
3. An incentive fee of $\frac{1}{4}$ of 1 percent per year of each account whose
performance exceeds twice the Standard and Poor's 425 Industrial Stock Index.

IAC's relatively low advisory fees plus the "pay-for-performance" plan has
had great appeal to both large and small investors. The company has often
produced profits for its clients above those of the stock averages. IAC's success
in its business operation is indicated by the fact that earnings have risen from
deficits in 19x5 and 19x6 to $.11, $.12, and $.34 in the next three successive
years.

One of the objectives management had in mind when the business became a
corporation was to adopt the most modern techniques in the handling and
processing of accounts. In addition, management felt that the continued success
of IAC was dependent upon the modernization of the company's techniques for
selecting stocks for purchase and sale. Many large pension funds, mutual funds,

and investment advisory services use the computer extensively in their investment decision processes. Newer approaches, such as those by Markowitz and Sharpe, utilize sophisticated statistical techniques. When many stocks are evaluated, the large quantity of calculations required by the newer techniques make extensive use of the computer mandatory.

Mr. Tomson, however, intends to understand the nature of the new techniques and their value to IAC's operations before he leads his firm into a major commitment of time and resources. With this in mind, he has asked a new employee, who was recently graduated from a large, well-known business school, to utilize one of the simpler of the new techniques in making portfolio recommendations to one of the firm's clients. The new employee, a Mr. James Jacobs, will be asked to explain the procedures and results to Mr. Tomson.

Mr. Jacobs has decided to use Sharpe's responsiveness model.

QUESTIONS

Objective Function:
$$\text{Max } (1 - \lambda) E_i - \lambda b_i$$

where λ = a value from 0 to 1.0

E_i = expected return on security i ($HPRi - 1.0$)

b_i = expected responsiveness of security i (slope value with Standard and Poor's Industrial Stock Index)

1. Plot the objective function on two widely spaced parallel vertical axes for λ = 0 on the left axis and λ = 1 on the right axis for each of the first four firms of Part II B identifying each security. (In the absence of expected values derived from the case data themselves, use the respective historical averages.)

2. (a) Connect with linear lines the E_is and b_is for each security.
   (b) What is the basis for the assumed linear relationship between the E_is and b_is?

3. Based upon the linear lines of 2(a) representing each security's return/risk combination between λ = 0 and λ = 1, generate all of the efficient corner portfolio for [i.e., select the top n lines corresponding to the number of securities in the portfolio, noting the particular securities represented in each instance as one moves from the left vertical axis (λ = 0) to the right vertical axis (λ = 1)]:
   (a) A portfolio consisting of one security.
   (b) A portfolio consisting of two securities.
   (c) A portfolio consisting of three securities.

4. (a) Assuming an equal dollar investment in each security, calculate the corresponding expected portfolio returns (E_ps) for each of the corner portfolios in question 3.
   (b) Calculate the portfolio risks (b_ps) corresponding to the E_ps of question 4(a).

(c) Plot on a graph the E_ps and b_ps determined in 4(a) and 4(b) for the two-security case with E_p on the vertical axis and b_p on the horizontal axis.

5. (a) Given the information of 3(b) and 4(c) what rate of return could one receive if the same risk as that of the S & P Index were taken?
   (b) Which securities and security proportions would comprise the situation of 5(a)?

6. (a) Explain the basic assumptions which underlie the practical relevance of the above portfolio return and risk measures.
   (b) Critically assess the usefulness of Sharpe's responsiveness model to IAC's management.

Case 24: Markowitz's Covariance Model

Investment Advisory Consultants II

Trends which used to take years to run their course now do so in months—It all, of course, reflects the growing sophistication of investment decision-making. (Barron's.)

The management of IAC is highly pleased with the firm's record of growth in number of clients serviced and in earnings. Mr. Tomson, president of the company, is firmly convinced that the successful record is the result of using better analytical techniques than most competing firms. IAC has followed the policy of carefully testing different analytical techniques to determine if their incorporation into IAC's system of analysis would improve the performance of the portfolios of the firm's clients. If tests indicate that a new technique improves performance in most cases it is incorporated into the IAC system.

During the past year, the firm has been testing the Sharpe responsiveness model. The results have been favorable, and the model is now being applied to the portfolios of the firm's clients. However, management has been told that the model is not as precise in its handling of some portfolio risks as a model proposed earlier by a Professor Harry Markowitz.

Mr. Tomson first heard of the Markowitz model several years ago, but he was told that it is not feasible when applied to portfolios which include a large number of stocks. His informant stated that the vast number of computations required makes the model impractical even when a large-scale computer is used.

Mr. Tomson has reasoned, however, that since most of the accounts managed by IAC involve an investment of around $40,000 and, therefore, only 5 to 10 securities, the Markowitz full covariance model should be considered for use by the firm. With this in mind, he recently requested the security analysis section of IAC to establish and manage hypothetical securities' portfolios utilizing the model. Each portfolio would have a different return/risk objective. At the end of one year, the results would then be compared with the results obtained from the actual portfolios currently managed by IAC.

QUESTIONS

1. (a) How many different portfolio combinations can be formed with four securities?

   (b) How many portfolios can be formed? Explain.

2. (a) Calculate the rates of return, their variances and standard deviations for Richardson Chemicals, Klimate Control, Central Processing, and Fashion Faire Cosmetics. (In the absence of expectational answers, use the historical data.)

   (b) Calculate all of the simple correlation coefficients among the security returns of 2(a).

3. (a) Assuming an equal dollar investment in each security, for each portfolio combination calculate (1) the portfolio return and (2) the portfolio variance.

   (b) Plot each portfolio return against its corresponding variance. Put the variances on the vertical axis and the expected returns on the horizontal axis.

   (c) Sketch the efficient frontier.

   (d) Must the efficient frontier always be convex to the horizontal axis? Why or why not?

   (e) How many portfolios of the above four securities fall on the efficient frontier?

4. (a) Given a lending-borrowing rate of 6 percent, add the capital market line to your graph.

   (b) Which portfolio combination is closest to the tangency of the capital market line and the efficient frontier?

5. (a) What are the limitations of the above analyses?

   (b) How useful is Markowitz's covariance model to IAC's management? Discuss.

Case 25: Latané's Portfolio Building Model

Diversified, Incorporated

*If at first you don't succeed, try, try again; then quit—there's no use being a damn fool about it. (*W. C. Fields.*)*

Diversified, Inc. (DI), was incorporated in 1894 as Specialized Investors, Inc., for the principal purpose of issuing face-amount installment certificates. The present name was adopted in 1949 after the company had expanded extensively into the mutual fund field. DI has since diversified widely and is currently the parent of a large investment complex comprised of six mutual funds and nine other subsidiaries involved in various types of financial activities. These activities include the issuance of face amount savings certificates; the sale of a wide variety of life, annuity, and health insurance; the leasing of equipment to business and industry; and the making of home improvement, residential, and commercial loans. The company also offers shares in oil and gas exploration ventures and manages mutual funds with assets currently valued at over $6 billion. The first subsidiary fund began operations in 1940, and five other fund subsidiaries have been organized up to the present time. Last year DI acquired a municipal bond underwriter and an institutional brokerage concern.

National Investors, a financial holding company, exercises control over DI through the ownership of 43 percent of the latter company's outstanding common. DI's capitalization consists of 4.4 million shares of class A common, 10.6 million shares of class B common, and 50,000 shares of $3.50 preferred issued in exchange for a brokerage subsidiary. The preferred is convertible into common at varying rates from 1.6 to 5.2 shares depending upon the subsequent earnings performance of the brokerage firm.

DI currently owns or manages businesses with a total of $7.8 billion in assets, about 80 percent of which is comprised of mutual fund assets. Sales of mutual fund shares totaled $510 million in 19x9, a slight increase from the $503 million in 19x8. Face-amount savings certificates increased sharply in 19x9 to over $270 million from $210 million in 19x8, an increase of 29 percent. Life insurance in force also increased by 23 percent during the same period.

DI's net operating income is thus derived from 5 principal sources: face certificates, mutual funds, finance, brokerage, and insurance. In 19x9, face certificates accounted for nearly 60 percent of total net operating income, and revenues from the management of mutual funds comprised nearly 25 percent. Each of the remaining sources contributed less than 5 percent to income. A sharp decline in brokerage income in 19x9 resulted from decreased trading volume on the stock exchanges. (See Exhibit 2.)

The mutual funds owned and managed by DI have not performed well recently, partly because of a sluggish stock market, but also because of the company's relatively outmoded methods of portfolio analyses. Several competing funds have been using the computer extensively in applying the newer techniques of portfolio analysis such as those suggested by Professors Markowitz, Sharpe, and Latané.

The management of DI is becoming increasingly concerned that the firm may not be competitive in its portfolio selecting process in the future. The management is aware that investors are becoming more and more conscious of the relative performances of mutual funds. Hence, the management of DI has decided to explore the merits of the portfolio model recently developed by Professors Latané and Tuttle. It was believed that one of the particular advantages of the model would be that it permits qualified judgments to be introduced by the analyst at various stages in the development of the portfolio. In addition, the model is relatively easy to understand. Thus, due to both its ease of comprehension and relative simplicity in computation, DI has moved to explore preliminary results of the model using a small group of securities. If the results prove profitable, DI's management intends to adopt the model in the company portfolio selection process.

QUESTIONS

1. (a) For the securities listed below, calculate good year ($\overline{HPR}_G$) and bad year ($\overline{HPR}_B$) expected holding period returns. Assume that it is equally likely for the HPR for Standard and Poor's Industrial Stock Index to be 1.30 or .90 and that the historical slope value between each security's HPRs with respect to the index remains unchanged. (In the absence of expectational data use the respective historical values.)

   1. National Aircraft   (NA)   4. Hercules Minerals   (HM)
   2. Computer Systems   (CS)   5. Richardson Chemicals   (RC)
   3. Proprietary Drug   (PD)   6. Fashion Faire Cosmetics (FF)

   (b) Drop all dominated stocks, i.e., those for which the expected HPRs in both good market years and bad market years are exceeded by one or more other securities.

   (c) Calculate the nondiversifiable risk (NS) and diversifiable risk (DS) for each remaining security.
   Note: $NS = HPR_G - \overline{HPR}$ [or slope value (b) times the average market variability (S_{mkt})].

2. (a) Calculate the pure risk yield (PRY) for each remaining security, assuming a 7 percent riskless rate (r), and then rank all of the securities in order from the highest to the lowest.

$$\text{Note: } PRY = \frac{E_i - r}{NS_i}$$

where E_i = expected return on security i (i.e., $E_i = \overline{HPR} - 1.0$).

(b) Appraise the desirability of each of the securities in question 2(a) for inclusion in the final portfolio.

3. Allocate the portfolio, assuming $100,000 of investible funds:
(a) Using equal dollar weights (w_i).

$$w_i = \frac{1}{n}$$

(b) On the basis of weights inversely proportional to each stock's diversifiable risk (round the weights to the nearest thousand dollars).

$$w_i = \frac{(1/DS_i)}{\sum_{i=1}^{n} (1/DS_i)}$$

4. Using each set of weights derived in question 3:
(a) Calculate the portfolio's pure risk yields.

$$PRY_p = \frac{\sum_{i=1}^{n} w_i (E_i - r)}{\sum_{i=1}^{n} w_i (NS)_i}$$

(b) Estimate the optimum leverage ratios (q), i.e., the optimum investment in risk assets per dollar of market valued net worth.

$$q = \frac{PRY_p}{NS_p}$$

(c) Calculate the portfolios (1) arithmetic mean return and (2) geometric mean return.

$$G = [I^2 + (PRY)^2 (2I-1) + (PRY)^4]^{1/2} \qquad I = 1.0 + r$$

5. Based upon Exhibit 5 evaluate the results derived from question 4.

6. Discuss the advantages and limitations of the above portfolio procedures.

EXHIBIT 1

Gross Income (millions of dollars)   DIVERSIFIED, INCORPORATED

	19x9	19x8
Distribution fees (before compensation to sales representatives)	$ 47.9	$ 45.5
Interest	40.7	36.8
Cash Dividends	10.9	10.5
Life insurance premiums and other considerations	27.7	23.5
Investment advisory and service fees from associated mutual funds and related net brokerage income	24.3	23.9
Income from other brokerage operations	14.2	14.9
Real Estate:		
Rent and Service income	8.8	8.0
Hotel, restaurant and parking ramp revenue	6.1	5.6
Sales of real estate	3.2	----
Discount earned on installment loans	12.4	11.3
Finance charges on leasing contracts	10.5	9.7
Other income	6.4	5.7
Gross Income	$213.2	$195.4

EXHIBIT 2

Major Sources of Income (000)   DIVERSIFIED, INCORPORATED

	19x9		19x8	
	Amount	%	Amount	%
Certificates	$13,622	58.6	$12,739	49.5
Mutual funds	5,801	24.9	6,678	26.0
Insurance	871	3.7	1,166	4.5
Finance Group	1,134	4.9	1,888	7.3
Brokerage	1,074	4.6	2,392	9.3
Unclassified	760	3.3	849	3.4
Total net operating income	$23,262	100.0	$25,712	100.0

EXHIBIT 3

Comparative Data (millions)   DIVERSIFIED, INCORPORATED

	19x9	19x8	19x7	19x6	19x5
Total Net Assets Managed	$7,826.0	$7,975.2	$7,246.8	$6,132.2	$6,310.4
Total Fund Assets Managed	6,253.8	6,655.5	6,121.2	5,125.6	5,335.2
Life Insurance in Force	2,707.6	2,156.3	1,841.4	1,609.0	1,402.6
Sales of Fund Shares	510.0	503.0	420.2	536.4	602.3
Contractual Plan Sales Face Amount	280.6	209.5	179.6	194.3	64.7
Subsidiaries' Sales of Certificates	270.3	218.9	206.6	159.7	212.2

EXHIBIT 4

Selected per Share Data   DIVERSIFIED, INCORPORATED

	19x9	19x8	19x7	19x6	19x5
Net Operating Income* per Share					
Class A	3.27	3.62	3.27	3.12	2.84
Class B	.82	.91	.82	.78	.71
Dividends per Share					
Preferred	.875	----	----	----	----
Class A	1.80	1.80	1.80	1.60	1.60
Class B	.45	.45	.45	.41	.40
Price Range (bid) Class A Common Stock					
High	58.75	62.00	41.75	47.00	57.13
Low	36.00	32.63	30.00	26.00	41.63
Last	36.00	53.00	36.50	30.13	44.50
*Excludes realized security profits of:					
Class A	.44	.41	.42	.45	.39
Class B	.11	.10	.10	.11	.07

EXHIBIT 5

Resulting Portfolio q and G Based on Selected
Combination of Package PRYs and NSs   DIVERSIFIED, INCORPORATED

I = 1.07

Portfolio NS

Portfolio PRY	.2	.3	.4	.5	G
			q		
.1	.54	.36	.27	.22	1.075
.2	1.11	.74	.56	.44	1.092
.3	1.76	1.18	.88	.70	1.122
.4	2.55	1.70	1.27	1.02	1.167
.5	3.57	2.38	1.78	1.43	1.236

Source: Henry A. Latané and Donald L. Tuttle, *Security Analysis and Portfolio Management*, The Ronald Press Company, New York, 1970, p. 667.

Case 26: Treynor's Fund Performance Model

Portfolio Planning, Inc.

The current trend is away from the "go-go" to the "go-slow's."
(Barron's.)

Portfolio Planning, Inc. (PPI), was originally organized in 1940 as an unincorporated investment trust with several classes of shares. It now operates as an open-end investment company which is segregated into several different funds. The company's trust agreement terminates either when all shares have been liquidated or in the year 2065, whichever comes first. The trust may be terminated even sooner if a qualified trustee is not appointed as provided in the trust agreement. Upon termination, the trustee will liquidate each of the specialized funds and distribute the underlying assets of each fund to its own shareholders.

The company's management group, Portfolio Advisors, Inc. (PAI), receives a fee of $\frac{1}{2}$ of 1 percent of the first $410 million of the combined net assets of PPI and $\frac{3}{8}$ of 1 percent of the combined net assets exceeding $410 million. PAI expanded its operation in 19x7 by acquiring a majority interest in General Advisory Service. A year later PAI organized Nationwide Management Corp., an asset management company which manages a separate fund named Tri-Capital Fund, Inc.

PPI has on occasion discontinued some of its specialized funds, e.g., its low-priced common stock series in 19x7 and its selected group series in 19x8. Currently, the company has seven investment funds. The following three of the seven account for the bulk of the firm's operations: (1) Income Series, (2) Stock Series, and (3) Growth Stock Series. Exhibit 1 contains a statistical listing of each of these three series.

The portfolio of the Income Series is generally diversified among bonds, preferred stocks, and common stocks. All investments for this portfolio are selected on the basis of their relatively high current yield. During the past year, 19x9, the fund's holdings of bonds and preferred stocks were at their highest level in the past decade, whereas holdings in common stocks were at their lowest level. Holdings in four industry groups comprised a total of 20.1 percent of the assets of the fund: banks and finance, 5.8 percent of the assets; oils, 5.2 percent;

iron and steels, 5.1 percent; and rails, 4.0 percent. The next largest industry holding was retail trade which accounted for only 1.0 percent. The largest single common stock investment was in Standard Oil of New Jersey which comprised 3.8 percent of the fund's assets. Kaiser Steel, GAC Corporation, Chesapeake and Ohio Railway, and Inland Steel comprised a total of 8.9 percent of the assets. Unrealized capital appreciation at the end of the year amounted to about 1.0 percent of the dollar value of assets.

The Stock Series is the largest of PPI's funds. This series consists of a diversified group of stocks purchased with the dual objectives of obtaining a relatively good current income and reasonable capital growth. The series is restricted to stocks of financial, industrial, railroad, and/or public utility corporations. The five largest industry groups in 19x9 were: oils, 13.2 percent; public utilities, 12.2 percent; retail trade, 6.6 percent; finance, 6.4 percent; and automotive, 6.2 percent. Major individual holdings aggregating about 11 percent of the series' total assets were in duPont, Continental Can, Philip Morris, Beneficial Finance, and Gulf Oil. Unrealized capital appreciation at year end in this fund amounted to about 12 percent of asset value.

The Growth Stock Series is comprised of a diversified group of common stocks with better than average growth prospects. The objective of this fund is long-term capital appreciation. Major industry holdings at the end of 19x9 were: automation, computers, and office equipment, 9.5 percent; utilities, 9.1 percent; banks and finance, 8.7 percent; oils, 7.6 percent; and metals and metallurgy, 6.6 percent. Major individual holdings were in IBM, Pabst Brewing, Texas Utilities, Southern Co., and Kennecott Copper, with percentage of asset holdings in each firm ranging down from 4.2 percent to 2.5 percent. Unrealized capital appreciation at the end of 19x9 amounted to 8.3 percent of asset value.

PPI offers several special services for its shareholders. A voluntary accumulation plan allows an investor to invest at his discretion in any of the seven funds of PPI upon making a minimum initial investment of $250 and subsequent periodic investments of at least $25. Shareholders of any series may have their dividends automatically reinvested at the offering price of the series and their capital gains reinvested at the net asset value of the series. The Growth Stock Series offers both 10-year and 15-year payment periods on a contractual basis. A monthly or quarterly withdrawal plan is available without charge to accounts of $5,000 or more, subject to a $25 minimum withdrawal rule. Shares of one series may be exchanged at net asset value for those of any other series as well as any of the other funds owned and managed by the management company, PAI. A nominal clerical fee of $5.00 is charged for this service. Finally, a Keogh plan agreement is available for self-employed persons. This plan allows the investor to select any combination of the PPI funds without affecting his tax exempt status.

The trustee will redeem any fund shares at their net asset value within 5 days of receipt of certificates. No charge is made for liquidation.

All of PPI's funds are offered at net asset value plus a load charge of 8.5 percent of the offering price. The charge is reduced for single investments of

$12,500 or more. PPI's total net assets at the end of 19x9 amounted to approximately $880 million.

QUESTIONS

1. Briefly discuss PPI as a vehicle for serving the needs of investors.

2. (a) On separate graphs, plot the rates of return ($HPR - 1.0$) before commissions for each of PPI's three principal funds against the annual rates of return of the Dow Jones Industrial Average (DJIA) for the period 19x0 through 19x9. (Use end-of-year price data and identify each year's return on the graph.)

   (b) Calculate the respective characteristic (regression) lines, average rates of return, and correlation coefficients between each fund's HPRs and the HPRs of the DJIA.

   (c) Briefly discuss the return/risk implications of each fund's characteristic line.

   (d) Is each fund sufficiently diversified? Explain.

3. (a) Plot on a graph the characteristic line of each fund in comparison with the DJIA, with fund rate of return denoted on the vertical axis and market rate of return denoted on the horizontal axis.

   (b) On another graph, plot each fund's expected return against its slope value (b) with the DJIA, assuming a market rate of return of 10 percent.

   (c) Repeat 3(b) assuming a market return of 30 percent.

   (d) Assuming a 5 percent riskless rate, sketch the portfolio possibility lines for both 3(b) and 3(c).

   (e) Discuss the implications revealed by the portfolio possibility lines of 3(d).

4. (a) Based upon the graph of 3(a), and assuming a riskless rate of interest of 5 percent, denote by the use of Treynor's method each fund's performance rating.

   (b) How can an individual investor's particular portfolio return and risk preferences be satisfied if he chooses to invest in one of PPI's funds? Explain.

5. Explain the limitations of the Treynor method for rating the performance of funds.

EXHIBIT 1

Income Series Fund Statistical History

PORTFOLIO PLANNING, INC.

			AT YEAR-ENDS						ANNUAL DATA			
	Total Net Assets (millions)	Number of Share-holders (thousands)	Cash & Equiva-lent	% of Assets in Bonds & Pre-ferreds*	Common Stocks	Net Asset Value Per Share	Offer-ing Price	Yield (%)	Divi-dend Distribu-tions	Capital Gains Distribu-tions	Offering Price High	Low
19x9	$ 82.1	24.3	5	73	22	$5.20	$5.68	4.6	$ .28	$ .35	$7.17	$5.64
19x8	100.2	24.9	2	56	42	6.53	7.14	3.8	.28	.27	7.33	6.36
19x7	94.7	25.8	3	49	48	6.20	6.78	4.1	.28	.25	7.01	6.23
19x6	86.5	26.7	4	50	46	5.68	6.21	4.3	.27	.23	7.51	5.87
19x5	99.1	27.5	4	38	58	6.56	7.17	3.7	.27	.21	7.22	6.57
19x4	94.1	28.8	2	39	59	6.30	6.89	3.7	.26	.17	7.08	6.55
19x3	89.5	30.1	2	39	59	5.98	6.54	3.9	.26	.10	6.68	6.01
19x2	79.8	30.9	5	36	59	5.49	6.00	4.7	.29	.21	6.91	5.46
19x1	84.7	30.8	1	33	66	6.19	6.77	4.0	.28	.20	6.91	6.21
19x0	74.3	30.8	2	34	64	5.68	6.21	4.5	.29	.20	7.02	5.99

*Mainly convertible issues.

PORTFOLIO PLANNING, INC.

EXHIBIT 2

Stock Series Fund Statistical History

| | | | AT YEAR-ENDS | | | | | | ANNUAL DATA | | | |
	Total Net Assets (millions)	Number of Share-holders (thousands)	Cash & Equiva-lent	% of Assets in Bonds & Pre-ferreds*	Common Stocks	Net Asset Value Per Share	Offer-ing Price	Yield (%)	Divi-dend Distribu-tions	Capital Gains Distribu-tions	Offering Price High	Offering Price Low
19x9	$329.8	59.1	10	14	76	$ 8.08	$ 8.83	3.6	$ .34	$ .52	$11.72	$8.62
19x8	415.7	59.2	7	10	83	10.72	11.72	2.9	.35	.44	12.00	9.45
19x7	347.7	60.9	8	6	86	9.16	10.01	3.3	.34	.40	10.27	8.94
19x6	302.3	62.8	8	4	88	8.17	8.93	3.6	.33	.42	10.80	8.13
19x5	336.9	62.2	5	4	91	9.57	10.46	3.0	.32	.37	10.46	9.06
19x4	288.7	60.9	2	...	98	8.92	9.75	3.0	.30	.35	9.93	8.92
19x3	236.7	59.4	3	...	97	8.13	8.89	3.3	.30	.32	9.01	8.15
19x2	197.7	58.6	9	...	91	7.44	8.13	4.0	.34	.31	9.99	7.08
19x1	227.0	58.0	1	...	99	9.10	9.95	3.4	.35	.30	10.09	8.47
19x0	182.2	57.7	2	...	98	7.75	8.47	4.2	.37	.30	9.91	7.89

*Mainly convertible issues.

EXHIBIT 3

Growth Stocks Series Fund Statistical History

PORTFOLIO PLANNING, INC.

| | | | AT YEAR-ENDS | | | | | | ANNUAL DATA | | | |
| | Total Net Assets (millions) | Number of Share-holders (thousands) | Cash & Equiva-lent | Bonds & Pre-ferreds* | Common Stocks | Net Asset Value Per Share | Offer-ing Price | Yield (%) | Divi-dend Distribu-tions | Capital Gains Distribu-tions | Offering Price High | Low |
			% of Assets in									
19x9	$258.9	65.3	12	1	87	$ 9.09	$ 9.93	2.2	$ .25	$1.25	$13.11	$ 9.44
19x8	280.3	62.6	7	2	91	11.88	12.98	1.7	.24	1.55	13.57	11.64
19x7	236.3	61.5	12	2	86	12.21	13.34	1.7	.23	.92	13.38	10.48
19x6	170.1	62.5	9	1	90	9.66	10.56	1.4	.15	.52	11.79	8.84
19x5	174.3	63.8	5	1	94	10.42	11.39	1.0	.12	.42	11.39	9.05
19x4	145.0	66.1	3	0	97	8.87	9.69	1.1	.11	.38	10.04	9.14
19x3	136.8	69.8	3	0	97	8.42	9.20	1.2	.11	.36	9.23	8.26
19x2	118.3	72.1	5	0	95	7.63	8.34	1.2	.10	.35	10.85	6.59
19x1	137.9	68.9	1	0	99	9.96	10.89	.9	.10	.21	11.10	9.50
19x0	106.9	60.4	1	0	99	8.84	9.66	1.2	.12	.21	10.07	8.25

*Mainly convertible issues.

EXHIBIT 4

Dow Jones Industrial Average
PORTFOLIO PLANNING, INC.

YEAR	HIGH	LOW	CLOSE	DIVIDEND
19x0	685.47	566.05	615.89	21.36
19x1	734.91	610.25	731.14	22.71
19x2	726.01	535.76	652.10	23.30
19x3	767.21	646.79	762.95	23.41
19x4	891.71	766.08	874.13	31.24
19x5	969.26	840.59	969.26	28.61
19x6	995.15	744.32	785.69	31.89
19x7	943.08	786.41	905.11	30.19
19x8	985.21	825.13	943.75	31.34
19x9	943.75	769.93	800.36	33.90

Case 27: Comprehensive Case—Comparison of Capital Asset Models of Treynor, Sharpe, Jensen

Management Capital, Inc.

Accordingly, computer experts have come up with a way of measuring the risk (or volatility) factor in a portfolio—the so-called Beta factor. (Barron's.)

Management Capital, Inc. (MCI), manages the four mutual funds of American Investors Group (AIG). MCI's basic annual fee is .425 of one percent of the value of the average net assets of each of AIG's funds. However, MCI's overall fee is dependent upon its managerial performance, since the fee increases by .075 of one percent of net asset value for each 2 percent better performance than the Dow Jones Industrial Stock Average for the year. On the other hand, the fee decreases by .075 of one percent for each 2 percent poorer performance than the Dow Jones Industrial Average (to a minimum of .25 of one percent).

MCI supervises all of the investments of the AIG funds. In addition, analytical and statistical information as well as research and administrative personnel and services are provided for AIG.

The management of MCI is well aware that the company has been successful financially over the past decade because the assets it manages have increased significantly. Of more significance to MCI, however, is the fact that each of the fund's specified objectives were essentially met; each fund's returns were commensurate with the risks taken. The first fund—Balanced Incorporated—emphasizes reasonable income, preservation of value, and long-term appreciation. The second fund—Investment Growth—emphasizes growth via heavy concentration of investments in "quality" growth stocks. The third fund—Fixed Income—is comprised of investments solely in bonds and preferred stocks; hence, current income and preservation of capital are the primary objectives of this fund. The fourth fund—Variable Growth—has long-term capital growth as its primary objective. This fund was designed for an investor whose goal is building up the equity of a retirement fund or an estate. The fund requires all dividends and capital gains distributions to be automatically reinvested in additional shares. Investments of the fund primarily include common stocks of companies which invest heavily in research, the development of new products and services, and/or the expansion of existing operations which have good potential. Variable Growth has been the most popular of AIG's funds.

Critics have recently been pointing out to MCI's management that the basis upon which its incentive compensation plan is figured does not adequately take fund performance into consideration. MCI is compensated only on the basis of rate of return criteria. Several academicians, notably Professors Treynor, Sharpe, and Jensen, have suggested that proper evaluation would also include risk considerations. Indeed, empirical studies have shown that most mutual funds have tended to live up to their promises that they provide lower risks than the combinations of stocks comprising the market averages. Consequently, it is only reasonable that their return performances be judged in view of the corresponding risks rather than solely on the basis of comparisons with an average such as the DJIA.

MCI's management agrees that it seems unfair to treat all of its funds on the same basis when, in fact, each fund's return/risk objectives differ widely. The management team believes that the company's fees would have been higher if the newer criteria had been used, i.e., if risk had been included explicitly as a part of the performance rating.

QUESTIONS

1. (a) Based upon MCI's current fee schedule, estimate total fee collected in 19x1 and 19x9.
   (b) Compute the average annual rate of growth in the fees [based upon the answer to 1(a)].

2. (a) Rate the performance before commissions of each of AIG's funds by the Treynor, Sharpe, and Jensen methods. Assume a 5 percent riskless rate of interest (use end-of-year price data).
   (b) Has MCI done a creditable job for each of its fund's investors? Discuss.

3. Are AIG's funds well diversified? Explain.

4. Based upon the above analyses, would MCI's fees have been higher if they had been based upon a performance rating which included risk? Why or why not?

5. Which of the three measures of performance of 2(a) is the most relevant in evaluating AIG's funds? Discuss.

EXHIBIT 1

Balanced Fund Statistical History

MANAGEMENT CAPITAL, INC.

	Total Net Assets (millions)	Number of Shareholders (thousands)	% of Assets in			Net Asset Value Per Share	Offering Price	Yield (%)	Dividend Distributions	Capital Gains Distributions	Offering Price	
			Cash & Equivalent	Bonds & Preferreds	Common Stocks						High	Low
19x9	$2,681.1	405.1	3	30	67	$ 9.85	$10.70	3.6	$ .40	$ .44	$12.32	$10.53
19x8	2,998.0	417.4	5	26	69	11.21	12.18	3.3	.42	.53	12.81	11.67
19x7	2,987.5	436.8	4	29	67	11.32	12.31	3.4	.43	.26	12.87	11.60
19x6	2,760.7	446.6	5	36	59	10.68	11.61	3.8	.44	.17	13.38	10.93
19x5	2,976.7	435.3	4	33	63	12.27	13.33	3.2	.43	.29	13.81	12.96
19x4	2,674.4	405.1	3	35	62	12.30	13.36	3.1	.41	.24	13.59	12.57
19x3	2,257.7	373.7	4	33	63	11.59	12.60	3.1	.39	.20	12.87	11.61
19x2	1,870.9	344.9	0	39	61	10.71	11.64	3.3	.39	.35	13.08	10.57
19x1	1,915.1	329.6	0	35	65	11.97	13.01	2.9	.37	.17	13.25	11.46
19x0	1,599.2	319.2	0	36	64	10.58	11.50	3.2	.37	.08	11.59	10.77

EXHIBIT 2

Investment Growth Fund Statistical History

MANAGEMENT CAPITAL, INC.

	Total Net Assets (millions)	Number of Share- holders (thousands)	% of Assets in			Net Asset Value Per Share	Offer- ing Price	Yield (%)	Divi- dend Distribu- tions	Capital Gains Distribu- tions	Offering Price	
			Cash & Equiva- lent	Bonds & Pre- ferreds*	Common Stocks						High	Low
19x9	$2,221.4	373.6	4	3	93	$19.29	$20.97	2.3	$ .50	$ .88	$24.39	$20.09
19x8	2,340.8	367.2	5	3	92	22.42	24.37	2.2	.57	1.10	25.78	21.35
19x7	2,148.3	368.6	4	1	95	22.28	24.22	2.4	.59	.49	24.61	20.65
19x6	1,736.0	370.9	8	1	91	19.04	20.69	2.8	.60	.40	24.44	19.08
19x5	1,801.2	346.3	4	0	96	22.25	24.18	2.2	.55	.32	24.65	21.85
19x4	1,467.1	302.9	3	1	96	21.06	22.89	2.1	.49	.38	23.63	20.84
19x3	1,192.6	275.7	3	1	96	19.19	20.86	2.1	.44	.40	21.37	18.58
19x2	998.6	266.8	4	2	94	17.19	18.68	2.2	.40	.10	22.10	15.64
19x1	1,025.0	234.2	3	2	96	20.44	22.22	1.8	.39	.24	22.55	18.17
19x0	713.1	199.2	2	1	97	16.86	18.33	2.2	.41	.20	19.16	16.60

*Mainly convertible issues.

EXHIBIT 3

Fixed Income Fund Statistical History

MANAGEMENT CAPITAL, INC.

	AT YEAR-ENDS									ANNUAL DATA			
	Total Net Assets (millions)	Number of Share-holders (thousands)	Cash & Equiva-lent	Bonds	Preferred Stocks	Net Asset Value Per Share	Offer-ing Price	Yield (%)	Divi-dend Distribu-tions	Capital Gains Distribu-tions	Offering Price High	Low
			% of Assets in									
19x9	$30.8	5.1	4	86	10	$ 8.80	$ 9.46	5.7	$ .54	$ .00	$10.11	$ 9.44
19x8	34.9	5.6	6	85	9	9.35	10.16	5.1	.52	.02	10.35	9.97
19x7	36.1	6.1	5	85	10	9.35	10.05	5.0	.51	.01	10.69	10.02
19x6	40.4	6.7	6	83	11	9.57	10.29	4.9	.51	.00	11.04	10.20
19x5	46.1	7.5	4	82	14	10.22	10.99	4.5	.50	.04	11.27	10.96
19x4	44.9	7.5	8	71	21	10.39	11.17	4.4	.49	.05	11.30	11.08
19x3	36.4	6.8	11	53	36	10.41	11.19	4.5	.50	.04	11.32	11.00
19x2	32.8	6.4	6	45	49	10.23	11.00	4.6	.51	.02	11.13	10.89
19x1	30.4	6.4	4	34	62	10.19	10.96	4.6	.50	.02	11.06	10.73
19x0	28.5	6.5	6	23	71	9.98	10.73	4.6	.49	.00	10.86	10.51

EXHIBIT 4
Variable Growth Fund Statistical History

MANAGEMENT CAPITAL, INC.

	Total Net Assets (millions)	Number of Shareholders (thousands)	Cash & Equivalent	Bonds & Preferred*	Common Stocks	Net Asset Value Per Share	Offering Price	Yield (%)	Income Dividends	Capital Gains Distributions	Offering Price High	Offering Price Low
			% of Assets in									
19x9	$1,050.7	254.5	7	3	90	$7.88	$ 8.56	1.8	$ .15	$ .00	$10.17	$7.83
19x8	1,182.7	248.2	8	7	85	9.35	10.16	1.5	.16	.48	11.06	8.39
19x7	949.3	208.3	7	2	91	9.19	9.99	1.4	.15	.53	10.63	8.06
19x6	588.5	171.2	14	---	86	7.44	8.09	1.8	.15	.40	9.87	7.19
19x5	469.2	127.5	3	1	96	8.44	9.17	1.7	.16	.25	9.58	7.90
19x4	374.9	120.0	3	2	95	7.46	8.11	1.8	.15	.24	8.76	7.44
19x3	322.5	118.3	2	2	96	6.84	7.43	1.5	.12	.31	7.87	6.63
19x2	275.3	120.9	8	2	90	6.14	6.67	1.3	.09	.00	8.15	5.47
19x1	277.0	106.2	3	2	95	7.51	8.16	1.0	.08	.04	8.52	6.59
19x0	166.1	83.3	1	1	98	6.12	6.55	1.5	.10	.02	6.72	5.93

————AT YEAR-ENDS———— ————ANNUAL DATA————

*Mainly convertible issues.

Case 28:   Comprehensive Case—Comparison of the Models of Markowitz, Sharpe, and Latané

Growth Incorporated

Believe it or not, some people almost always make money in the stock market. (G. M. Loeb.)

Growth Incorporated (GI), which currently manages the investment accounts of three mutual funds with a total market value of over $1.5 billion, has been one of the most successful money management enterprises in the U. S. The company's outstanding success is generally accredited to 73-year old Terrance D. Bondfield, one of the most astute money men of all time. Mr. Bondfield entered the mutual fund business in 1950 with his Capital Appreciation Fund. Since this fund was a "no-load fund" its future was keyed to performance rather than to aggressive promotion by mutual fund salesmen. GI was created to serve as the investment management for the fund.

Mr. Bondfield's investment philosophy is predicated on his keen and far reaching insight with respect to trends emerging in the capital markets. For example, he became convinced in the 1930s that inflation was going to become a trademark of the 1940s and 1950s. After many year's service as an investment advisor, he organized the Capital Appreciation Fund which was to meet the threat of inflation by concentrating its investments in the stocks of "quality" growth companies. While most investment managers at that time simultaneously invested their funds in fixed income securities and bemoaned the fact that inflation was eroding away their earnings, T. D. Bondfield was busy selecting stocks of companies which had high earnings growth potentials. He reasoned that if he bought stocks whose earnings were growing faster than the economy he could protect both himself and his clients against inflation. He discarded the prevailing rule of investing for cyclical swings as old fashioned and not relevant for the trends emerging.

After a decade of very successfully applying his philosophy, Mr. Bondfield reevaluated the investment horizon. He came to the conclusion that many of the traditional growth stocks which had made his Capital Appreciation Fund such a success were now substantially overpriced. Hence, he decided the thing to do was to switch to small companies which would eventually become growth stocks. With this in mind, he formed Emerging Growth Stock Fund. Within 2 years the stock market had crashed, and the new fund became known by cynics as the "Lost Growth" Fund. Not long after, however, as the data of Exhibits 1 and 2 indicate, the "old philosopher" had come up with appropriate investment decisions again. Soon everybody was trying to get into the act and the age of the "Go-Go" funds was born.

At the end of the past decade, Mr. Bondfield formulated the third phase in the evolution of his investment philosophy. He believed that the world was ending an era of rapid growth. He reasoned that the capitalistic nations had outgrown the international monetary structure and now do not know what to do about it—hence, the gold crises and accelerating inflation. Accordingly, he began to delve deeply into the question of the type of investment program that would be best during the coming decade. He believed there would be a flight from the dollar and thus earnings growth of U. S. companies would be meager. One thing was certain: he did not want to own dollars or bonds. The technology stocks that had become a Bondfield trademark were also avoided in favor of "real" assets. Mr. Bondfield believes that as the dollar depreciates and the population swells, real assets will emerge as the best new investment vehicle. Accordingly, he recently formed Natural Resource Fund to capitalize on his idea. The new fund, as was true for the two earlier funds, does not have a load charge and is managed by GI. Natural Resource Fund will include some technology companies, but most of the capital will be invested in gold stocks, silver stocks, uranium, copper and, especially, stocks backed by large amounts of undeveloped land such as forest products companies. Thus, Mr. Bondfield has for the third time in the past two decades launched a new era of fund management. His past successes have had much to do with his ability to command sizeable commitments from investors.

As was true also in the case of Emerging Growth Fund, Mr. Bondfield was a year or two ahead of his time as the stock market suffered one of its sharpest drops in history after the formation of Natural Resource Fund. However, this time he managed to hold losses to a minimum.

While the investment philosophy of Mr. Bondfield has carried Growth, Inc. to substantial successes thus far, management of the company realizes that because of his age, he may not be around much longer. And, although Mr. Bondfield's keen insight has generally produced portfolio returns higher than the stock averages and other mutual funds, there exist portfolio evaluation techniques which may achieve similar or perhaps better results. These techniques provide a more formal approach to portfolio aggregation.

QUESTIONS

1. (a) Do you agree with Mr. Bondfield's investment philosophy? Why or why not?

   (b) How relevant is his "natural resource" philosophy in today's investment climate? Discuss.

2. (a) Apply the portfolio models of Markowitz, Sharpe, and Latané for AF, GL, COG, and CS. Use the following procedures: (1) In the absence of expectational data, use historical return/risk values; (2) compute and graph efficient frontiers and capital market lines when relevant; (3) assume a lending rate of .06 and a borrowing rate of .10; (4) for Latané's model, assume an equally probable variation of .90 to 1.30 in the *HPR*s of the Standard and Poor's Industrial Stock Index; (5) assume an equal dollar investment in each security comprising the corresponding portfolios.

   (b) Compare and contrast the above portfolio models.

3. How relevant is the borrowing rate in GI's case? Explain.

EXHIBIT 1

Capital Appreciation Fund Statistical History

GROWTH INCORPORATED

| | At YEAR-ENDS | | | | | ANNUAL DATA | | | | | |
| | Total Net Assets (millions) | Number of Shareholders (thousands) | Cash & Equivalent | Bonds & Preferreds* | Common Stocks | Net Asset Value Per Share | Yield (%) | Dividend Distributions | Capital Gains Distributions | Offering Price High | Low |
				% of Assets in							
Current	$657.5	128.9	5	4	91	$23.09	1.8	.42	.57	$26.36	$17.55
19x9	612.9	111.2	11	3	86	26.14	1.4	.39	.77	26.84	22.56
19x8	514.1	95.1	8	0	92	26.45	.7	.18	0	27.42	21.47
19x7	393.3	73.8	5	1	94	24.57	1.6	.39	.53	24.70	20.06
19x6	246.6	56.7	11	0	89	20.10	1.8	.38	.50	22.40	17.73
19x5	196.8	42.4	12	1	87	21.16	1.6	.34	.60	21.68	17.51
19x4	128.9	32.3	6	0	94	17.60	1.7	.30	.34	18.37	16.38
19x3	104.2	28.6	5	0	95	16.30	1.7	.28	.28	16.53	14.14
19x2	79.3	25.4	9	1	90	14.23	1.9	.27	.25	16.89	11.82
19x1	71.8	18.2	7	1	92	16.89	1.4	.25	.50	17.60	14.03
19x0	39.9	11.0	13	0	87	14.15	1.7	.25	.40	14.45	12.60

*Mainly convertible issues.

EXHIBIT 2

Emerging Growth Fund Statistical History

GROWTH INCORPORATED

| | | | AT YEAR–ENDS | | | | | ANNUAL DATA | | | |
| | Total Net Assets (millions) | Number of Share-holders (thousands) | % of Assets in | | | Net Asset Value Per Share | Yield (%) | Divi-dend Distribu-tions | Capital Gains Distribu-tions | Offering Price | |
			Cash & Equiva-lent	Bonds & Pre-ferreds*	Common Stocks					High	Low
Current	$187.2	24.5	12	2	86	$24.36	.8	$.21	$1.20	$29.45	$16.69
19x9	159.6	21.0	9	3	88	29.15	.6	.18	1.72	33.24	24.59
19x8	163.0	21.1	9	1	90	33.24	0	0	0	34.28	22.75
19x7	123.0	21.4	17	1	82	26.97	.5	.15	1.43	27.43	15.17
19x6	26.6	5.0	18	4	78	15.29	.6	.09	.50	15.44	2.52
19x5	15.3	2.7	14	3	83	13.40	.3	.04	.59	13.40	9.65
19x4	9.3	2.1	13	2	85	9.77	0	.02	.33	10.19	9.25
19x3	9.2	2.1	5	2	93	9.94	0	0	0	10.12	9.02
19x2	7.6	2.1	3	6	91	9.06	0	0	0	12.69	7.58
19x1	8.2	1.8	4	5	91	12.76	0	0	0	13.25	10.94
19x0	.6	.1	4	4	92	10.92	0	0	0	10.94	9.41

*Mainly convertible issues.

EXHIBIT 3

Natural Resource Fund Statistical History   GROWTH INCORPORATED

	AT YEAR-ENDS			ANNUAL DATA	
Year	Total Net Assets (millions)	Net Asset Value Per Share	Yield (%)	Dividend Distributions	Capital Gains Distributions
Current	$89.4	$9.49	1.7	$0.16	0
19x9	43.1	9.73	0	0	0

IV APPENDIXES

A Definitions

$$\text{Average collection period} = \frac{\text{receivables}}{\text{sales}} \times 360$$

$$\text{Book value per share} = \frac{\text{common stock equity}}{\text{number of common shares}}$$

Borrowing rate:
Before-tax rate which must be paid for the use of funds by investors. The borrowing rate is usually higher than the lending rate.

$$\text{Capital turnover} = \frac{\text{sales}}{\text{total assets}}$$

Capitalization rate:
Discount rate used to determine the present value of an infinite stream of constant receipts.

Coefficient of correlation:
A relative measure of the extent to which two series of numbers tend to vary together.

Common stock equity = common stock plus surplus accounts

Convertible security:
Either a bond or preferred stock wherein a fixed number of shares of common stock of the firm may be obtained per bond or share of preferred stock, usually upon request of the security holder.

Corner portfolio:
Maximum return of a group of securities for a given risk level.

$$\text{Cost of debt (before taxes)} = \frac{\text{interest}}{\text{current + long-term debt}}$$

$$\text{Cost of preferred stock (before taxes)} = \frac{\text{preferred dividends}}{\text{preferred stock} (1 - \text{tax rate})}$$

Covariance:
An absolute measure of the extent to which two sets of numbers vary together (see Appendix B).

Debt leverage:
The amount of earnings per share due to the use of debt in the financial structure:

$$(1 - TXR) \, [(RBIT - I)DEQ] \, B.V.$$

where TXR = tax rate
$RBIT$ = rate of return on assets before interest and taxes
DEQ = debt to equity ratio
$B.V.$ = book value per share of common

$$\text{Debt to equity} = \frac{\text{current debt + long-term debt}}{\text{common stock equity}}$$

Dependent variable:
A variable whose value is at least partially influenced by the value of some other variable in an equation or model.

Depreciation:
Amortization of the costs of assets over their useful lives. *Straight-line depreciation SL* = investment cost I minus net salvage value SV divided by expected years N of useful life; that is,

$$SL = \frac{I - SV}{N}$$

Sum of the years digits depreciation SYD = allocation of cost of assets minus net salvage on the basis of the ratio of the years of useful life divided by the sum of the years; for example,

$$SYD_1 = \left[\frac{N}{\sum\limits_{i=1}^{N} (\text{year}_i)} \right] (I - SV) \quad SYD_2 = \left[\frac{N - 1}{\sum\limits_{i=1}^{N} (\text{year}_i)} \right] (I - SV)$$

If $N = 5$, then

$$SYD_1 = \frac{5}{1 + 2 + 3 + 4 + 5} \, (I - SV) = 1/3 \, (I - SV)$$

$$SYD_2 = \frac{5 - 1}{1 + 2 + 3 + 4 + 5} = 4/15 \, (I - SV)$$

Declining balance depreciation DB = amortization of asset cost less salvage at a rate which when applied to the net book value of the asset at the beginning of each period will result in writing the asset down to salvage value by decreasing charges throughout its estimated service life. For example, if the asset cost is $10,000, the useful life is 5 years, and the estimated net salvage is $778, the asset will be fully depreciated in 5 years by applying a rate which in this instance is twice that of the straight-line rate. $DB_1 = 2(.20)I = .4I$ and $DB_2 = .4(I - .4I)$, etc. At the end of the fifth year depreciation will have totaled $9,222, leaving the salvage value of $778. For tax purposes the *DB* rate cannot exceed twice the straight-line rate.

Discount rate:

Rate at which a stream of actual or expected receipts is adjusted for the time value of money.

Diversifiable risk (DS_i):

Unsystematic risk; random risk; variation in a security price due solely to factors related only to a particular firm. Usually measured by the standard error of the estimate of the regression of the *HPR*s of a stock against the *HPR*s of a market index.

$$\text{Dividend payout} = \frac{\text{common dividends per share}}{\text{common earnings per share}}$$

$$\text{Dividend yield} = \frac{\text{annual dividend per share}}{\text{share price}}$$

Dominated security:

A security whose expected *HPR*s in both good and bad market years are exceeded by the expected *HPR*s of another security.

Efficient capital market:

Refers to the adjustment of stock prices to new information. The market is efficient if it fully reflects all available information. Weak, semistrong, and strong form tests of an efficient capital market refer to the type of information analyzed: weak data are merely historical price data, semistrong data are other published data, and strong data are those data available only to "insiders."

Efficient frontier:

A series of corner portfolios.

Expected return (E):
Expected percentage increment (resulting from dividends and capital gains) in an investment holding for the next period.

Financial leverage:
This term is defined in three different ways in financial literature:

(1) The use of borrowed funds. This is the most usual meaning.

(2) $\dfrac{\text{Long-term debt}}{\text{Total assets}}$ or $\dfrac{\text{long-term debt}}{\text{common stock equity}}$

(3) $\dfrac{\% \text{ change in common earnings}}{\% \text{ change in earnings before interest and taxes}}$

Flow-through accounting:
Fully accounting for in one year (via inclusion in the income statement) an expense or revenue item. An alternative to amortizing the item over a period of time.

Holding period return (HPR):
Value of an investment holding ratioed to the initial cost of the investment; refers to a specified period of time. For example,

$$\text{Annual } HPR_{19x9} = \frac{P_{19x9} + D_{19x9}}{P_{19x8}} \text{ for a share of common stock}$$

$$= \frac{P_{19x9} + D_{19x9} + C.G._{19x9}}{P_{19x8}} \text{ for a mutual fund}$$

where P = price per share (may be average over period of time or price as of specified point in time)

D = annual cash dividends paid to shareholder over holding period

$C.G.$ = capital gains distributed to shareholder over holding period

Independent variable:
A variable whose value is unaffected by the value of the other variables in an equation or model.

$$\text{Interest coverage} = \frac{\text{earnings before taxes} + \text{interest (i.e., } EBIT)}{\text{interest}}$$

$$\text{Inventory turnover} = \frac{\text{cost of goods sold}}{\text{average inventory}}$$

Investment company:
A firm specializing in security investments for the benefit of investors who do not desire to select their own securities. Mutual funds are open-end investment companies wherein the number of fund shares varies with investor's demand. Closed-end funds have a fixed number of shares outstanding.

Lending rate:
Rate at which funds can be safely invested, i.e., with no systematic or random risk; comparable to the riskless rate.

$$\textbf{Market-book value} = \frac{\text{market price of a share of stock}}{\text{book value of the share}}$$

Market index:
An index or average of a group of common stocks such as the Standard and Poor's 425 Industrials (S & P_{425}) or the Dow Jones 30 Industrials (DJIA). Each of these market indexes is comprised of different securities and each is usually calculated differently.

Non-diversifiable risk (NS_i):
Systematic risk; covariation of the returns of a security with the returns of the market index; the slope value, commonly referred to as β coefficient defined as $(V_i)S_{mkt}$ by Latané and Tuttle, where V_i = slope value of the returns of a security with the returns of the market index and S_{mkt} = average of expected variability of returns of the market index. Defined by Sharpe as $\beta_i \sigma_m$, where β_i = the change in security i's rate of return relative to a change in the market rate of return and σ_m = standard deviation of the return of the market index.

Operating leverage:
The percent change in net operating income resulting from a change in sales divided by the percent change in sales. A leverage figure greater than 1 is caused by fixed costs. Operating leverage is a measure of the relative volatility of operating income to sales.

Portfolio possibility line:
Linear relationship between the return of a portfolio or a mutual fund and the return of a market index, with the line of relationship originating on the dependent (vertical) axis at the riskless rate of interest.

Portfolio responsiveness:

$$(\beta_p) = \sum_{i=1}^{n} X_i \beta_i$$

where X_i = proportion of portfolio invested in security i
β_i = slope value between *HPR*s of security i and market index

Portfolio return $(E_p) = \displaystyle\sum_{i=1}^{n} X_i E_i$

where X_i = proportion of portfolio invested in security i
E_i = expected return on security i
n = number of securities in portfolio

Preferred leverage in dollars per share:
The amount of earnings per share due to the use of preferred stock in the financial structure.

$$(1 - TXR)[(RBIT - PFR)PFQ]B.V.$$

where TXR = tax rate
$RBIT$ = rate of return on assets before interest and taxes
PFR = cost of preferred stock, expressed as a rate
PFQ = preferred to equity ratio
$B.V.$ = book value per share of common

Price-earnings ratio $= \dfrac{\text{share price of common stock}}{\text{earnings per share for the year}}$

Prior charge coverage $= \dfrac{\text{earnings before taxes + interest + net lease charges}}{\text{interest + net lease charges + preferred div. } (1/1 - TXR)}$

Random walk:
Refers to short-run stock price movements wherein such movements are "statistically independent" of past price actions (i.e., current or future price fluctuations cannot be predicted from any history of past price changes). Advocates of the random walk theory also usually assume that successive price changes are identically distributed.

Relative debt leverage $= \dfrac{\text{debt leverage in dollars}}{\text{common earnings per share}}$ (see **Debt leverage**)

Relative preferred leverage $= \dfrac{\text{preferred leverage in dollars}}{\text{common earnings per share}}$ (see **Preferred leverage**)

Required return (k):
Marginal rate of return demanded by investors to warrant investment in a security.

Responsiveness:
Slope value between a security's *HPR*s (or *E*s) and a market index *HPR*s (*E*s).

$$\text{Return on assets} = \frac{\text{common earnings}}{\text{total assets}}$$

$$\text{Return on equity} = \frac{\text{common earnings}}{\text{common stock equity}}$$

$$\text{Return on sales} = \frac{\text{common earnings}}{\text{sales}}$$

Riskless rate of interest (r):
Rate of interest under certainty; rate of return on an investment with no risk of default; rate of interest on federal government obligations.

Scatter diagram:
Plot of a finite number of observations of a dependent variable (Y) against the same number of observations of an independent variable (X), with the dependent variable on the vertical axis.

$$\text{Tax rate} = \frac{\text{taxes}}{\text{earnings before taxes}}$$

Volatility:
Referred to as the slope value β between security or portfolio returns and the returns of a market index.

B Statistical Formulas

$$\text{Arithmetic mean} = \frac{\sum\limits_{i=1}^{n} X_i}{n}$$

where X_i = a number taken from a series of numbers
n = total number of numbers in series

Coefficient of correlation (r):

Product moment formula for the compution of r:

$$r_{xy} = \frac{E_{xy}}{\sqrt{E_x{}^2 E_y{}^2}}$$

where x = observation of variable X minus mean of variable X
y = observation of variable Y minus mean of variable Y

$$\text{Coefficient of variation} = \frac{\text{standard deviation}}{\text{arithmetic mean}}$$

$$\text{Covariance} = \frac{\sum\limits_{i=1}^{n} (X_i - \overline{X})(Y_i - \overline{Y})}{n - 1} = r_{xy} S_x S_y$$

where X_i and Y_i = individual numbers, each taken from a set of numbers
X and Y = means of number sets X and Y
r = correlation between X and Y
S_x and S_y = standard deviations of X and Y
n = total number of numbers in the sets

$$\text{Geometric mean } (G) = \sqrt[n]{a \cdot b \cdot c \ldots n}$$

where a, b, c, etc., are numbers and n = total number of numbers.

Growth rate (g):

Average annual rate of increase in the value of a variable. For example

$$1 + g = \sqrt[n]{\frac{\text{most recent value}}{\text{beginning value}}}$$

where n is the number of periods over which the increase has taken place. The g can also be obtained easily from a compound interest table. For example

$$V = P(1 + g)^n \qquad \text{then} \qquad (1 + g)^n = \frac{V}{P}$$

where V is the most recent value, P is the beginning value and n is the number of periods during which growth has occurred; g can be read directly from the table.

Optimum leverage ratio (q):

The optimum investment in risk assets per dollar of market valued net worth of the investor. Symbolically

$$q = \frac{PRY_p}{NS_p}$$

where PRY_p = pure risk yield of portfolio
NS_p = nondiversifiable risk of portfolio

Portfolio variance $(V_p) = \sum_{i=1}^{n} X_i^2 \, var(E_i) + 2\sum_{j=1}^{n-1} \sum_{k=j+1}^{n} X_j X_k \, cov(E_j, E_k)$

where X_i = proportion of portfolio invested in security i
$var\, E_i$ = expected variance in return of security i
X_j, X_k = proportions invested in securities j and k respectively
$cov(E_j, E_k)$ = covariance between returns of securities j and k
n = number of securities in portfolio

Since $cov(E_j, E_k) = r_{jk} S_j S_k$, where r_{jk} is the correlation between the returns of securities j and k and $S_j S_k$ is the product of the standard deviations of the returns of securities j and k, then portfolio variance also equals

$$\sum_{i=1}^{n} X_i^2 \, var(E_i) + 2\sum_{j=1}^{n-1} \sum_{k=j+1}^{n} X_j X_k r_{jk} S_j S_k$$

Pure risk yield (PRY):

Expected return of a security (E_i for security i) or of a portfolio (E_p) minus the riskless rate of interest (r) divided by nondiversifiable risk of the security or portfolio (NS_i or NS_p). Thus

$$PRY_i = \frac{E_i - r}{NS_i} \quad \text{and} \quad PRY_p = \frac{E_p - r}{NS_i}$$

Regression equation (simple linear):

$$y = a + bx$$
$$na + b\Sigma x = \Sigma y$$
$$a\Sigma x + b\Sigma x^2 = \Sigma xy$$

or

$$b = \frac{\Sigma xy}{\Sigma x^2} \quad \text{or} \quad b = \frac{n\Sigma XY - \Sigma X \Sigma Y}{n\Sigma X^2 - (\Sigma X)^2}$$

$$a = \overline{Y} - b\overline{X}$$

where $y = Y - \overline{Y}$
  $x = X - \overline{X}$
  Y = dependent variable
  $\overline{Y}$ = mean of dependent variable
  X = independent variable
  $\overline{X}$ = mean of dependent variable
  a = origin of equation
  b = average change in Y per unit of X; slope value
  n = number of observations

Standard deviation (S_x) = square root of variance   (see **Variance**)

Standard error of estimate ($S_y \cdot x$):

$$S_y \cdot x = \sqrt{\frac{\sum_{i=1}^{n} (Y_i - Y_c)^2}{n-2}}$$

where Y_i = an observation of dependent variable
  Y_c = computed value of dependent variable

Shortcut formula

$$Sy \cdot x \sqrt{\frac{\sum Y_i^2 - a \sum Y_i - b \sum X_i Y_i}{n-2}}$$

Variance (S_x^2) = $\dfrac{\sum\limits_{i=1}^{n} (X_i - \bar{X})^2}{n-1}$ or $\dfrac{\sum X_i^2}{n-1} - \dfrac{\sum X_i^2}{n(n-1)}$

where X_i = one number taken from series of numbers
X = mean of series
n = total number of numbers in series

C Selected Stock Valuation Models

Gordon's dividend model:
$$P_O = \frac{D_O}{K_e - g} \qquad\qquad g = br$$

where P_O = current market price per share
D_O = current dividends per share in dollars
K_e = required rate of return on stock
g = average annual growth rate in dividends per share expected by investors at margin
b = percentage of earnings retained in firm
r = rate of return expected to be earned on new equity funds invested by firm

Holt's model:
$$\frac{P_g(0)/E_g(0)}{P_a(0)/E_a(0)} = \left(\frac{1 + \Delta E_g + D_g}{1 + \Delta E_a + D}\right)^T$$

where $P_g(0)$ = current share price of growth stock
$P_a(0)$ = current share price of nongrowth stock of comparable risk
$E_g(0)$ = current year's earnings of growth stock
$E_a(0)$ = current year's earnings of nongrowth stock
ΔE_g = percent per annum growth rate of earnings per share of growth stock
ΔE_a = percent per annum growth rate of earnings per share of non-growth stock
D_g = constant (and current) dividend yield of growth stock
D_a = constant (and current) dividend yield of nongrowth stock
T = duration of growth in years

Malkiel's growth stock valuation and price earnings models:

Growth stock valuation model:

$$P = \frac{D(1+g)}{1+r} + \frac{D(1+g)^2}{(1+r)^2} + \cdots + \frac{D(1+g)^N}{(1+r)^N} + \frac{m_sE(1+g)^N}{(1+r)^N}$$

where P = present value of future stream of receipts; current price
    D = dividends per share in past fiscal year
    E = earnings per share in past fiscal year
    g = expected growth rate of earnings per share and dividends per share over next N years
    m_S = standard earnings multiple, or price earnings ratio of the S & P 425 Industrial Stock Index
    r = apparent marginal efficiency of representative standard share
    N = number of years of rapid growth

Price earnings model:

$$m = \frac{D\,(1+g)}{E\,(\bar{r}-g)} - \frac{D\,(1+g)^{N-1}}{E\,(\bar{r}-g)\,(1+\bar{r})^{N}} + \frac{\overline{m}_S\,(1+g)^{N}}{(1+\bar{r})^{N}}$$

where $m = P/E$ = current price-earnings ratio of a growth stock
    D = dividends per share in past fiscal year
    E = earnings per share in past fiscal year
    g = expected growth rate of earnings per share and dividends per share over next N years
    $\overline{m}_S$ = standard earnings multiple, or price earnings ratio of the S & P 425 Industrial Stock Index
    $\bar{r}$ = apparent marginal efficiency of representative standard share
    N = number of years of rapid growth

Walter's model:

$$V_c = \frac{D + (R_a/R_c)\,(E-D)}{R_c}$$

where V_c = present value of share of stock
    D = cash dividends per share
    E = earnings per share
    R_a = rate of return on additional equity investment
    R_c = market capitalization rate or investors' required rate of return on stock

EXHIBIT C 1

Graham and Dodd's Earnings Multipliers (based upon a 7-year growth horizon)

Industrials [*]

Expected Rate of Growth	Multiplier of Current Earnings
3.5	15
5.0	17
7.2	20
10.0	23.5
12.0	27
14.3	31
17.0	35.5
20.0	41.5

Utilities [†]

Expected Rate of Growth	Multiplier of Current Earnings
2	15
4	17
5	18
6	19
8	22
10	25
12	28
14	32

*Benjamin Graham et al., *Security Analysis,* 4th Ed., McGraw-Hill Book Company, New York, 1962, p. 537
†*Ibid.,* p. 591.

D Portfolio Evaluation Models

Jensen's portfolio evaluation model:

$$\delta_j = E_j - [E_O + B_j (M - E_O)]$$

where δ_j = performance measure applicable to portfolio of fund j
E_j = average annual rate of return of portfolio or fund j
E_O = riskless rate of interest
M = average annual rate of return of market index
B_j = slope value between returns of fund j and market returns; volatility

Sharpe's portfolio evaluation model:

$$\phi = \frac{Y - E}{S_y}$$

where ϕ = excess portfolio yield per unit of ex-post risk
Y = average annual ex-post yield
E_O = riskless rate of interest
S_y = standard deviation of the ex-post yields

Treynor's portfolio evaluation model:

$$\psi = \frac{E_O - A}{B}$$

where ψ = fund performance index
E_O = riskless rate of interest

A = vertical intercept between the returns of a particular fund and returns of the market index

B = slope value between the rates of return of the fund and rates of return of the market index, or the average change in the fund return per unit change of market return; also called "volatility"

Treynor's composite measure of fund performance, using volatility as a risk measure, is given by:

$$\psi' = \frac{E_j - E_O}{B}$$

where E_j is the historical rate of return of fund and other terms are as defined above.

E Market Indexes

Dow Jones Industrial Average

YEAR	HIGH	LOW	CLOSE	DIVIDEND
19X0	685.47	566.05	615.89	21.36
19X1	734.91	610.25	731.14	22.71
19X2	726.01	535.76	652.10	23.30
19X3	767.21	646.79	762.95	23.41
19X4	891.71	766.08	874.13	31.24
19X5	969.26	840.59	969.26	28.61
19X6	995.15	744.32	785.69	31.89
19X7	943.08	786.41	905.11	30.19
19X8	985.21	825.13	943.75	31.34
19X9	943.75	769.93	800.36	33.90

EXHIBIT E2

Standard and Poor's Index of Selected per Share Accounting and Price Data for 425 Industries

	19x9	19x8	19x7	19x6	19x5	19x4	19x3	19x2	19x1	19x0
Sales	108.34	101.49	91.86	88.46	80.69	73.19	68.50	64.63	59.51	59.47
Depreciation	4.84	4.56	4.25	3.87	3.52	3.24	3.04	2.89	2.66	2.56
Income Taxes	5.13	5.14	4.11	4.35	4.14	3.70	3.51	3.16	2.80	2.87
Common Earnings	6.13	6.16	5.62	5.87	5.50	4.85	4.24	3.83	3.37	3.40
Common Dividends	3.25	3.16	2.97	2.95	2.82	2.58	2.36	2.20	2.07	2.00
Price Index:										
High	116.24	118.03	106.15	100.60	98.55	91.29	79.25	75.22	76.69	65.02
Low	97.75	95.05	85.31	77.89	86.43	79.74	65.48	54.80	60.87	55.34
Average	107.00	106.54	95.73	89.25	92.49	85.52	72.37	65.01	68.78	60.18
Price/Earnings Ratio:										
High	19.0	19.2	18.9	17.1	17.9	18.8	18.7	19.6	22.8	19.1
Low	15.9	15.4	15.2	13.3	15.7	16.4	15.4	14.3	18.1	16.3
Average	17.4	17.3	17.0	15.2	16.8	17.6	17.0	16.9	20.4	17.7
Book Value Per Share	52.53	50.21	47.78	45.59	43.50	40.23	38.17	36.37	34.85	33.74
Book Value - % Return	11.67	12.27	11.76	12.88	12.64	12.06	11.11	10.53	9.67	10.08

Source: *S & P Analyst's Handbook.*

EXHIBIT E3

Standard and Poor's Index of Industrial Stocks

Weekly Price Data

Year 19x4 Week	S&P Average	Year 19x5 Week	S&P Average
January 6	80.31	January 4	89.75
13	80.85	11	90.68
20	81.27	18	91.52
27	81.39	25	92.20
February 3	81.44	February 1	92.52
10	81.93	8	91.32
17	82.15	15	90.74
24	82.36	22	92.07
March 2	82.84	March 1	92.06
9	83.65	8	91.73
16	84.14	15	91.98
23	83.87	22	91.68
30	84.33	29	91.08
April 6	84.78	April 5	91.74
13	85.12	12	93.21
20	85.35	19	93.81
27	84.69	26	94.32
May 4	86.08	May 3	95.05
11	86.13	10	95.36
18	85.64	17	94.75
25	85.37	24	93.60
June 1	84.22	31	92.50
8	84.09	June 7	90.76
15	85.51	14	90.11
22	86.09	21	89.40
29	87.06	28	88.54
July 6	88.23	July 5	90.22
13	88.49	12	90.77
20	88.49	19	89.40
27	87.86	26	89.37
August 3	86.75	August 2	90.80
10	86.80	9	91.33
17	86.95	16	92.10
24	86.32	23	92.15
31	87.08	30	92.75
September 7	87.94	September 6	94.21
14	88.30	13	95.18
21	88.90	20	95.62
28	89.17	27	95.87
October 5	89.89	October 4	96.23
12	89.72	11	97.11
19	89.93	18	97.69
26	89.69	25	98.12
November 2	90.09	November 1	98.22
9	89.96	8	97.96
16	91.05	15	98.34
23	90.55	22	97.71
30	88.84	29	95.93
December 7	88.50	December 6	97.17
14	88.36	13	97.94
21	89.09	20	98.01
28	88.85	27	97.72

EXHIBIT E3 (continued)

Standard and Poor's Index of Industrial Stocks

Year 19x6 Week		S&P Average	Year 19x7 Week		S&P Average
January	3	98.79	January	2	86.27
	10	99.33		9	88.97
	17	99.95		16	90.73
	24	100.03		23	91.82
	31	99.03		30	92.56
February	7	100.27	February	6	93.13
	14	99.46		13	94.02
	21	97.70		20	93.28
	28	96.15		27	93.45
March	7	94.74	March	6	95.02
	14	93.98		13	95.75
	21	95.48		20	97.13
	28	95.63		27	97.31
April	4	97.92	April	3	95.89
	11	98.21		10	95.42
	18	98.58		17	98.34
	25	98.06		24	100.29
May	2	95.50	May	1	101.23
	9	92.48		8	100.88
	16	90.56		15	99.49
	23	93.01		22	97.71
	30	92.10		29	96.51
June	6	91.40	June	5	96.88
	13	92.89		12	99.60
	20	92.80		19	99.60
	27	91.42		26	98.34
July	4	93.08	July	3	98.44
	11	93.11		10	99.69
	18	92.08		17	100.80
	25	89.68		24	101.60
August	1	89.00		31	103.21
	8	89.26	August	7	103.26
	15	86.89		14	102.21
	22	83.54		21	100.98
	29	81.94		28	100.59
September	5	81.61	September	4	101.92
	12	84.50		11	103.31
	19	83.71		18	104.78
	28	82.24		25	105.56
October	3	79.21	October	2	105.21
	10	80.89		9	105.19
	17	82.90		16	103.68
	24	84.43		23	103.21
	31	85.67		30	101.49
November	7	86.46	November	6	99.77
	14	86.88		13	100.25
	21	85.22		20	101.33
	28	85.46		27	102.65
December	5	86.67	December	4	103.94
	12	87.65		11	103.92
	19	86.48		18	103.58
	26	85.50		25	104.44

EXHIBIT E3 (continued)

Standard and Poor's Index of Industrial Stocks

Year 19x8 Week	S&P Average	Year 19x9 Week	S&P Average
January 1	104.13	January 6	110.54
8	104.77	13	110.21
15	103.80	20	110.98
22	101.43	27	111.53
29	100.45	February 3	111.98
February 5	98.91	10	112.37
12	97.33	17	109.75
19	98.44	24	106.71
26	97.36	March 3	107.74
March 4	96.66	10	107.43
11	97.27	17	107.95
18	96.59	24	109.62
25	97.23	31	110.60
April 1	101.56	April 7	110.21
8	104.44	14	110.49
15	105.38	21	110.53
22	105.41	28	112.95
29	107.26	May 5	114.77
May 6	107.90	12	115.64
13	106.93	19	114.40
20	105.89	26	113.49
27	106.95	June 2	112.26
June 3	109.95	9	109.20
10	110.90	16	106.80
17	109.30	23	106.05
24	108.74	30	108.18
July 1	108.79	July 7	106.53
8	111.25	14	104.14
15	110.36	21	101.43
22	107.33	28	99.50
29	105.69	August 4	102.66
August 5	105.54	11	102.26
12	107.01	18	104.62
19	107.57	25	104.22
26	107.63	September 1	103.95
September 2	109.36	8	103.26
9	109.94	15	104.46
16	110.75	22	104.50
23	111.65	29	102.32
30	112.53	October 6	102.58
October 7	112.96	13	105.31
14	113.46	20	107.04
21	114.05	27	106.94
28	112.90	November 3	107.26
November 4	112.82	10	107.50
11	114.48	17	105.24
18	115.39	24	102.85
25	116.99	December 1	101.70
December 2	117.67	8	99.92
9	117.18	15	99.62
16	116.36	22	99.99
23	114.35		
30	113.08		

EXHIBIT E3 (continued)

Standard and Poor's Index of Industrial Stocks

Current
Year

Week		S&P Average
January	5	102.30
	12	100.80
	19	98.72
	26	95.31
February	2	94.74
	9	95.03
	16	95.80
	23	97.50
March	2	98.19
	9	96.67
	16	95.41
	23	97.03
	30	98.13
April	6	96.77
	13	94.65
	20	92.20
	27	88.97
May	4	86.81
	11	84.29
	18	80.93
	25	79.42
June	1	84.98
	8	82.60
	15	83.52
	22	82.13
	29	80.07
July	6	79.88
	13	82.81
	20	84.95
	27	85.48
August	3	84.60
	10	82.62
	17	84.66
	24	89.34
	31	89.83
September	7	90.75
	14	89.98
	21	90.95
	28	92.91
October	5	94.71
	12	92.82
	19	91.82
	26	91.64
November	2	88.53
	9	90.71
	16	91.33
	23	93.34
	30	96.88
December	7	98.57
	14	98.61
	21	98.93
	28	99.30

F Compound Interest, Present Value

EXHIBIT F1

Compound Sum of $1

Year	1%	2%	3%	4%	5%	6%	7%
1	1.010	1.020	1.030	1.040	1.050	1.060	1.070
2	1.020	1.040	1.061	1.082	1.102	1.124	1.145
3	1.030	1.061	1.093	1.125	1.158	1.191	1.225
4	1.041	1.082	1.126	1.170	1.216	1.262	1.311
5	1.051	1.104	1.159	1.217	1.276	1.338	1.403
6	1.062	1.126	1.194	1.265	1.340	1.419	1.501
7	1.072	1.149	1.230	1.316	1.407	1.504	1.606
8	1.083	1.172	1.267	1.369	1.477	1.594	1.718
9	1.094	1.195	1.305	1.423	1.551	1.689	1.838
10	1.105	1.219	1.344	1.480	1.629	1.791	1.967
11	1.116	1.243	1.384	1.539	1.710	1.898	2.105
12	1.127	1.268	1.426	1.601	1.796	2.012	2.252
13	1.138	1.294	1.469	1.665	1.886	2.133	2.410
14	1.149	1.319	1.513	1.732	1.980	2.261	2.579
15	1.161	1.346	1.558	1.801	2.079	2.397	2.759
16	1.173	1.373	1.605	1.873	2.183	2.540	2.952
17	1.184	1.400	1.653	1.948	2.292	2.693	3.159
18	1.196	1.428	1.702	2.026	2.407	2.854	3.380
19	1.208	1.457	1.754	2.107	2.527	3.026	3.617
20	1.220	1.486	1.806	2.191	2.653	3.207	3.870
25	1.282	1.641	2.094	2.666	3.386	4.292	5.427
30	1.348	1.811	2.427	3.243	4.322	5.743	7.612

Year	8%	9%	10%	12%	14%	15%	16%
1	1.080	1.090	1.100	1.120	1.140	1.150	1.160
2	1.166	1.188	1.210	1.254	1.300	1.322	1.346
3	1.260	1.295	1.331	1.405	1.482	1.521	1.561
4	1.360	1.412	1.464	1.574	1.689	1.749	1.811
5	1.469	1.539	1.611	1.762	1.925	2.011	2.100
6	1.587	1.677	1.772	1.974	2.195	2.313	2.436
7	1.714	1.828	1.949	2.211	2.502	2.660	2.826
8	1.851	1.993	2.144	2.476	2.853	3.059	3.278
9	1.999	2.172	2.358	2.773	3.252	3.518	3.803
10	2.159	2.367	2.594	3.106	3.707	4.046	4.411
11	2.332	2.580	2.853	3.479	4.226	4.652	5.117
12	2.518	2.813	3.138	3.896	4.818	5.350	5.936
13	2.720	3.066	3.452	4.363	5.492	6.153	6.886
14	2.937	3.342	3.797	4.887	6.261	7.076	7.988
15	3.172	3.642	4.177	5.474	7.138	8.137	9.266
16	3.426	3.970	4.595	6.130	8.137	9.358	10.748
17	3.700	4.328	5.054	6.866	9.276	10.761	12.468
18	3.996	4.717	5.560	7.690	10.575	12.375	14.463
19	4.316	5.142	6.116	8.613	12.056	14.232	16.777
20	4.661	5.604	6.728	9.646	13.743	16.367	19.461
25	6.848	8.623	10.835	17.000	26.462	32.919	40.874
30	10.063	13.268	17.449	29.960	50.950	66.212	85.850

EXHIBIT F1 (continued)

Compound Sum of $1

Year	18%	20%	24%	28%	32%	36%
1	1.180	1.200	1.240	1.280	1.320	1.360
2	1.392	1.440	1.538	1.638	1.742	1.850
3	1.643	1.728	1.907	2.067	2.300	2.515
4	1.939	2.074	2.364	2.684	3.036	3.421
5	2.288	2.488	2.932	3.436	4.007	4.653
6	2.700	2.986	3.635	4.398	5.290	6.328
7	3.185	3.583	4.508	5.629	6.983	8.605
8	3.759	4.300	5.590	7.206	9.217	11.703
9	4.435	5.160	6.931	9.223	12.166	15.917
10	5.234	6.192	8.594	11.806	16.060	21.647
11	6.176	7.430	10.657	15.112	21.199	29.439
12	7.288	8.916	13.215	19.343	27.983	40.037
13	8.599	10.699	16.386	24.759	36.937	54.451
14	10.147	12.839	20.319	31.691	48.757	74.053
15	11.974	15.407	25.196	40.565	64.359	100.712
16	14.129	18.488	31.243	51.923	84.954	136.97
17	16.672	22.186	38.741	66.461	112.14	186.28
18	19.673	26.623	48.039	85.071	148.02	253.34
19	23.214	31.948	59.568	108.89	195.39	344.54
20	27.393	38.338	73.864	139.38	257.92	468.57
25	62.669	95.396	216.542	478.90	1033.6	2180.1
30	143.371	237.376	634.820	1645.5	4142.1	10143.

Year	40%	50%	60%	70%	80%	90%
1	1.400	1.500	1.600	1.700	1.800	1.900
2	1.960	2.250	2.560	2.890	3.240	3.610
3	2.744	3.375	4.096	4.913	5.832	6.859
4	3.842	5.062	6.544	8.352	10.498	13.032
5	5.378	7.594	10.486	14.199	18.896	24.761
6	7.530	11.391	16.777	24.138	34.012	47.046
7	10.541	17.086	26.844	41.034	61.222	89.387
8	14.758	25.629	42.950	69.758	110.200	169.836
9	20.661	38.443	68.720	118.588	198.359	322.688
10	28.925	57.665	109.951	201.599	357.047	613.107
11	40.496	86.498	175.922	342.719	642.684	1164.902
12	56.694	129.746	281.475	582.622	1156.831	2213.314
13	79.372	194.619	450.360	990.457	2082.295	4205.297
14	111.120	291.929	720.576	1683.777	3748.131	7990.065
15	155.568	497.894	1152.921	2862.421	6746.636	15181.122
16	217.795	656.84	1844.7	4866.1	12144.	28844.0
17	304.914	985.26	2951.5	8272.4	21859.	54804.0
18	426.879	1477.9	4722.4	14063.0	39346.	104130.0
19	597.630	2216.8	7555.8	23907.0	70824.	197840.0
20	836.683	3325.3	12089.0	40642.0	127480.	375900.0
25	4499.880	25251.	126760.0	577060.0	2408900.	9307600.0
30	24201.432	191750.	1329200.	8193500.0	45517000.	230470000.0

EXHIBIT F2

Present Value of $1

Year	1%	2%	3%	4%	5%	6%	7%	8%	9%	10%	12%	14%	15%
1	.990	.980	.971	.962	.952	.943	.935	.926	.917	.909	.893	.877	.870
2	.980	.961	.943	.925	.907	.890	.873	.857	.842	.826	.797	.769	.756
3	.971	.942	.915	.889	.864	.840	.816	.794	.772	.751	.712	.675	.658
4	.961	.924	.889	.855	.823	.792	.763	.735	.708	.683	.636	.592	.572
5	.951	.906	.863	.822	.784	.747	.713	.681	.650	.621	.567	.519	.497
6	.942	.888	.838	.790	.746	.705	.666	.630	.596	.564	.507	.456	.432
7	.933	.871	.813	.760	.711	.665	.623	.583	.547	.513	.452	.400	.376
8	.923	.853	.789	.731	.677	.627	.582	.540	.502	.467	.404	.351	.327
9	.914	.837	.766	.703	.645	.592	.544	.500	.460	.424	.361	.308	.284
10	.905	.820	.744	.676	.614	.558	.508	.463	.422	.386	.322	.270	.247
11	.896	.804	.722	.650	.585	.527	.475	.429	.388	.350	.287	.237	.215
12	.887	.788	.701	.625	.557	.497	.444	.397	.356	.319	.257	.208	.187
13	.879	.773	.681	.601	.530	.469	.415	.368	.326	.290	.229	.182	.163
14	.870	.758	.661	.577	.505	.442	.388	.340	.299	.263	.205	.160	.141
15	.861	.743	.642	.555	.481	.417	.362	.315	.275	.239	.183	.140	.123
16	.853	.728	.623	.534	.458	.394	.339	.292	.252	.218	.163	.123	.107
17	.844	.714	.605	.513	.436	.371	.317	.270	.231	.198	.146	.108	.093
18	.836	.700	.587	.494	.416	.350	.296	.250	.212	.180	.130	.083	.070
19	.828	.686	.570	.475	.396	.331	.276	.232	.194	.164	.116	.083	.070
20	.820	.673	.554	.456	.377	.319	.258	.215	.178	.149	.104	.073	.061
25	.780	.610	.478	.375	.295	.233	.184	.146	.116	.092	.059	.038	.030
30	.742	.552	.412	.308	.231	.174	.131	.099	.075	.057	.033	.020	.015

Year	16%	18%	20%	24%	28%	32%	36%	40%	50%	60%	70%	80%	90%
1	.862	.847	.833	.806	.781	.758	.735	.714	.667	.625	.588	.556	.526
2	.743	.718	.694	.650	.610	.574	.541	.510	.444	.391	.346	.309	.277
3	.641	.609	.579	.524	.477	.435	.398	.364	.296	.244	.204	.171	.146
4	.552	.516	.482	.423	.373	.329	.292	.260	.198	.153	.120	.095	.077
5	.476	.437	.402	.341	.291	.250	.215	.186	.132	.095	.070	.053	.040
6	.410	.370	.335	.275	.227	.189	.158	.133	.088	.060	.041	.029	.021
7	.354	.314	.279	.222	.178	.143	.116	.095	.059	.037	.024	.016	.011
8	.305	.266	.233	.179	.139	.108	.085	.068	.039	.023	.014	.009	.006
9	.263	.226	.194	.144	.108	.082	.063	.048	.026	.015	.008	.005	.003
10	.227	.191	.162	.116	.085	.062	.046	.035	.017	.009	.005	.003	.002
11	.195	.162	.135	.094	.066	.047	.034	.025	.012	.006	.003	.002	.001
12	.168	.137	.112	.076	.052	.036	.025	.018	.008	.004	.002	.001	.001
13	.145	.116	.093	.061	.040	.027	.018	.013	.005	.002	.001	.001	.000
14	.125	.099	.078	.049	.032	.021	.014	.009	.003	.001	.001	.000	.000
15	.108	.084	.065	.040	.025	.016	.010	.006	.002	.001	.000	.000	.000
16	.093	.071	.054	.032	.019	.012	.007	.005	.002	.001	.000	.000	
17	.080	.060	.045	.026	.015	.009	.005	.003	.001	.000	.000		
18	.069	.051	.038	.021	.012	.007	.004	.002	.001	.000	.000		
19	.060	.043	.031	.017	.009	.005	.003	.002	.000	.000			
20	.051	.037	.026	.014	.007	.004	.002	.001	.000	.000			
25	.024	.016	.010	.005	.002	.001	.000	.000					
30	.012	.007	.004	.002	.001	.000	.000						

EXHIBIT F3

Sum of an Annuity of $1

Year	1%	2%	3%	4%	5%	6%
1	1.000	1.000	1.000	1.000	1.000	1.000
2	2.010	2.020	2.030	2.040	2.050	2.060
3	2.030	3.060	3.091	3.122	3.152	3.184
4	4.060	4.122	4.184	4.246	4.310	4.375
5	5.101	5.204	5.309	5.416	5.526	5.637
6	6.152	6.308	6.468	6.633	6.802	6.975
7	7.214	7.434	7.662	7.898	8.142	8.394
8	8.286	8.583	8.892	9.214	9.549	9.897
9	9.369	9.755	10.159	10.583	11.027	11.491
10	10.462	10.950	11.464	12.006	12.578	13.181
11	11.567	12.169	12.808	13.486	14.207	14.972
12	12.683	13.412	14.192	15.026	15.917	16.870
13	13.809	14.680	15.618	16.627	17.713	18.882
14	14.947	15.974	17.086	18.292	19.599	21.051
15	16.097	17.293	18.599	20.024	21.579	23.276
16	17.258	18.639	20.157	21.825	23.657	25.673
17	18.430	20.012	21.762	23.698	25.840	28.213
18	19.615	21.412	23.414	25.645	28.132	30.906
19	20.811	22.841	25.117	27.671	30.539	33.760
20	22.019	24.297	26.870	29.778	33.066	36.786
25	28.243	32.030	36.459	41.646	47.727	54.865
30	34.785	40.568	47.575	56.085	66.439	79.058

Year	7%	8%	9%	10%	12%	14%
1	1.000	1.000	1.000	1.000	1.000	1.000
2	2.070	2.080	2.090	2.100	2.120	2.140
3	3.215	3.246	3.278	3.310	3.374	3.440
4	4.440	4.506	4.573	4.641	4.770	4.921
5	5.751	5.867	5.985	6.105	6.353	6.610
6	7.152	7.336	7.523	7.716	8.115	8.536
7	8.654	8.923	9.200	9.487	10.089	10.730
8	10.260	10.637	11.028	11.436	12.300	13.233
9	11.978	12.488	13.021	13.579	14.776	16.085
10	13.816	14.487	15.193	15.937	17.549	19.337
11	15.784	16.645	17.560	18.531	20.655	23.044
12	17.888	18.977	20.141	21.384	24.133	27.271
13	20.141	21.495	22.953	24.523	28.029	32.089
14	22.550	24.215	26.019	27.975	32.393	37.581
15	25.129	27.152	29.361	31.772	37.280	43.842
16	27.888	30.324	33.003	35.950	42.753	50.980
17	30.840	33.750	36.974	40.545	48.884	59.118
18	33.999	37.450	41.301	45.599	55.750	68.394
19	37.379	41.446	46.018	51.159	63.440	78.969
20	40.995	45.762	51.160	57.275	72.052	91.025
25	63.249	73.106	84.701	98.347	133.334	181.871
30	94.461	113.283	136.308	164.494	241.333	356.787

EXHIBIT F3 (continued)

Sum of an Annuity of $1

Year	16%	18%	20%	24%	28%	32%
1	1.000	1.000	1.000	1.000	1.000	1.000
2	2.160	2.180	2.200	2.240	2.280	2.320
3	3.506	3.572	3.640	3.778	3.918	4.062
4	5.066	5.215	5.368	5.684	6.016	6.362
5	6.877	7.154	7.442	8.048	8.700	9.398
6	8.977	9.442	9.930	10.980	12.136	13.406
7	11.414	12.142	12.916	14.615	16.534	18.696
8	14.240	15.327	16.499	19.123	22.163	25.678
9	17.518	19.086	20.799	24.712	29.369	34.895
10	21.321	23.521	25.959	31.643	38.592	47.062
11	25.733	28.755	32.150	40.238	50.399	63.122
12	30.850	34.931	39.580	50.985	65.510	84.320
13	36.786	42.219	48.497	64.110	84.853	112.303
14	43.672	50.818	59.196	80.496	109.612	149.240
15	51.660	60.965	72.035	100.815	141.303	197.997
16	60.925	72.939	87.442	126.011	181.87	262.36
17	71.673	87.068	105.931	157.253	233.79	347.31
18	84.141	103.740	128.117	195.994	300.25	459.45
19	98.603	123.414	154.740	244.033	385.32	607.47
20	115.380	146.628	186.688	303.601	494.21	802.86
25	249.214	342.603	471.981	898.092	1706.8	3226.8
30	530.312	790.948	1181.882	2640.916	5873.2	12941.0

Year	36%	40%	50%	60%	70%	80%
1	1.000	1.000	1.000	1.000	1.000	1.000
2	2.360	2.400	2.500	2.600	2.700	2.800
3	4.210	4.360	4.750	5.160	5.590	6.040
4	6.725	7.104	8.125	9.256	10.503	11.872
5	10.146	10.846	13.188	15.810	18.855	22.370
6	14.799	16.324	20.781	26.295	33.054	41.265
7	21.126	23.853	32.172	43.073	57.191	75.278
8	29.732	34.395	49.258	69.916	98.225	136.500
9	41.435	49.153	74.887	112.866	167.983	246.699
10	57.352	69.814	113.330	181.585	286.570	445.058
11	78.998	98.739	170.995	291.536	488.170	802.105
12	108.437	139.235	257.493	467.458	830.888	1444.788
13	148.475	195.929	387.239	748.933	1413.510	2601.619
14	202.926	275.300	581.859	1199.293	2403.968	4683.914
15	276.979	386.420	873.788	1919.869	4087.745	8432.045
16	377.69	541.99	1311.7	3072.8	6950.2	15179.0
17	514.66	759.78	1968.5	4917.5	11816.0	27323.0
18	700.94	1064.7	2953.8	7868.9	20089.0	49182.0
19	954.28	1491.6	4431.7	12591.0	34152.0	88528.0
20	1298.8	2089.2	6648.5	20147.0	58059.0	159350.0
25	6053.0	11247.0	50500.0	211270.0	824370.0	3011100.0
30	28172.0	60501.0	383500.0	2215400.0	11705000.0	56896000.0

EXHIBIT F4

Present Value of an Annuity of $1

Year	1%	2%	3%	4%	5%	6%	7%	8%	9%	10%
1	0.990	0.980	0.971	0.962	0.952	0.943	0.935	0.926	0.917	0.909
2	1.970	1.942	1.913	1.886	1.859	1.833	1.808	1.783	1.759	1.736
3	2.941	2.884	2.829	2.775	2.723	2.673	2.624	2.577	2.531	2.487
4	3.902	3.808	3.717	3.630	3.546	3.465	3.387	3.312	3.240	3.170
5	4.853	4.713	4.580	4.452	4.329	4.212	4.100	3.993	3.890	3.791
6	5.795	5.601	5.417	5.242	5.076	4.917	4.766	4.623	4.486	4.355
7	6.728	6.472	6.230	6.002	5.786	5.582	5.389	5.206	5.033	4.868
8	7.652	7.325	7.020	6.733	6.463	6.210	6.971	5.747	5.535	5.335
9	8.566	8.162	7.786	7.435	7.108	6.802	6.515	6.247	5.985	5.759
10	9.471	8.983	8.530	8.111	7.722	7.360	7.024	6.710	6.418	6.145
11	10.368	9.787	9.253	8.760	8.306	7.887	7.499	7.139	6.805	6.495
12	11.255	10.575	9.954	9.385	8.863	8.384	7.943	7.536	7.161	6.814
13	12.134	11.348	10.635	9.986	9.394	8.853	8.358	7.904	7.487	7.103
14	13.004	12.106	11.296	10.563	9.899	9.295	8.745	8.244	7.786	7.367
15	13.865	12.849	11.938	11.118	10.380	9.712	9.108	8.559	8.060	7.606
16	14.718	13.578	12.561	11.652	10.838	10.106	9.447	8.851	8.312	7.824
17	15.562	14.292	13.166	12.166	11.274	10.477	9.763	9.122	8.544	8.022
18	16.398	14.992	13.754	12.659	11.690	10.828	10.059	9.372	8.756	8.201
19	17.226	15.678	14.324	13.134	12.085	11.158	10.336	9.604	8.950	8.365
20	18.046	16.351	14.877	13.590	12.462	11.470	10.594	9.818	9.128	8.514
25	22.023	19.523	17.413	15.622	14.094	12.783	11.654	10.675	9.823	9.077
30	25.808	22.397	19.600	17.292	15.373	13.765	12.409	11.258	10.274	9.427

Year	12%	14%	16%	18%	20%	24%	28%	32%	36%
1	0.893	0.877	0.862	0.847	0.833	0.806	0.781	0.758	0.735
2	1.690	1.647	1.605	1.566	1.528	1.457	1.392	1.332	1.276
3	2.402	2.322	2.246	2.174	2.106	1.981	1.868	1.766	1.674
4	3.037	2.914	2.798	2.690	2.589	2.404	2.241	2.096	1.966
5	3.605	3.433	3.274	3.127	2.991	2.745	2.532	2.345	2.181
6	4.111	3.889	3.685	3.498	3.326	3.020	2.759	2.534	2.339
7	4.564	4.288	4.039	3.812	3.605	3.242	2.937	2.678	2.455
8	4.968	4.639	4.344	4.078	3.837	3.421	3.076	2.786	2.540
9	5.328	4.946	4.607	4.303	4.031	3.566	3.184	2.868	2.603
10	5.650	5.216	4.833	4.494	4.193	3.682	3.269	2.930	2.650
11	5.988	5.453	5.029	4.656	4.327	3.776	3.335	2.978	2.683
12	6.194	5.660	5.197	4.793	4.439	3.851	3.387	3.013	2.708
13	6.424	5.842	5.342	4.910	4.533	3.912	3.427	3.040	2.727
14	6.628	6.002	5.468	5.008	4.611	3.962	3.459	3.061	2.740
15	6.811	6.142	5.575	5.092	4.675	4.001	3.483	3.076	2.750
16	6.974	6.265	5.669	5.162	4.730	4.033	3.503	3.088	2.758
17	7.120	5.373	5.749	4.222	4.775	4.059	3.518	3.097	2.763
18	7.250	6.467	5.818	5.273	4.812	4.080	3.529	3.104	2.767
19	7.366	6.550	5.877	5.316	4.844	4.097	3.539	3.109	2.770
20	7.469	6.623	5.929	5.353	4.870	4.110	3.546	3.113	2.772
25	7.843	6.873	6.097	5.467	4.948	4.147	3.564	3.122	2.776
30	8.055	7.003	6.177	5.517	4.979	4.160	3.569	3.124	2.778

EXHIBIT F5

Table of Five-place Common Logarithms (1 to 100 by tenths)

No.	0	1	2	3	4	5	6	7	8	9
0	--∞	00 000	30 103	47 712	60 206	69 897	77 815	84 510	90 309	95 424
1	00 000	04 139	07 918	11 394	14 613	17 609	20 412	23 045	25 527	27 875
2	30 103	32 222	34 242	36 173	38 021	39 794	41 497	43 136	44 716	46 240
3	47 712	49 136	50 515	51 851	53 148	54 407	55 630	56 820	57 978	59 106
4	60 206	61 278	62 325	63 347	64 345	65 321	66 276	67 210	68 124	69 020
5	69 897	70 757	71 600	72 428	73 239	74 036	74 819	75 587	76 343	77 085
6	77 815	78 533	79 239	79 934	80 618	81 291	81 954	82 607	83 251	83 885
7	84 510	85 126	85 733	86 332	86 923	87 506	88 081	88 649	89 209	89 763
8	90 309	90 848	91 381	91 908	92 428	92 942	93 450	93 952	94 448	94 939
9	95 424	95 904	96 379	96 848	97 313	97 772	98 227	98 677	99 123	99 564
10	00 000	00 432	00 860	01 284	01 703	02 119	02 531	02 938	03 342	03 743
11	04 139	04 532	04 922	05 308	85 690	06 070	06 446	06 819	07 188	07 555
12	07 918	08 279	08 636	08 991	09 342	09 691	10 037	10 380	10 721	11 059
13	11 394	11 727	12 057	12 385	12 710	13 033	13 354	13 672	13 988	14 301
14	14 613	14 922	15 299	15 534	15 836	16 137	16 435	16 732	17 026	17 319
15	17 609	17 898	18 184	18 469	18 752	19 033	19 312	19 590	19 866	20 140
16	20 412	20 683	20 951	21 219	21 484	21 748	22 011	22 272	22 531	22 789
17	23 045	23 300	23 553	23 805	24 055	24 304	24 551	24 797	25 042	25 285
18	25 527	25 768	26 007	26 245	26 482	26 717	26 951	27 184	27 416	27 646
19	27 865	28 103	28 330	28 556	28 780	29 003	29 226	29 447	29 667	29 885
20	30 103	30 320	30 535	30 750	30 963	31 175	31 387	31 597	31 806	32 015
21	32 222	32 428	32 634	32 838	33 041	33 244	33 445	33 646	33 846	34 044
22	34 242	34 439	34 635	34 830	35 025	35 218	35 411	35 603	35 793	35 984
23	36 173	36 361	36 549	36 736	36 922	37 107	37 291	37 475	37 658	37 840
24	38 021	38 202	38 382	38 561	38 739	38 917	39 094	39 270	39 445	39 620
25	39 794	39 967	40 140	40 312	40 483	40 654	40 824	40 993	41 162	41 330
26	41 497	41 664	41 830	41 996	42 160	42 325	42 488	42 651	42 813	42 975
27	43 136	43 297	43 457	43 616	43 775	43 933	44 091	44 248	44 404	44 560
28	44 716	44 871	45 025	45 179	45 332	45 484	45 637	45 788	45 939	46 090
29	46 240	46 389	46 538	46 687	46 835	46 982	47 129	47 276	47 422	47 567
30	47 712	47 857	48 001	48 144	48 287	48 430	48 572	48 714	48 855	48 996
31	49 136	49 276	49 415	49 554	49 693	49 831	49 969	50 106	50 243	50 379
32	50 515	50 651	50 786	50 920	51 054	51 188	51 322	51 455	51 587	51 720
33	51 851	51 983	52 114	52 244	52 375	52 504	52 634	52 763	52 892	53 020
34	53 148	53 275	53 403	53 529	53 656	53 782	53 908	54 033	54 158	54 283
35	54 407	54 531	54 654	54 777	54 900	55 023	55 145	55 267	55 388	55 509
36	55 630	55 751	55 871	55 991	56 110	56 229	56 348	56 467	56 585	56 703
37	56 820	56 937	57 054	57 171	57 287	57 403	57 519	57 634	57 749	57 864
38	57 978	58 092	58 206	58 320	58 433	58 546	58 659	58 771	58 883	58 995
39	59 106	59 218	59 329	59 439	59 550	59 660	59 770	59 879	59 988	60 097
40	60 206	60 314	60 423	60 531	60 638	60 745	60 853	60 959	61 066	61 172
41	61 278	61 384	61 490	61 595	61 700	61 805	61 909	62 014	62 118	62 221
42	62 325	62 428	62 531	62 634	62 737	62 839	62 941	63 043	63 144	63 246
43	63 347	63 448	63 548	63 649	63 749	63 849	63 949	64 048	64 147	64 246
44	64 345	64 444	64 542	64 640	64 738	64 836	64 933	65 031	65 128	65 225
45	65 321	65 418	65 514	65 610	65 706	65 801	65 896	65 992	66 087	66 181
46	66 276	66 370	66 464	66 558	66 652	66 745	66 839	66 932	67 025	67 117
47	67 210	67 302	67 394	67 486	67 578	67 669	67 761	67 852	67 943	68 034
48	68 124	68 215	68 305	68 395	68 485	68 574	68 664	68 753	68 842	68 931
49	69 020	69 108	69 197	69 285	69 373	69 461	69 548	69 636	69 723	69 810
50	69 897	69 984	70 070	70 157	70 243	70 329	70 415	70 501	70 586	70 672

EXHIBIT F5 (continued)

Table of Five-place Common Logarithms (1 to 100 by tenths)

No.	0	1	2	3	4	5	6	7	8	9
51	70 757	70 842	70 927	71 012	71 096	71 181	71 265	71 349	71 433	71 517
52	71 600	71 684	71 767	71 850	71 933	72 016	72 099	72 181	72 263	72 346
53	72 428	72 509	72 591	72 673	72 754	72 835	72 916	72 997	73 078	73 159
54	73 239	73 320	73 400	73 480	73 560	73 640	73 719	73 799	73 878	73 957
55	74 036	74 115	74 194	74 273	74 351	74 429	74 507	74 586	74 663	74 741
56	74 819	74 896	74 974	75 051	75 128	75 205	75 282	75 358	75 435	75 511
57	75 587	75 664	75 740	75 815	75 891	75 967	76 042	76 118	76 193	76 268
58	76 343	76 418	76 492	76 567	76 641	76 716	76 790	76 864	76 938	77 012
59	77 985	77 159	77 232	77 305	77 379	77 452	77 525	77 597	77 670	77 743
60	77 815	77 887	77 960	78 032	78 104	78 176	78 247	78 319	78 390	78 462
61	78 533	78 604	78 675	78 746	78 817	78 888	78 958	79 029	79 099	79 169
62	79 239	79 309	79 379	79 449	79 518	79 588	79 657	79 727	79 796	79 865
63	79 934	80 003	80 072	80 140	80 209	80 277	80 346	80 414	80 482	80 550
64	80 618	80 686	80 754	80 821	80 889	80 956	81 023	81 090	81 157	81 224
65	81 291	81 358	81 425	81 491	81 558	81 624	81 690	81 757	81 823	81 889
66	81 954	82 020	82 086	82 151	82 217	82 282	82 347	82 413	82 478	82 543
67	82 607	82 672	82 737	82 802	82 866	82 930	82 995	83 059	83 123	83 187
68	83 251	83 315	83 378	83 442	83 506	83 569	83 632	83 696	83 759	83 822
69	83 885	83 948	84 011	84 073	84 136	84 198	84 261	84 323	84 386	84 448
70	84 510	84 572	84 634	84 696	84 757	84 819	84 880	84 942	85 003	85 065
71	85 126	85 187	85 248	85 309	85 370	85 431	85 491	85 552	85 612	85 673
72	85 733	85 794	85 854	85 914	85 974	86 034	86 094	86 153	86 213	86 273
73	86 332	86 392	86 451	86 510	86 570	86 629	86 688	86 747	86 806	86 864
74	86 923	86 982	87 040	87 099	87 157	87 216	87 274	87 332	87 390	87 448
75	87 506	87 564	87 622	87 679	87 737	87 795	87 852	87 910	87 967	88 024
76	88 081	88 138	88 195	88 252	88 309	88 366	88 423	88 480	88 536	88 593
77	88 649	88 705	88 762	88 818	88 874	88 930	88 986	89 042	89 098	89 154
78	89 209	89 265	89 321	89 376	89 432	89 487	89 542	89 597	89 653	89 708
79	89 763	89 818	89 873	89 927	89 982	90 037	90 091	90 146	90 200	90 255
80	90 309	90 363	90 417	90 472	90 526	90 580	90 634	90 687	90 741	90 795
81	90 848	90 902	90 956	91 009	91 062	91 116	91 169	91 222	91 275	91 328
82	91 381	91 434	91 487	91 540	91 593	91 645	91 698	91 751	91 803	91 855
83	91 908	91 960	92 012	92 064	92 117	92 169	92 221	92 273	92 324	92 376
84	92 428	92 480	92 531	92 583	92 634	92 686	92 737	92 788	92 840	92 891
85	92 942	92 993	93 044	93 095	93 146	93 197	93 247	93 298	93 349	93 399
86	93 450	93 500	93 551	93 601	93 651	93 702	93 752	93 802	93 852	93 902
87	93 952	94 002	94 052	94 101	94 151	94 201	94 250	94 300	94 349	94 399
88	94 448	94 498	94 547	94 596	94 645	94 694	94 743	94 792	94 841	94 890
89	94 939	94 988	95 036	95 085	95 134	95 182	95 231	95 279	95 328	95 376
90	95 424	95 472	95 521	95 569	95 617	95 665	95 713	95 761	95 809	95 856
91	95 904	95 952	95 999	96 047	96 095	96 142	96 190	96 237	96 284	96 332
92	96 379	96 426	96 473	96 520	96 567	96 614	96 661	96 708	96 755	96 802
93	96 848	96 895	96 942	96 988	97 035	97 081	97 128	97 174	97 220	97 267
94	97 313	97 359	97 405	97 451	97 497	97 543	97 589	97 635	97 681	97 727
95	97 772	97 818	97 864	97 909	97 955	98 000	98 046	98 091	98 137	98 182
96	98 227	98 272	98 318	98 363	98 408	98 453	98 498	98 543	98 588	98 632
97	98 677	98 722	98 767	98 811	98 856	98 900	98 945	98 989	99 034	99 078
98	99 123	99 167	99 211	99 255	99 300	99 344	99 388	99 432	99 476	99 520
99	99 564	99 607	99 651	99 695	99 739	99 782	99 826	99 870	99 913	99 957
100	00 000	00 043	00 087	00 130	00 173	00 217	00 260	00 303	00 346	00 389

EXHIBIT F6

New York and American Stock Exchange Commission Rates (effective 19x0-19x9)

Shares Selling at $	Even	1/8	1/4	3/8	1/2	5/8	3/4	7/8	Odd lot max. shrs. $6 min.
1	6.00	6.00	6.00	6.00	6.00	6.25	6.50	6.75	..
2	7.00	7.25	7.50	7.75	8.00	8.25	8.50	8.75	..
3	9.00	9.25	9.50	9.75	10.00	10.25	10.50	10.75	83
4	11.00	11.13	11.25	11.38	11.50	11.63	11.75	11.88	62
5	12.00	12.13	12.25	12.38	12.50	12.63	12.75	12.88	50
6	13.00	13.13	13.25	13.38	13.50	13.63	13.75	13.88	41
7	14.00	14.13	14.25	14.38	14.50	14.63	14.75	14.88	35
8	15.00	15.13	15.25	15.38	15.50	15.63	15.75	15.88	31
9	16.00	16.13	16.25	16.38	16.50	16.63	16.75	16.88	27
10	17.00	17.13	17.25	17.38	17.50	17.63	17.75	17.88	25
11	18.00	18.13	18.25	18.38	18.50	18.63	18.75	18.88	22
12	19.00	19.13	19.25	19.38	19.50	19.63	19.75	19.88	20
13	20.00	20.13	20.25	20.38	20.50	20.63	20.75	20.88	17
14	21.00	21.13	21.25	21.38	21.50	21.63	21.75	21.88	17
15	22.00	22.13	22.25	22.38	22.50	22.63	22.75	22.88	16
16	23.00	23.13	23.25	23.38	23.50	23.63	23.75	23.88	15
17	24.00	24.13	24.25	24.38	24.50	24.63	24.75	24.88	14
18	25.00	25.13	25.25	25.38	25.50	25.63	25.75	25.88	13
19	26.00	26.13	26.25	26.38	26.50	26.63	26.75	26.88	13
20	27.00	27.13	27.25	27.38	27.50	27.63	27.75	27.88	12
21	28.00	28.13	28.25	28.38	28.50	28.63	28.75	28.88	11
22	29.00	29.13	29.25	29.38	29.50	29.63	29.75	29.88	11
23	30.00	30.13	3 025	30.38	30.50	30.63	30.75	30.88	10
24	31.00	31.06	31.13	31.19	31.25	31.31	31.38	31.44	10
25	31.50	31.56	31.63	31.69	31.75	31.81	31.88	31.94	10
26	32.00	32.06	32.13	32.19	32.25	32.31	32.38	32.44	9
27	32.50	32.56	32.63	32.69	32.75	32.81	32.88	32.94	9
28	33.00	33.06	33.13	33.19	33.25	33.31	33.38	33.44	8
29	33.50	33.56	33.63	33.69	33.75	33.81	33.88	33.94	8
30	34.00	34.06	34.13	34.19	34.25	34.31	34.38	34.44	8
31	34.50	34.56	34.63	34.69	34.75	34.81	34.88	34.94	8
32	35.00	35.06	35.13	35.19	35.25	35.31	35.38	35.44	7
33	35.50	35.56	35.63	35.69	35.75	35.81	35.88	35.94	7
34	36.00	36.06	36.13	36.19	36.25	36.31	36.38	36.44	7
35	36.50	36.56	36.63	36.69	36.75	36.81	36.88	36.94	7
36	37.00	37.06	37.13	37.19	37.25	37.31	37.38	37.44	6
37	37.50	37.56	37.63	37.69	37.75	37.81	37.88	37.94	6
38	38.00	38.06	38.13	38.19	38.25	38.31	38.38	38.44	6
39	38.50	38.56	38.63	38.69	38.75	38.81	38.88	38.94	6
40	39.00	39.06	39.13	39.19	39.25	39.31	39.38	39.44	6
41	39.50	39.56	39.63	39.69	39.75	39.81	39.88	39.94	6
42	40.00	40.06	40.13	40.19	40.25	40.31	40.38	40.44	5
43	40.50	40.56	40.63	40.69	40.75	40.81	40.88	40.94	5
44	41.00	41.06	41.13	41.19	41.25	41.31	41.38	41.44	5
45	41.50	41.56	41.63	41.69	41.75	41.81	41.88	41.94	5
46	42.00	42.06	42.13	42.19	42.25	42.31	42.38	42.44	5
47	42.50	42.56	42.63	42.69	42.75	42.81	42.88	42.94	5
48	43.00	43.06	43.13	43.19	43.25	43.31	43.38	43.44	5
49	43.50	43.56	43.63	43.69	43.75	43.81	43.88	43.94	5
50	44.00	44.01	44.03	44.04	44.05	44.06	44.08	44.09	5

Round Lots Rates per 100 Shares

Source: *Standard and Poor's Stock Guide.*

EXHIBIT F6 (continued)

New York and American Stock Exchange Commission Rates (effective 19x0–19x9)

Shares Selling at $	Even	1/8	1/4	Round Lots Rates per 100 Shares 3/8	1/2	5/8	3/4	7/8	Odd lot max. shrs. $6 min.
51	44.10	44.11	44.13	44.14	44.15	44.16	44.18	44.19	4
52	44.20	44.21	44.23	44.24	44.25	44.26	44.28	44.29	4
53	44.30	44.31	44.33	44.34	44.35	44.36	44.38	44.39	4
54	44.40	44.41	44.43	44.44	44.45	44.46	44.48	44.49	4
55	44.50	44.51	44.53	44.54	44.55	44.56	44.58	44.59	4
56	44.60	44.61	44.63	44.64	44.65	44.66	44.68	44.69	4
57	44.70	44.71	44.73	44.74	44.75	44.76	44.78	44.79	4
58	44.80	44.81	44.83	44.84	44.85	44.86	44.88	44.89	4
59	44.90	44.91	44.93	44.94	44.95	44.96	44.98	44.99	4
60	45.00	45.01	45.03	45.04	45.05	45.06	45.08	45.09	4
61	45.10	45.11	45.13	45.14	45.15	45.16	45.18	45.19	4
62	45.20	45.21	45.23	45.24	45.25	45.26	45.28	45.29	4
63	45.30	45.31	45.33	45.34	45.35	45.36	45.38	45.39	4
64	45.40	45.41	45.43	45.44	45.45	45.46	45.48	45.49	4
65	45.50	45.51	45.53	45.54	45.55	45.56	45.58	45.59	4
66	45.60	45.61	45.63	45.64	45.65	45.66	45.68	45.69	4
67	45.70	45.71	45.73	45.74	45.75	45.76	45.78	45.79	4
68	45.80	45.81	45.83	45.84	45.85	45.86	45.88	45.89	4
69	45.90	45.91	45.93	45.94	45.95	45.96	45.98	45.99	4
70	46.00	46.01	46.03	46.04	46.05	46.06	46.08	46.09	4
71	46.10	46.11	46.13	46.14	46.15	46.16	46.18	46.19	4
72	46.20	46.21	46.23	46.24	46.25	46.26	46.28	46.29	4
73	46.30	46.31	46.33	46.34	46.35	46.36	46.38	46.39	4
74	46.40	46.41	46.43	46.44	46.45	46.46	46.48	46.49	4
75	46.50	46.51	46.53	46.54	46.55	46.56	46.58	46.59	4
76	46.60	46.61	46.63	46.64	46.65	46.66	46.68	46.69	4
77	46.70	46.71	46.73	46.74	46.75	46.76	46.78	46.79	4
78	46.80	46.81	46.83	46.84	46.85	46.86	46.88	46.89	4
79	46.90	46.91	46.93	46.94	46.95	46.96	46.98	46.99	4
80	47.00	47.01	47.03	47.04	47.05	47.06	47.08	47.09	4
81	47.10	47.11	47.13	47.14	47.15	47.16	47.18	47.19	4
82	47.20	47.21	47.23	47.24	47.25	47.26	47.28	47.29	4
83	47.30	47.31	47.33	47.34	47.35	47.36	47.38	47.39	4
84	47.40	47.41	47.43	47.44	47.45	47.46	47.48	47.49	4
85	47.50	47.51	47.53	47.54	47.55	47.56	47.58	47.59	4
86	47.60	47.61	47.63	47.64	47.65	47.66	47.68	47.69	4
87	47.70	47.71	47.73	47.74	47.75	47.76	47.78	47.79	4
88	47.80	47.81	47.83	47.84	47.85	47.86	47.88	47.89	4
89	47.90	47.91	47.93	47.94	47.95	47.96	47.98	47.99	4
90	48.00	48.01	48.03	48.04	48.05	48.06	48.08	48.09	4
91	48.10	48.11	48.13	48.14	48.15	48.16	48.18	48.19	4
92	48.20	48.21	48.23	48.24	48.25	48.26	48.28	48.29	4
93	48.30	48.31	48.33	48.34	48.35	48.36	48.38	48.39	4
94	48.40	48.41	48.43	48.44	48.45	48.46	48.48	48.49	4
95	48.50	48.51	48.53	48.54	48.55	48.56	48.58	48.59	4
96	48.60	48.61	48.63	48.64	48.65	48.66	48.68	48.69	4
97	48.70	48.71	48.73	48.74	48.75	48.76	48.78	48.79	4
98	48.80	48.81	48.83	48.84	48.85	48.86	48.88	48.89	4
99	48.90	48.91	48.93	48.94	48.95	48.96	48.98	48.99	4
100	49.00	49.01	49.03	49.04	49.05	49.06	49.08	49.09	4

EXHIBIT F6 (continued)

Formula for Minimum Commissions
Commissions may be quickly computed using the following formulae:
100 Share Lot

Price Between	Commission
$1 – $4	Add $3 to 2 times price of 1 shr.
$4 – $24	Add $7 to price of 1 shr.
$24 – $50	Add $19 to ½ of price of 1 shr.
$50 and over	Add $39 to 1/10 of price of 1 shr.

(Never more than $75 per 100 shares, nor less than $6)

Odd Lots

Amount Involved	Commission
$ 100 to $ 400	2% plus $ 1
$ 400 to $2,400	1% plus $ 5
$2,400 to $4,999	½% plus $17
$5,000 and over	1/10% plus $37

but never greater than $1.50 times number of shares, subject to minimum commission of $6 and maximum of $75.

In both cases above if the amount involved is less than $100, the commission is as mutually agreed.

New York and American Stock Exchange Commission Rates
Effective March 24, 1972

Stocks, Rights, and Warrants Selling at $1 Per Share and Above

The commission on stocks, rights, and warrants selling at $1 per share and above is to be computed on the basis of the amount of money involved in the order and subject to the definition of an "order." The rate schedules are:

1.   On 100 share orders and odd lot orders

      (a)   Dollar Amount of the Order

Dollar Amount of the Order	Commission
$100 but under $800	2.0% of money involved + $6.40
$800 but under $2,500	1.3% of money involved + $12.00
$2,500 and above	.9% of money involved + $22.00

            For each odd lot transaction subtract $2. The commission on a 100, share order shall not exceed $65.00.

      (b) Orders with value of less than $100

            Less than $100, 6% of money involved or as mutually agreed.

Source: Notice from Merrill Lynch, Pierce, Fenner, and Smith, Inc.